IMAGES
of America

BRADLEY

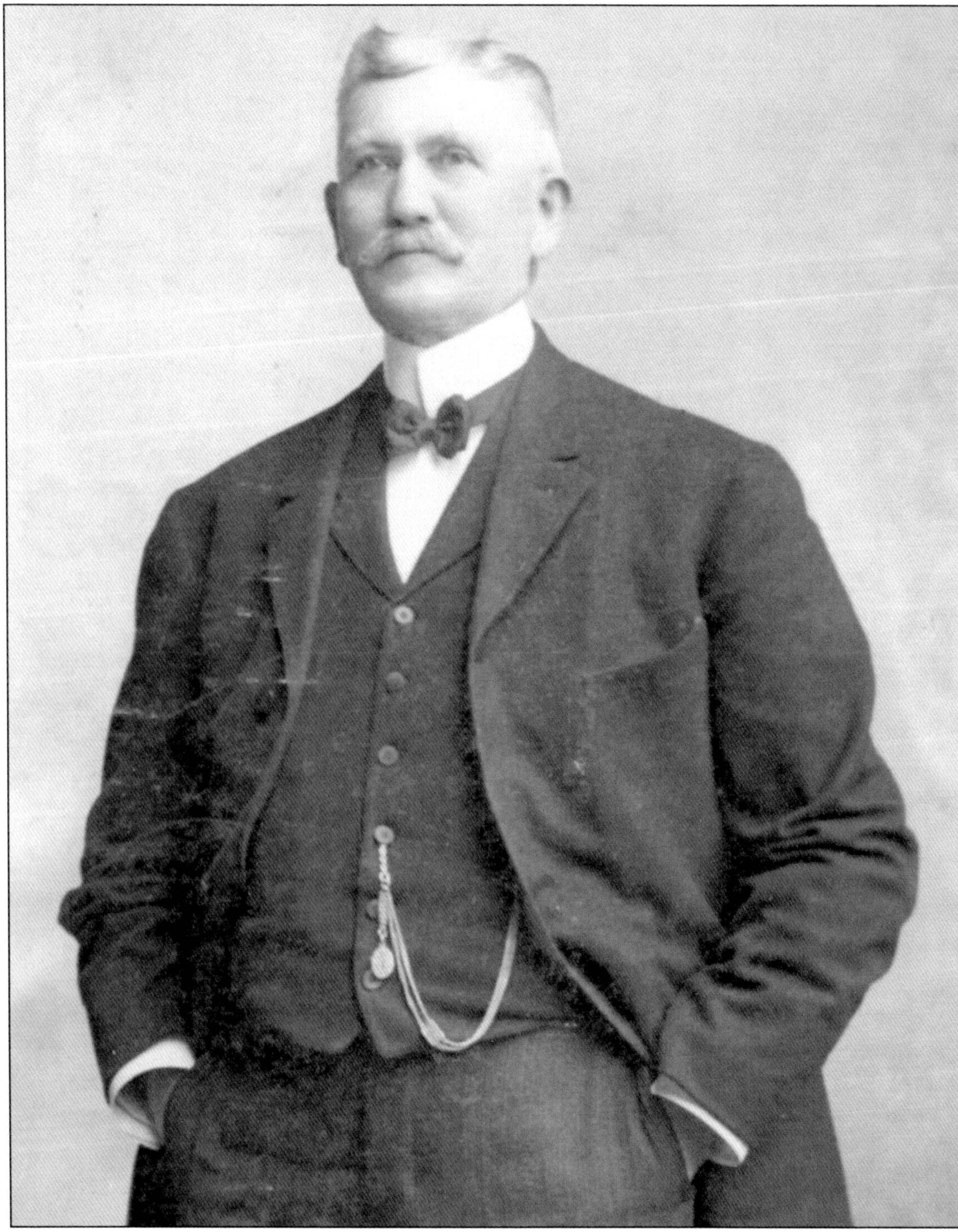

John Herman Hardebeck, commonly known as J. Herman, organized the North Kankakee Improvement Association in the spring of 1891. In the fall of 1892, Hardebeck reminded his friends, "On the first of September 1891, there was not a stick of timber nor a brick on the ground. Today there are three big factories, a machine shop, lumber yard, depot, brick store buildings, hotels, more than fifty residences, macadamized streets, streetcars, telephones, and a wide awake population." (Bradley Historical Society.)

On the cover: This photograph was taken during the Bradley Diamond Jubilee Celebration that took place from August 30 to September 4 in 1967. (Kankakee County Museum-Kankakee Daily Journal.)

IMAGES
of America

BRADLEY

Vic Johnson
and the Bradley Historical Society

ARCADIA
PUBLISHING

ISBN 978-0-7385-5173-9

Published by Arcadia Publishing
Charleston, South Carolina

Printed in the United States of America

Library of Congress Control Number: 2007932813

For all general information, please contact Arcadia Publishing:
Telephone 843-853-2070
Fax 843-853-0044
E-mail sales@arcadiapublishing.com
For customer service and orders:
Toll-Free 1-888-313-2665

Visit us on the Internet at www.arcadiapublishing.com

Dedicated to the memory of J. Herman Hardebeck.

CONTENTS

ACKNOWLEDGMENTS

The following people and organizations have contributed photographs and information used in the preparation of this history of Bradley, and their help is gratefully acknowledged: Mayor Gael Kent of the Bradley Board of Trustees and the Village of Bradley; State of Illinois Archives; executive director Norman Stevens of the Kankakee County Museum and the Kankakee County Historical Society; Pres. Nancy Arseneau of the Bourbonnais Grove Historical Society; Bradley Historical Society president Ryland Gagnon and members of the Bradley Historical Society; St. Joseph Grade School; the Kankakee Valley Genealogical Society; the Kankakee Daily Journal and the Small Publishing Group; the Bradley police and fire departments; the Bradley Public Library; Gagnon's Precision Video and Photography; and Mark Gravelin of G and G Printing.

Special thanks goes to village trustees Robert Martin and Robert Redmond for their continued support and for recognizing the need for a Bradley Historical Society.

A big thank-you goes to the people who have helped me put together this history in pictures and words, including Sue Forge Bainter, Robert Bell, Glenna Kolwelter Benoit, Francis Chamness, Steve Coy, Lori Clark, Harry Dandelles, Jeannie Colevris Dayhoff, Thomas Erickson, Marietta Frogge, Flossie Gulczynski, James Guiss, Elizabeth A. Keithcart, Kay LaChapelle, Donald LeBran, Thomas J. Lindsay, Mike Lyons, Randy Lowery, Shirley Vaughn Manley, Michelle Maier, William Maier, Dale Monte, Nelda Ravens, Boris Ruel Jr., Gail Hayes Schultz, Janice Brosseau Sims, Robert Simpson, Kenneth Smith, Marcia Stang, Rose Stefanich, Clayton Stillwell, Marietta Tanner, John J. Tofari, Dennis Vandenhaut, Jory Walters, and my wife, Theresa Johnson.

Photographs of businesses on Broadway taken by Richard Mulligan in the 1940s and donated by Carl Erickson made a valuable contribution to visual content of this book.

Photographs in this book are courtesy of the following sources unless otherwise noted: Bradley Historical Society (BHS), Robert Bell (RB), Steve Coy (SC), Carl Erickson (CE), Ryland Gagnon (RG), Kankakee County Museum (KCM), Kankakee County Museum-Kankakee Daily Journal (KCM-KDJ), Kankakee Daily Journal (KDJ), Dale Monte (DM), and Robert Simpson (RS).

INTRODUCTION

It was a time when ambitious men believed they could become Carnegies, Morgans, or Rockefellers, because, after all, these captains of industry and finance had not been born rich. Each of them had earned a fortune in his own lifetime.

It was a time of electromechanical miracles, such as the telephone and phonograph; a time when safety bicycles and pneumatic tires put millions of Americans on the road; a time when the sport of baseball became big business; and a time when the electric streetcar became an innovation in public transportation.

It was a time of wide horizons and big dreams; a time when something as new and startling as a factory town might be born and boom in the space of a single year.

It was a time for every man to stake a claim in some imminent plan for commercial improvement or expansion and, as the local newspaper proclaimed, "a time to be in it."

A man for whom that phrase was aptly applied was born in Hamilton County, Ohio, on September 1, 1842. J. Herman Hardebeck was the oldest son of Bernard and Elizabeth (Holt) Hardebeck. The senior Hardebeck and his wife had immigrated to the United States from Hanover, Germany.

Hardebeck grew up in Decatur County, Indiana, where, at an early age, he turned his attention to a career in manufacturing and the mercantile trade. At the age of 20, on September 11, 1862, Hardebeck married Elizabeth Schulte, daughter of J. B. and Catherine Schulte. The Schultes were natives of Prussia. Hardebeck and his family moved to Indianapolis in 1874, where he worked as a real estate agent for four years. From 1878 to 1883, Hardebeck engaged in agricultural pursuits near Fowler, Indiana, and he served several years as a Fowler trustee. Elizabeth died in 1880.

Hardebeck was a registered Democrat and a member of the Roman Catholic Church.

With his second wife, Philomena Schroeder, Hardebeck moved to Kankakee in 1889 and again applied his talents to the real estate business. He was instrumental in liquidating the large land holdings of Lemuel Milk. In the years from 1889 to 1891, as a member of the Kankakee Businessmens Association, Hardebeck played a leading roll in revitalizing Kankakee's stagnate economy. Charles Holt, publisher of the *Kankakee Gazette*, likened Hardebeck to a Moses leading Kankakee's businessmen out of the wilderness.

In the spring of 1891, Hardebeck organized a land syndicate called the North Kankakee Improvement Association. By May, he had an option on more than 1,000 acres of land. A full page advertisement in the August 27, 1891, issue of the *Kankakee Gazette*, announced "the North Kankakee Boom." A population of 4,000 was guaranteed by July 1, 1892, and "400 dwelling houses wanted at once."

Hardebeck had secured warranty deeds from Alva Perry and Hiram Goodwin for approximately 480 acres of land west of the Illinois Central Railroad tracks and south of North Road in June 1891. By September, this land had been subdivided into 78 blocks and platted as North Kankakee. Soon there were plans to build four large factories, a planning mill, and a machine shop. A lumberyard and a stone quarry were then located in North Kankakee to supply building materials.

In June 1892, Hardebeck subdivided 360 acres east of the Illinois Central Railroad tracks and transferred the title to a Chicago-based syndicate for resale. This money-raising scheme was required for financing the removal of the Demme and Dierkes furniture factory from Chicago to North Kankakee.

Although North Kankakee had been planned as a subdivision of Kankakee, and Hardebeck had offered to donate two lots, one on the east side and one on the west side for police and fire stations, Kankakee was short of money and delayed making a final decision.

After the Kankakee City Council failed to vote on the annexation of North Kankakee during several meetings in the summer of 1892, the citizens of North Kankakee decided to exercise the right of self determination. On September 14, 1892, a meeting was held at Morton Magruder's storeroom on the southeast corner of Broadway and Prairie Avenue. Among those in attendance was Dr. Preston Stebbings, a recent arrival from Bonfield, and E. C. Schumacher. A committee was formed with Stebbings as permanent chairman and Schumacher as secretary. It was decided by the committee to withdraw the annexation to Kankakee petition and to incorporate North Kankakee. "E. E. Day being present explained the necessary steps to be taken for incorporation," said the *Kankakee Gazette*, "and a petition was drawn up and signed by the legal voters for the same." E. E. Day was secured as attorney to carry the matter of incorporation through its legal course. An election for the incorporation of North Kankakee took place on October 7, 1892, at the lumber yard offices of Haymond and Wertz. According to the *Gazette*, "the election was a 'clean sweep' with 39 votes cast in favor."

"A caucus took place at Morton Magruder's store Saturday evening [October 8] to nominate six trustees. The following were chosen: E. Souligne, J. A. Levereau, E. C. Schumacher, Morton Magruder, Anton Munich, and Doctor Stebbings." On November 4, the nominees were elected by ballot. The next day, according to the newspaper account, "The Board of Trustees of the village of North Kankakee met in the office of Doctor P. Stebbings in a special meeting for the purpose of choosing a president of said board of trustees and appointing a treasurer, clerk, and village constable pro tem." The committee nominated Stebbings as temporary chairman and Schumacher to be the clerk. Then the committee nominated Stebbings as president of the board, and he was elected unanimously. H. M. Reynolds became village clerk and Charles Wertz became treasurer. At a meeting held that evening, committees for license and finance (Schumacher, Levereau, and Magruder), police (Magruder, Munich, and Levereau), street and alley (Schumacher, Levereau, and Souligne), and ordinance (Souligne, Schumacher, and Munich) were appointed.

The pioneer era was over long before Hardebeck platted North Kankakee. There is, however, a pioneer history of the Bradley area that begins in the early 1800s. A reminder of that early history is the Durham-Perry Farmstead (recently awarded National Register of Historic Places status), which is not within the municipal boundary of Bradley, but is contiguous with the western village limits.

One

The Jacques Jonveau Legacy

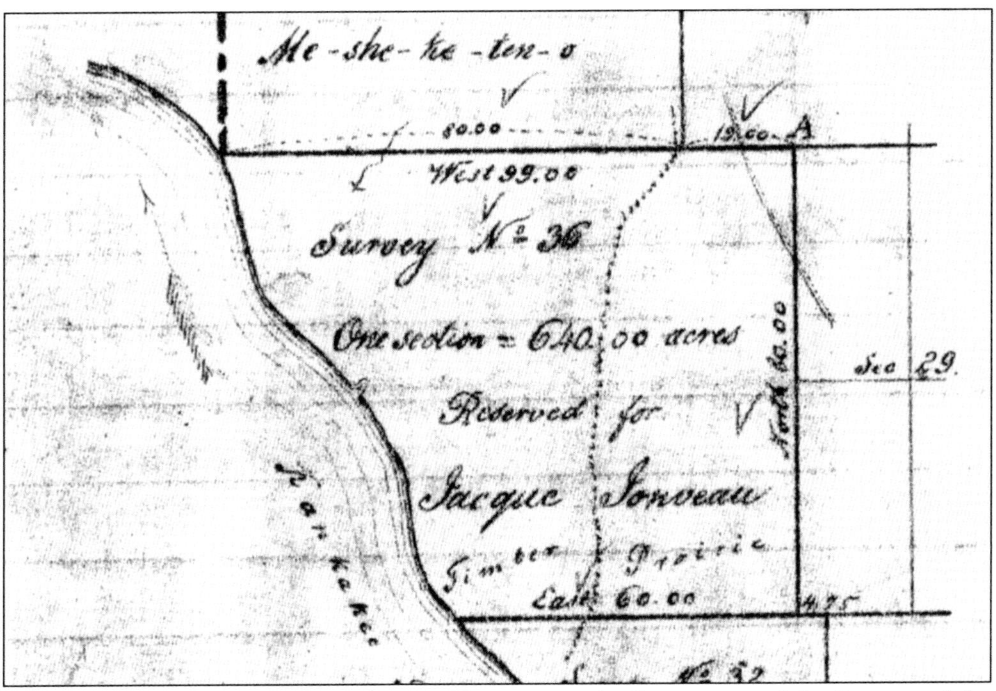

By the October 20, 1832, Treaty of Camp Tippecanoe, the Potawatomi of the Prairie and the Kankakee tribes ceded their Illinois lands to the federal government. A part of Bradley stands on a portion of the Jacques Vieau Jr. reserve. Vieau appears to have been in the employ of Gurdon S. Hubbard, who in 1825 had an American Fur Company trading post on the Iroquois River, some 26 miles southeast of the Kankakee River. In his autobiography, Hubbard mentions "my man Jombeau," and also referred to him as Jacques Jombeau. (State of Illinois Archives.)

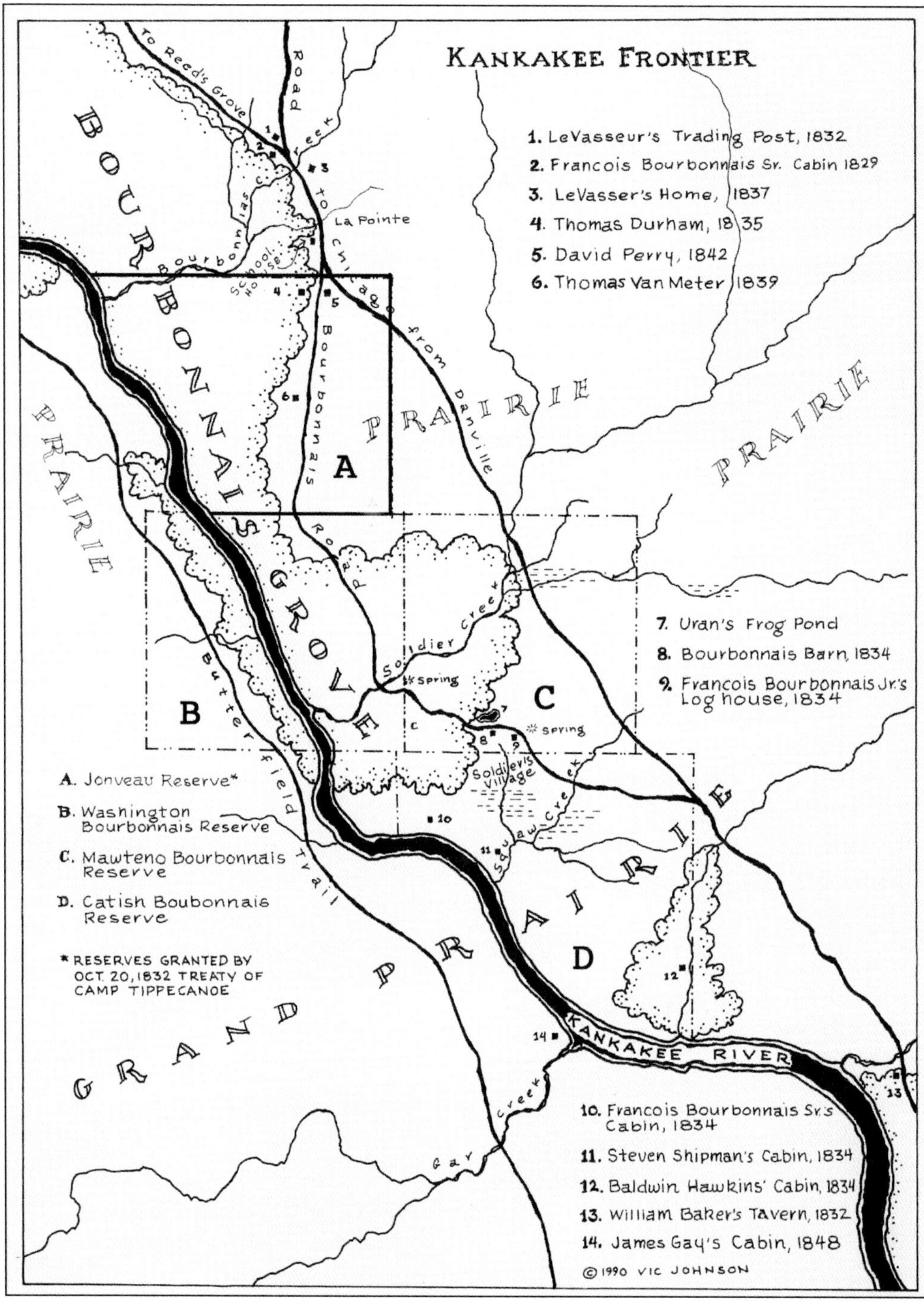

The Jonveau reserve (listed as A on the map) is 640 acres that was ceded to Jacques Vieau Jr. in October 1832. (Author's collection.)

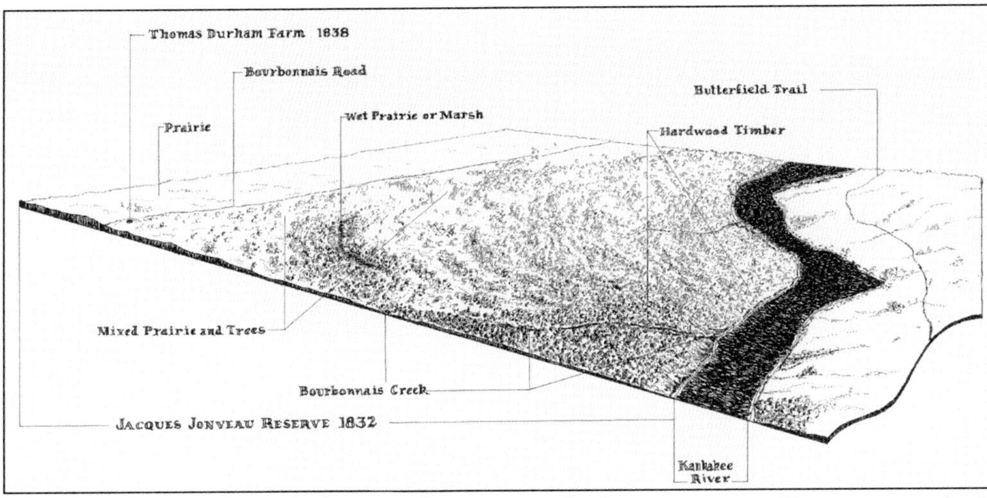

This is a perspective view looking southeast across the Jonveau reserve. Two warranty deeds dated January 29, 1838, gave Thomas Durham ownership of the north half (approximately 320 acres) of the reserve. John Blackstone owned the south half. Today the Perry Farm Park occupies 169 acres along the north boundary of the reserve. Barns that Durham built in the 1840s still stand south of the farmhouse on North Kennedy Drive, just west of the Bradley municipal limits. (Author's collection.)

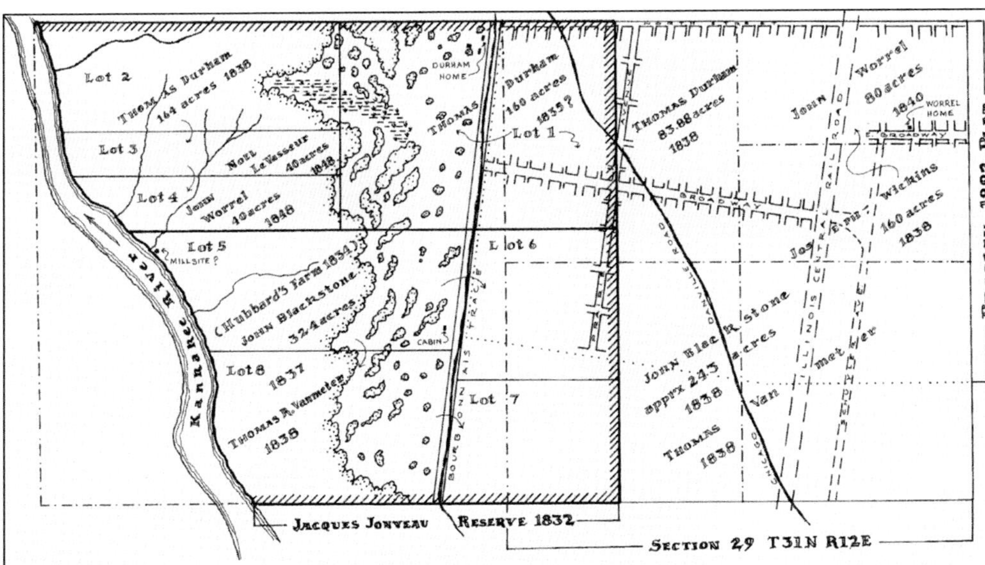

Subdivisions of the Jonveau reserve occurred as the property was purchased by pioneer settlers. On the left along the river is a grove of hardwood timber. Toward the center of the reserve lay a zone of mixed timber and prairie; beyond this grove to the east is open prairie. The Bourbonnais Trace is today known as Kennedy Drive. In 1892, the western part of North Kankakee (Bradley) was platted on the eastern portion of the reserve. (Author's collection.)

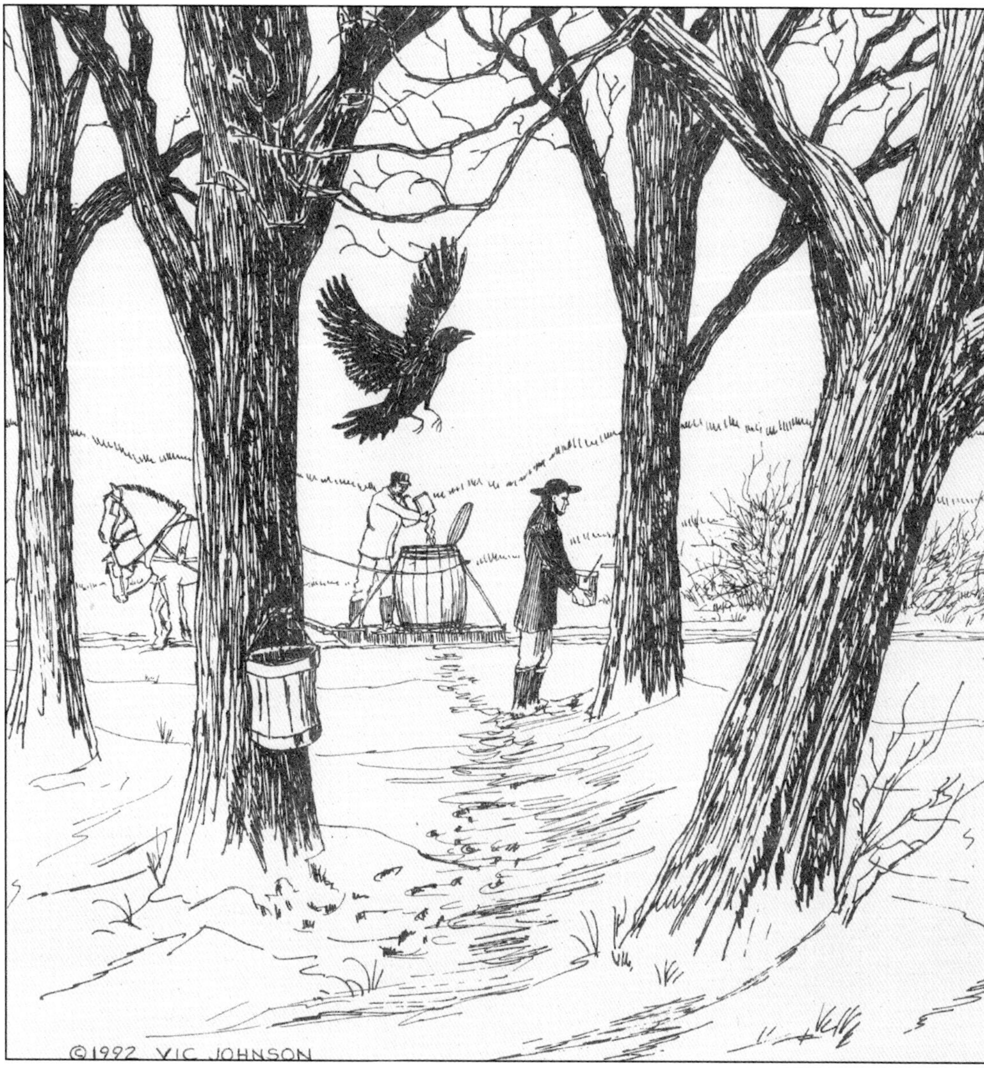

During February and early March, the Durham family collected sap from the many maple trees that grew near the river. They boiled it down to make maple sirup and maple sugar. Stephan Funk, whose family had been making syrup for over 150 years said syrup spelled with an *i* was preferred, and "the 'y' spelling of syrup refers to syrup made by adding sugar to fruit juices." Products derived from the maple sap were essential to the Native Americans of the old northwest. The sugar maple tree was known to the Potawatomis as *kisinamic* (cold tree) when used for medicine and *Inina'tig* (Indian tree) when used for food. Priscilla Mullin Sherard, a member of the Citizen Potawatomi Nation wrote, "The sugar maple and black sugar maple trees were found all over the north country and were the most valued food tree of the Potawatomis. The sugar was used in most of the cooking . . . Maple sap furnished sugar, and also vinegar. Venison was cooked with vinegar and sweetened afterwards with maple sugar . . . Two types of candy were made from the sap, taffy and snow candy. The last was made by placing nuts on the snow." The maple syrup was poured over the nuts and when it hardened it produced a candy much like Creole pralines. (Author's collection.)

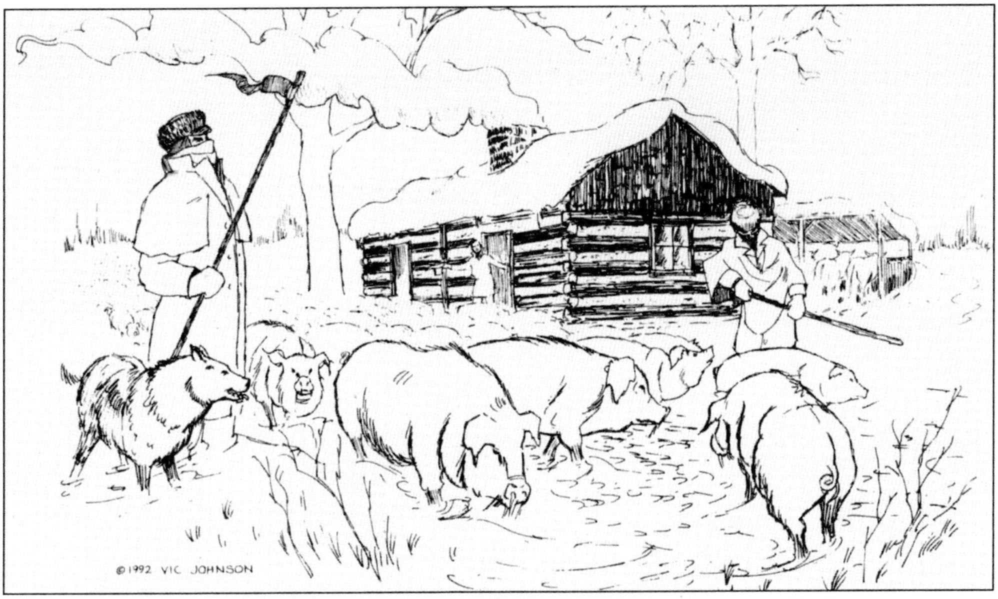

In May 1835, Thomas Durham moved his family from Vermilion Grove to the Jonveau reserve. There is some evidence in an 1837 John Blackstone deed of the south half of the property that Durham bought reserve land in 1834, but no official record has been found. The Durham's first home was a log cabin. The Durham farm soon became a place to stop for passing drovers and other travellers along the Bourbonnais Trace. (Author's collection.)

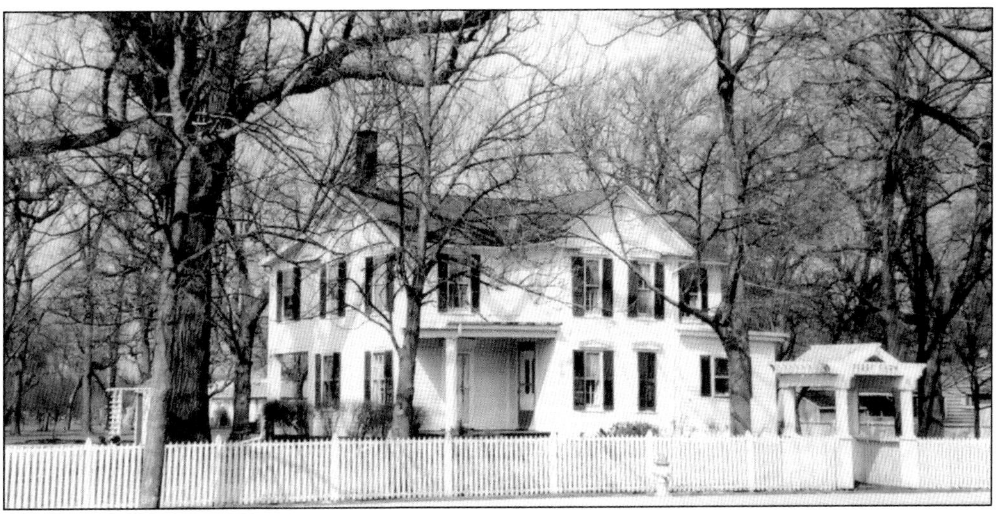

The exterior of this house was extensively remodelled about 1866 by Durham's son-in-law David Perry. In the 1840s, it was built as a two-story I-house by the Durham family. At that time, there were two rooms on the first floor with a central hall and stairway to the second floor, where a hallway also separated two rooms. Perry bought the Durham farm from the Durhams' sons and lived in the house with his wife, Margaret, and their family until he died in 1887. (Author's collection.)

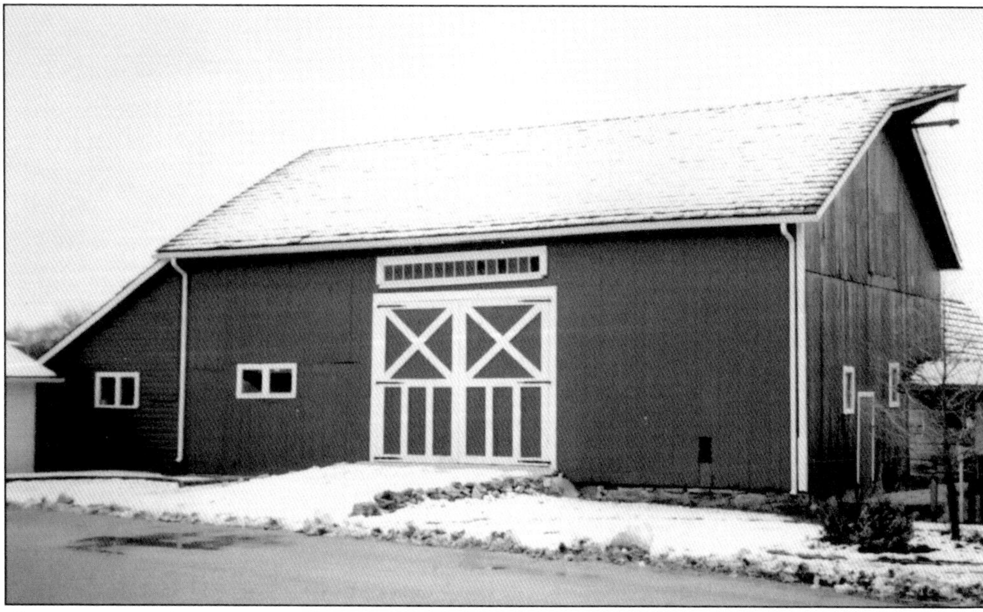

There are two barns (recently renovated) on the Durham-Perry Farmstead that were built between 1838 and 1845. Seen here, the larger barn, which is probably the oldest, reflects the design of the traditional three-bay English barn. Farmers once used the center bay as a threshing floor, and the two side bays were used either as storage or to shelter cows and horses. (Author's collection.)

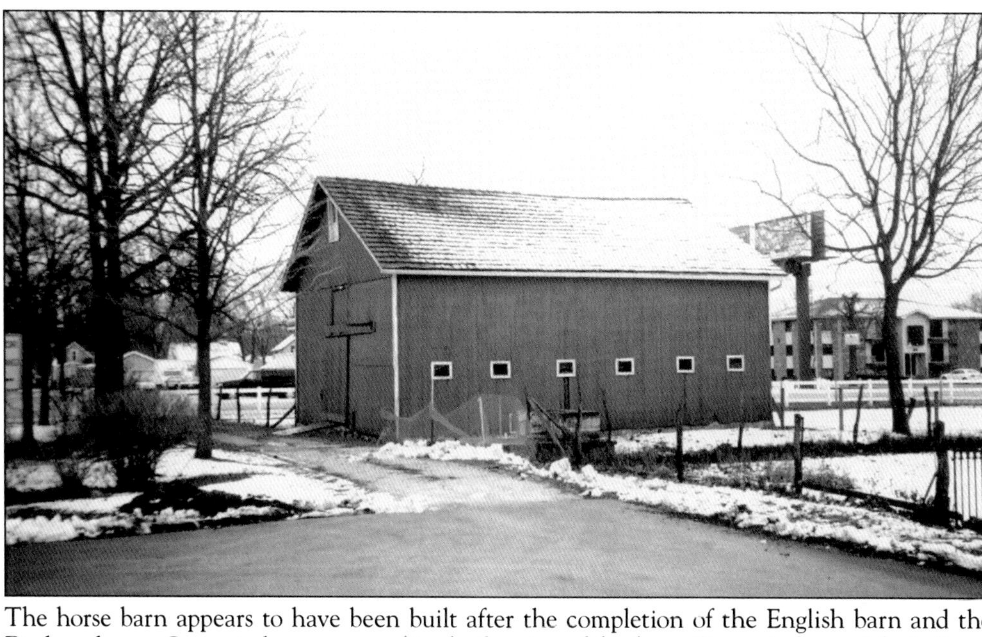

The horse barn appears to have been built after the completion of the English barn and the Durham house. Sawn timbers were used in the framing of this barn. Sawn timbers might indicate that the barn was built after the Perry-Worcester sawmill (see page 16) had begun operation. (Author's collection.)

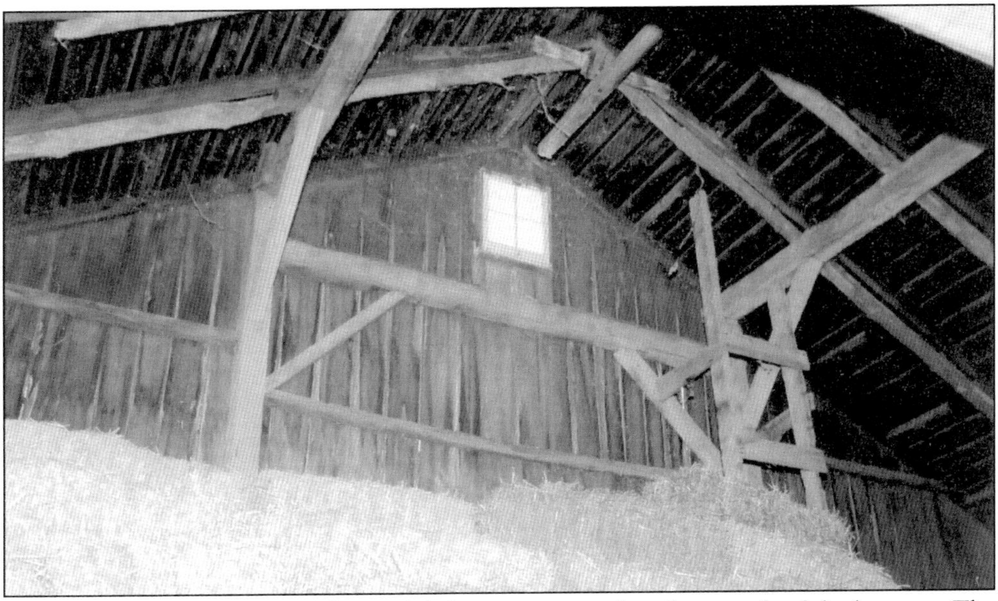

Timber frame construction of the English barn is seen in this photograph of the haymow. The roof rafters are the trunks of either pine or cedar trees and are not hewn. (RG.)

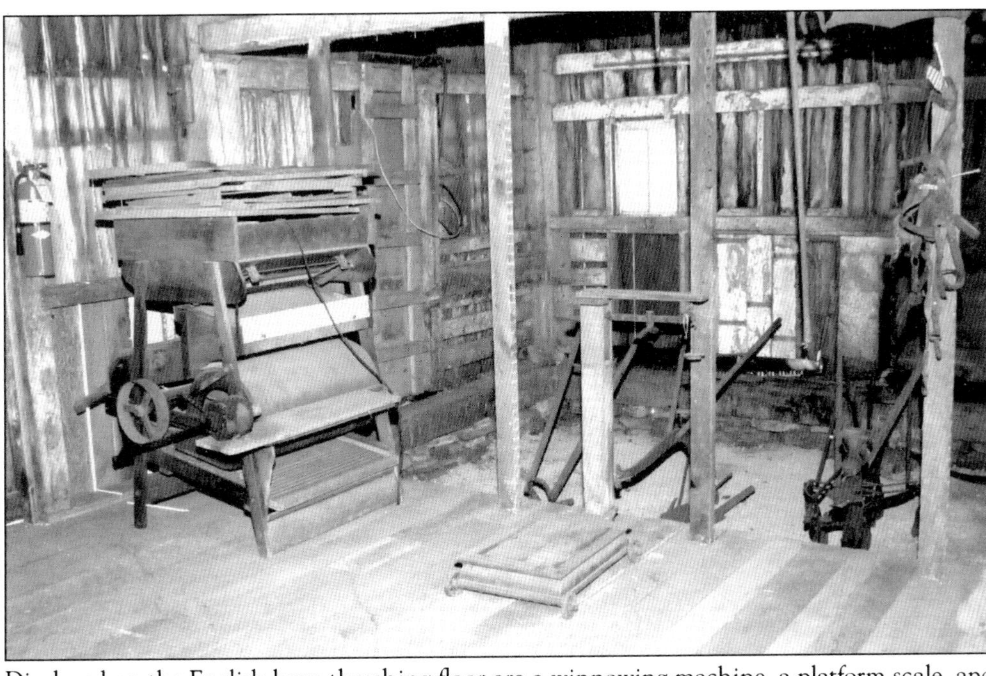

Displayed on the English barn threshing floor are a winnowing machine, a platform scale, and other tools used by farmers during the late 19th century and the early 20th century. The history of this farm from 1835 to 1986 records the transition from hand labor, horse powered farming to the mechanized farming in the 20th century. (RG.)

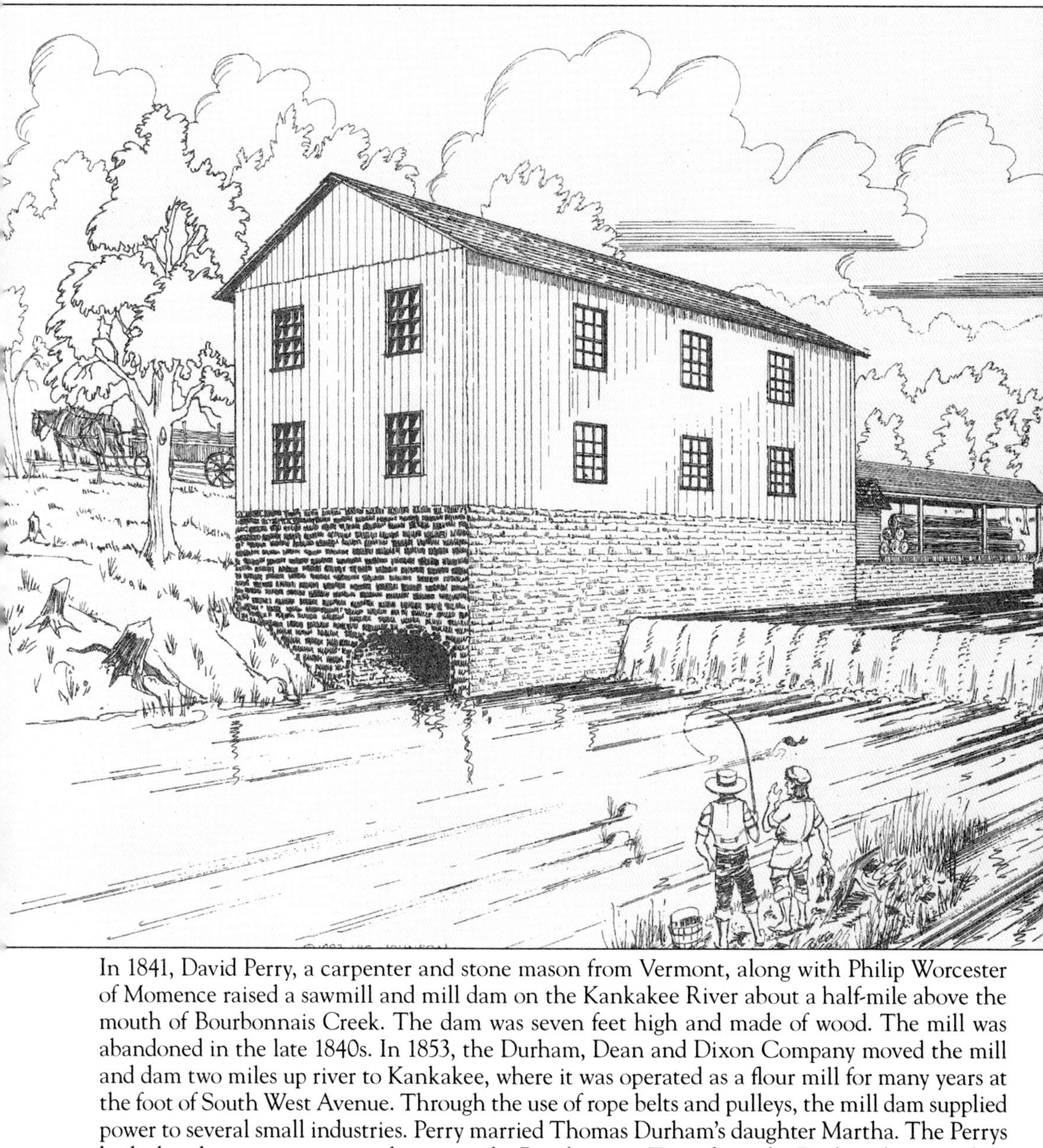

In 1841, David Perry, a carpenter and stone mason from Vermont, along with Philip Worcester of Momence raised a sawmill and mill dam on the Kankakee River about a half-mile above the mouth of Bourbonnais Creek. The dam was seven feet high and made of wood. The mill was abandoned in the late 1840s. In 1853, the Durham, Dean and Dixon Company moved the mill and dam two miles up river to Kankakee, where it was operated as a flour mill for many years at the foot of South West Avenue. Through the use of rope belts and pulleys, the mill dam supplied power to several small industries. Perry married Thomas Durham's daughter Martha. The Perrys built their home on a one-acre lot across the Bourbonnais Trace from the Durham home. When Perry's sole surviving heir, his granddaughter Lomira Perry, died in 1969, she left the farm in trust to the State of Illinois. In 1988, the state deeded the farm to the Bourbonnais Park District. The Durham-Perry Farmstead, part of the Perry Farm Park, was awarded National Register of Historic Places recognition in 2006. (Author's collection.)

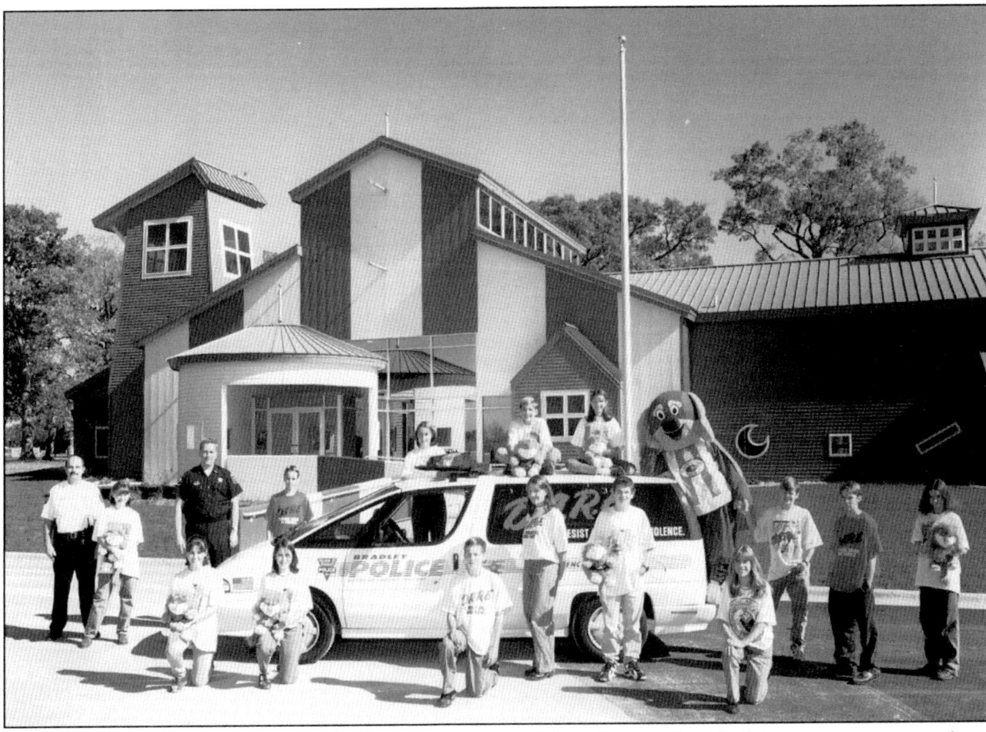

The Exploration Station is a children's museum. The idea to build this museum came from Marilyn O'Flaherty, a retired schoolteacher. She proposed the plan to the Bourbonnais Township Park District in the late 1980s. The building's exceptional, Distinguished Building Award–winning architecture was designed by Peter J. Exley in 1998. (RG.)

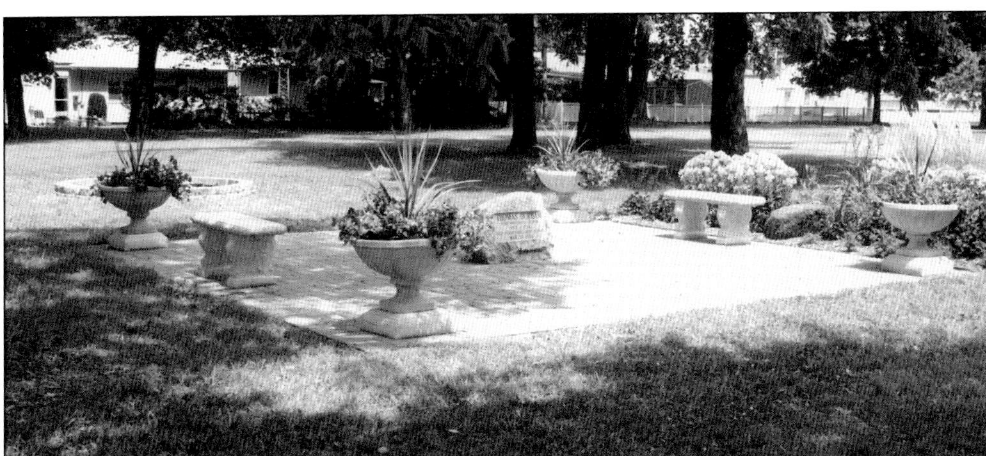

The last Perry farm tenant, Francis Duvoisin, recalled that as a child, Lomira told him that Thomas had been buried in the corner of his orchard. Archaeologist Robert Gergen, with the help of Duvoisin, found the long lost grave. The grave is now marked with a memorial stone. (Author's collection.)

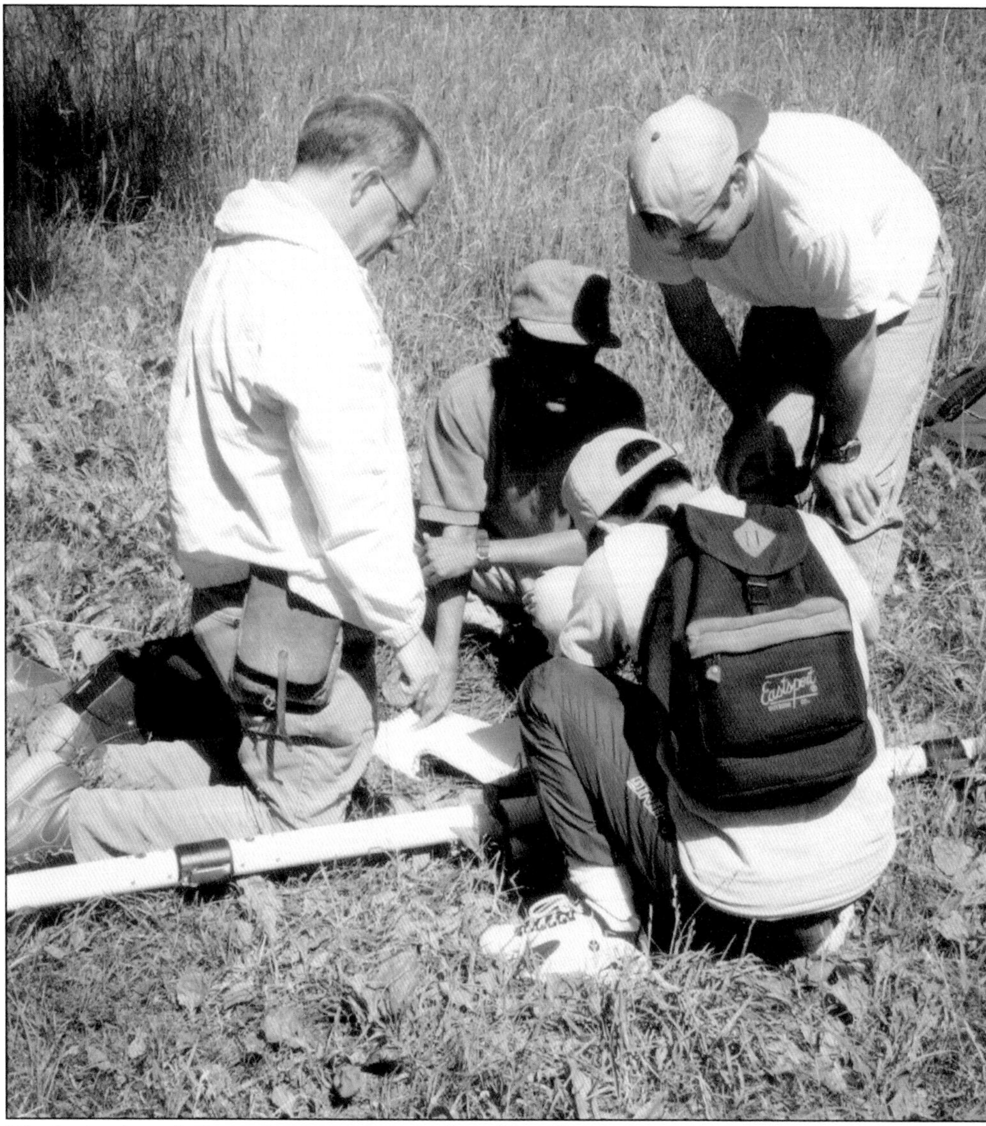

The bedrock underlying the Perry Farm Park and Bradley is 440- to 400-million-year-old Silurian limestone. The limestone contains fossils of animals and plants that once lived in a shallow, warm ocean. There are a few small sinkholes on the surface and numerous small caverns and channels eroded out by water within the limestone. In 1999, a team of student geologists from Northern Illinois University led by Prof. Philip J. Carpenter (on left) used electromagnetic conductivity profiling to trace these subsurface cavities. (Author's collection.)

Two

Birth of a Prairie Boomtown

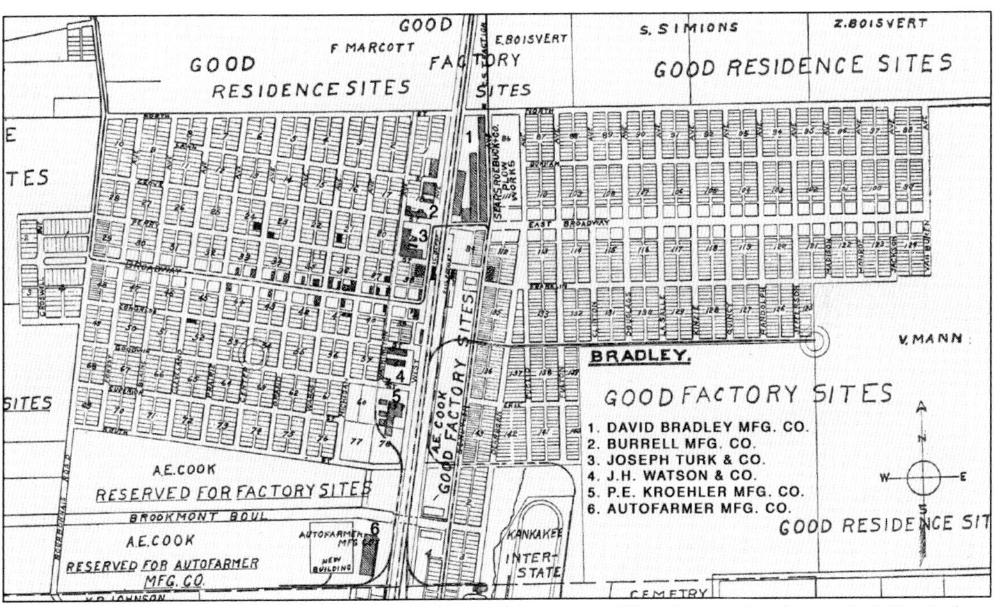

The Kankakee Commercial Association published this map of Bradley in a booklet titled, *Kankakee, Illinois: "Steady Growth—Not a Creation."* The Kankakee County Historical Society reprinted the booklet in 1985. Sites noted are West Bradley, platted September 7, 1891 (A); East Bradley, platted June 1, 1892 (B); Hardebeck's Park Addition (Woodlawn), platted February 21, 1893 (C); David Bradley Manufacturing Works (1); Burell Manufacturing Company (2); Joseph Turk Furniture Company (3); James A. Watson Sheet Metal Company (4); P. E. Kroehler Manufacturing Company (5); and Autofarmer Manufacturing Company (6). (Author's collection.)

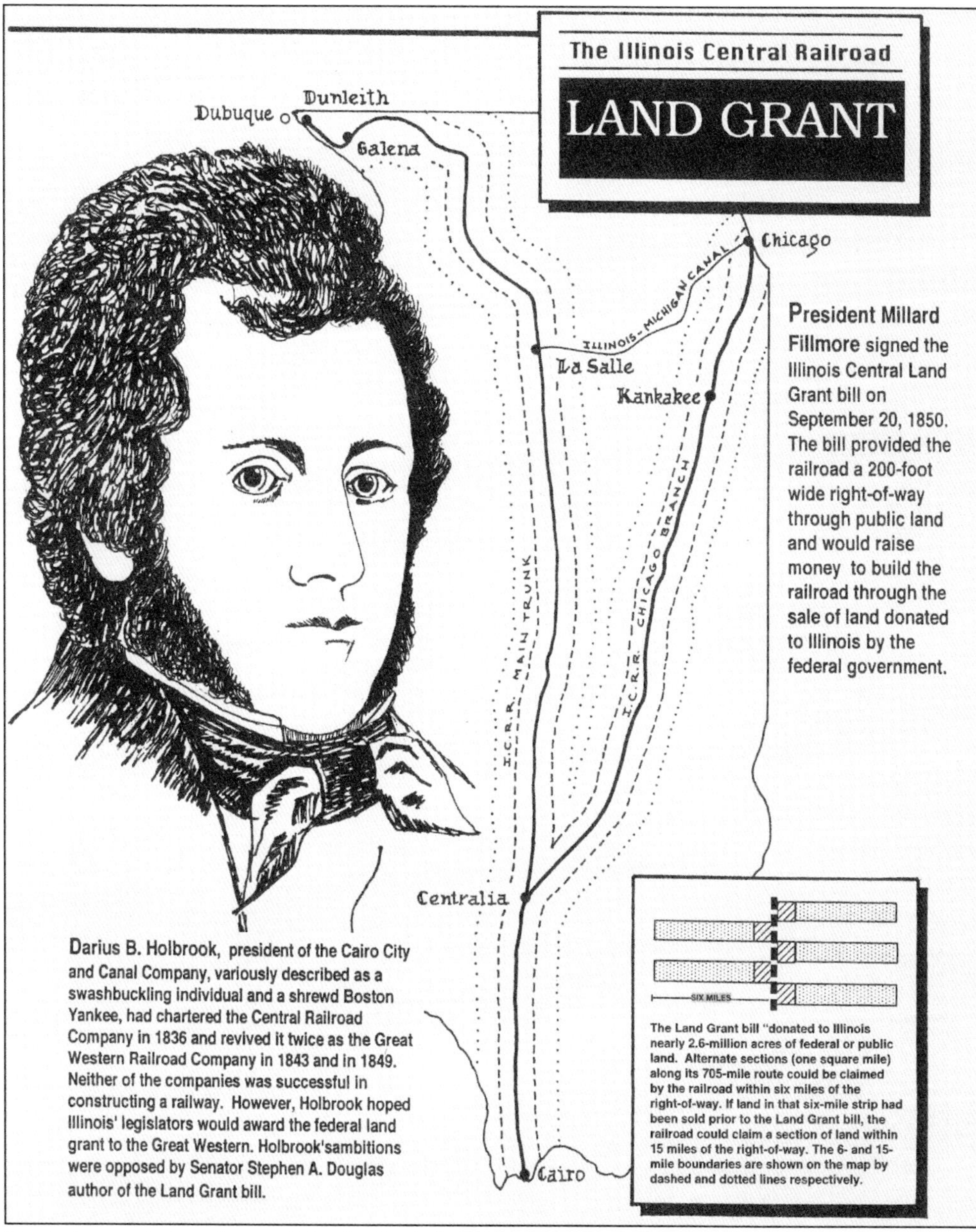

Kankakee and the village of North Kankakee (Bradley) were founded 39 years apart. Kankakee was founded when the country was largely agrarian, and North Kankakee was founded at the full tide of the industrial age. The Chicago branch of the Illinois Central Railroad played an important roll in the location of these settlements. In the 1850s, the proprietors of Kankakee saw the town's location in the heart of productive farmland as an ideal shipping point to send farm produce by rail into the Chicago markets. In the 1890s J. Herman Hardebeck realized the land could be better used for industrial expansion and capitalized on this idea by platting a factory town astride a main rail transportation artery. He then convinced manufacturers to remove from their crowded city sites to the hinterlands of Kankakee County. (Author's collection.)

Stephan A. Douglas, born in Vermont in 1813, was elected to the U.S. Senate from Illinois in 1847. He submitted a land grant bill in 1859 that paved the way for the building of the Illinois Central Railroad. Had Douglas not insisted that the plan include a "Chicago Branch," there probably would not have been a Kankakee or a Bradley. The original Cairo City and Canal Company plan called only for a railway from Cairo to Galena. The land grant proposal received significant support from John S. Wright, founder and editor of the *Prairie Farmer.* Abraham Lincoln, a member of the house, urged land grant aid for the proposed central railroad. Railroad quarry men took limestone from Wiley Creek to build the Kankakee River bridge buttresses (below). Railroad engineers used Wendell Bollman's revolutionary truss structure to span the river with two decks. Rail traffic used the upper deck; horses, wagons, and pedestrians crossed on the lower deck toll bridge. (Right, author's collection; below, KCM.)

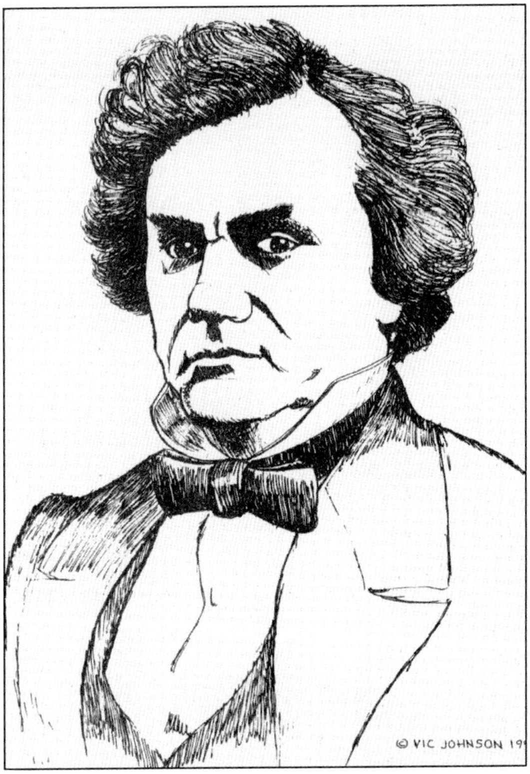

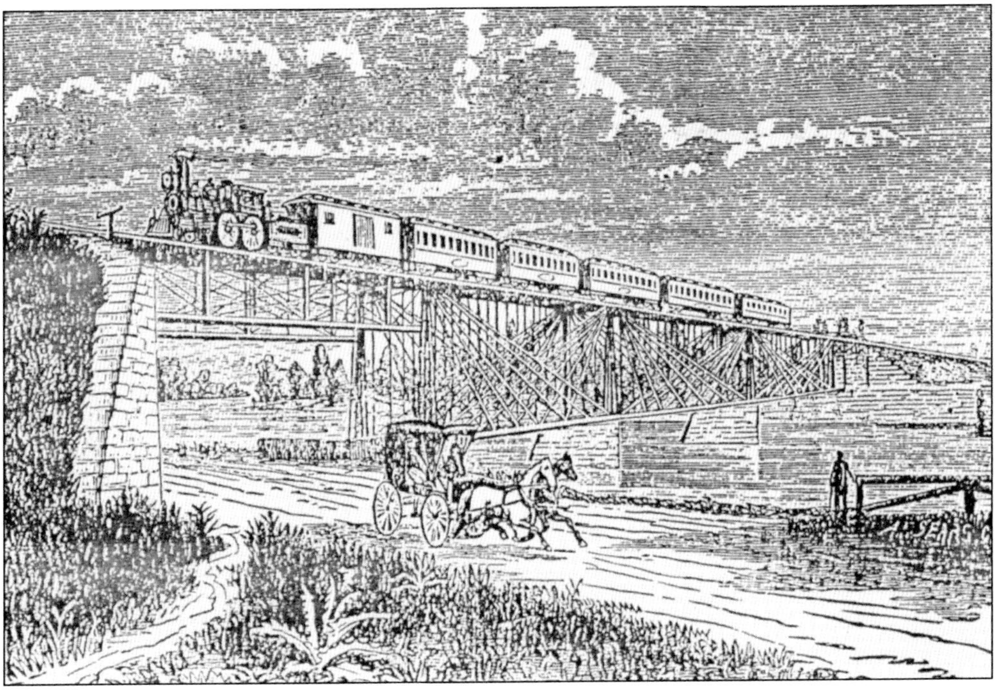

..THE..

NORTH KANKAKEE BOOM

THE GREATEST OPPORTUNITY OF A LIFE TIME
To Invest Your Surplus Funds and Savings and
MAKE SOME MONEY.

This Property will Double in Value in Twelve Months.
Get Some of This Property While it is Within Reach
AND MAKE MONEY.

This is the Best Location for a Manufacturing Town in Illinois.

...JUST PLATTED...

ELECTRIC LIGHTS-COMPLETE SYSTEM WATER WORKS

ADJOINS THE CITY OF KANKAKEE AND THE VILLAGE OF BOURBONNAIS

3 LARGE MANUFACTORIES
Already Located, with 300,000 Feet or
7 Acres of Floor Space.

3

3-MORE-MAMMOTH-FACTORIES
Already in Operation in Kankakee, turning
out Carloads of Manufactured Product.

AND MORE OF THEM ARE COMING...

...The Boom for Kankakee is Here to Stay

BETTER OPPORTUNITIES FOR INVESTMENTS AND FINE LOCATIONS
For Manufacturing Plants than is offered in Harvey or any other town in the State.

NORTH KANKAKEE joins Kankakee City on the north and the Village of Bourbonnais on the south, and is directly on the Illinois Central Railroad, and in connection with four other lines of road—the Big 4, K. & S., K. & S. W. and the Three I—the latter a belt line running around Chicago,

MAKING ITS SHIPPING FACILITIES BETTER

than can be offered by any other town in the State outside of the Metropolis, with Chicago rates to all points. The Central will build both Passenger and Freight depots here. An

ELECTRIC STREET RAILWAY

will run direct from Kankakee through the Plat to Bourbonnais in a direct line. The three factories already located will have a capacity of 1150 employes. All the factories located in the new town are under an iron clad guarantee contract to fulfill their part of the contract. Their pay roll will amount to between $15,000 to $30,000 per month, which is cash every two weeks. The land on which the site is located consists of as rich land as can be found anywhere, and will make beautiful building sites.

WANTED...
ALL KINDS OF BUSINESS

Grocers, Dry Goods, Hardware, Drug Stores, Bakers, Hotels, Boarding Houses Etc., to Locate Here Immediately.

A GOOD OPENING FOR A FIRST-CLSS BANK.

By the time their buildings are up and they are ready for business there will be
BUSINESS TO BE DONE.

BEING within easy reach of the Illinois Coal Mines, cheap fuel is assured. At Burbonnais is St. Viateur's College, one of the leading Educational Institutions of the State, with 300 students now enrolled, and an increase to 500 or 1000 in the near future expected, and which is rapidly becoming a strong competitor of Notre Dame in Indiana; and here also is Notre Dame Convent, while the Public Schools and St. Joseph's Convent at Kankakee offer

Unsurpassed Educational Advantages

Kankakee is nearly a "City of Churches," having thirteen of different denominations. The site is within a stone's throw of the beautiful Kankakee river, where is fine fishing and magnificent picnic grounds. The fare to Chicago by commutation tickets is 18 cents up, making a trip up to the metropolis possible every day, and there are eighteen passenger trains a day between these points. The best building stone and sand on the ground. The new Illinois Central round house and part of their shops are now building, all located within 1200 feet of this ground. Here you have all city advantages without the heavy city taxes. The price of lots will certainly advance when improvements begin. Investigate this at once. No more paying investment offered anywhere.

A POPULATION OF 4000 GUARANTEED BY JULY 1, 1892. 400 DWELLING HOUSES WANTED AT ONCE

Kankakee now has a Population of 10,000
which will soon be 20,000.

The Sale of Lots at Private Sale will begin
September 6, 1891.

FOR - FULL - INFORMATION
regarding North Kankakee and what it offers to investors call on or address - - - - - - -

J. H. HARDEBECK
ROOM 5 ARCADE BLDG, KANKAKEE, ILL.

DON'T WAIT.
Investigate Now. Strike while the Iron is Hot and Prices Low

Reprinted from the August 27, 1891, Kankakee Gazette
by the Bradley Centennial Book Committee
(C) 1991 Village of Bradley, Illinois

Full page advertisement printed in the August 7, 1891, edition of the *Kankakee Gazette.*

J. Herman Hardebeck used this full-page advertisement in the August 7, 1891, *Kankakee Gazette* to kick off the sale of property in North Kankakee. (BHS.)

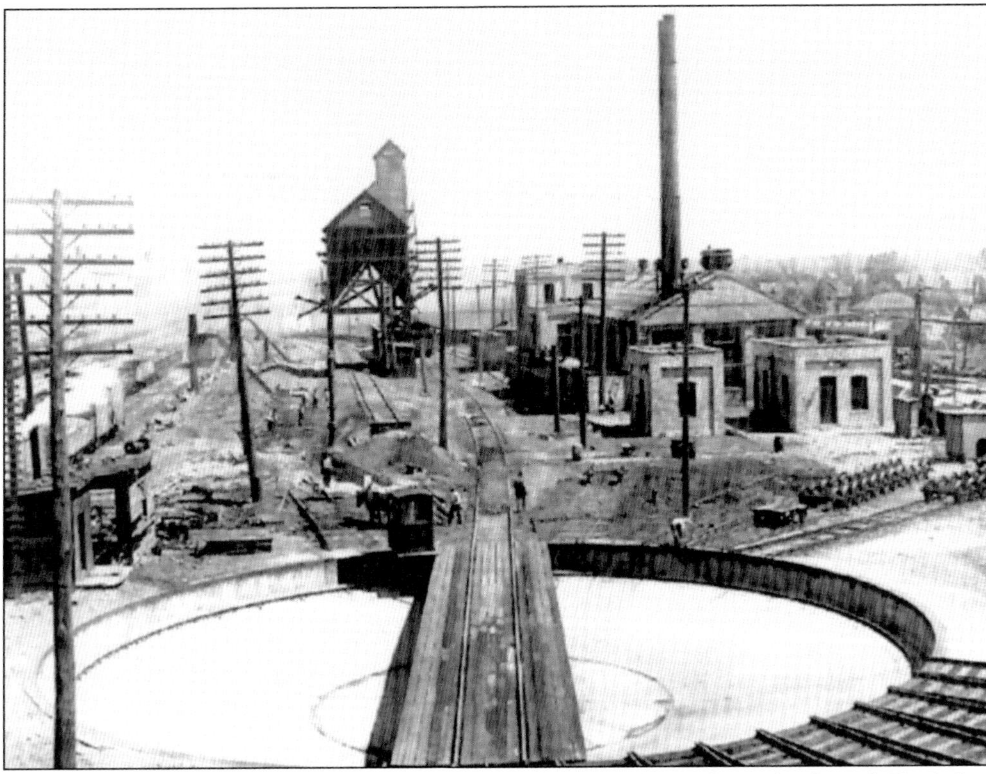

By December 1891, work on the Illinois Central Railroad freight yards south of North Kankakee was nearly finished. This photograph, taken in 1918, shows the yards, roundhouse turntable, coaling station, and machine shop. Dimly seen on the left between the telephone poles is the Kroehler Furniture Manufacturing Company. (ICRR Photo, ICHS Collection courtesy of the Illinois Central Historical Society.)

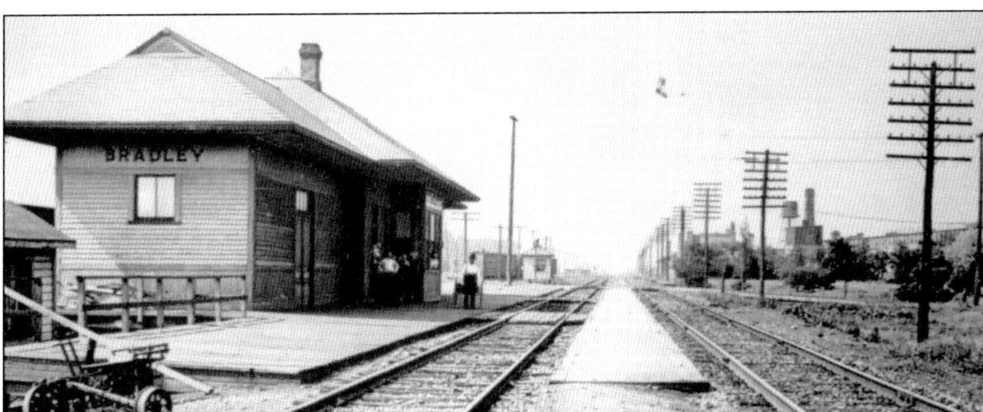

The North Kankakee Illinois Central Railroad depot was built on the east side of West Avenue between West Broadway and Perry Street in 1892. Four trains stopped there daily; two in the morning and two in the afternoon. The Bradley Manufacturing Works can be seen on the right. Until 1926, when the Broadway underpass opened, Perry Street was where the traffic and pedestrians crossed the railroad. Streetcars crossed one block further north on Grove Street. (BHS.)

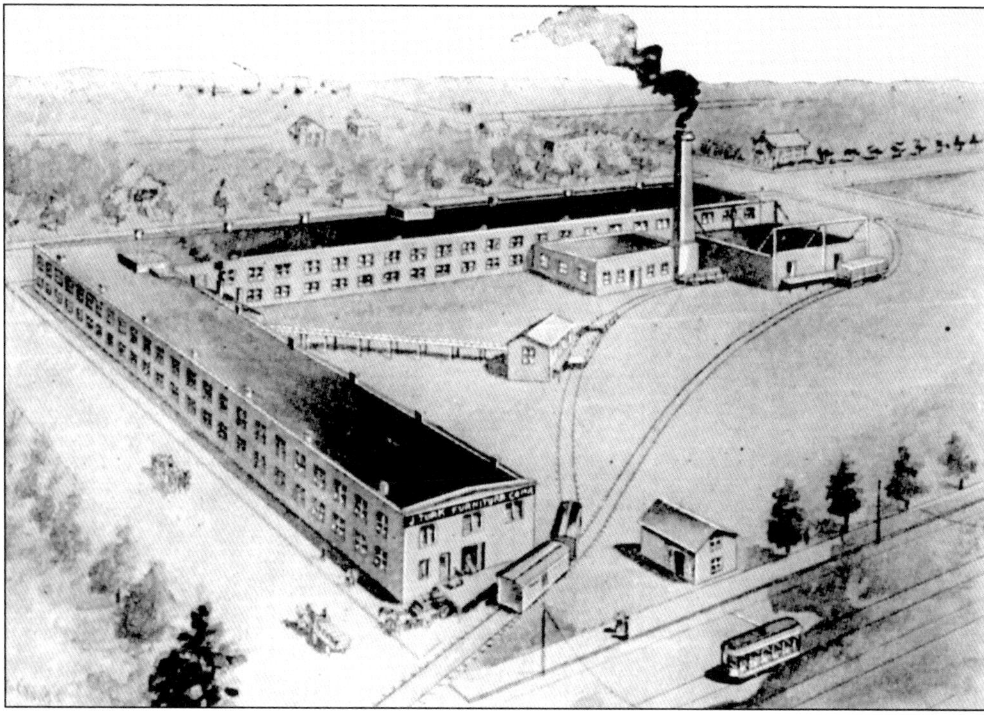

Turk and Lozier of Chicago broke ground for their North Kankakee factory in the 200 block of North Washington Avenue on October 8, 1891. This drawing is one of the earliest views of the factory. (BHS.)

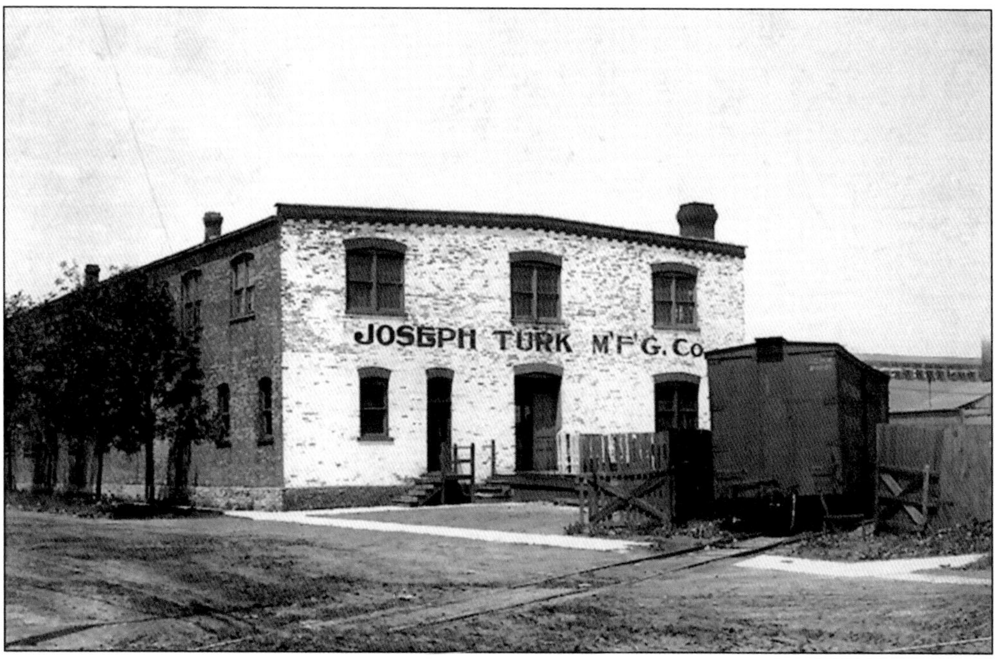

By August 25, 1892, gold leaf block letters on the front of the building said, "Joseph Turk Furniture Co." This photograph was taken at a later date. Over the years, the company manufactured bicycle frames, metal beds and furniture, and shower baths. (BHS.)

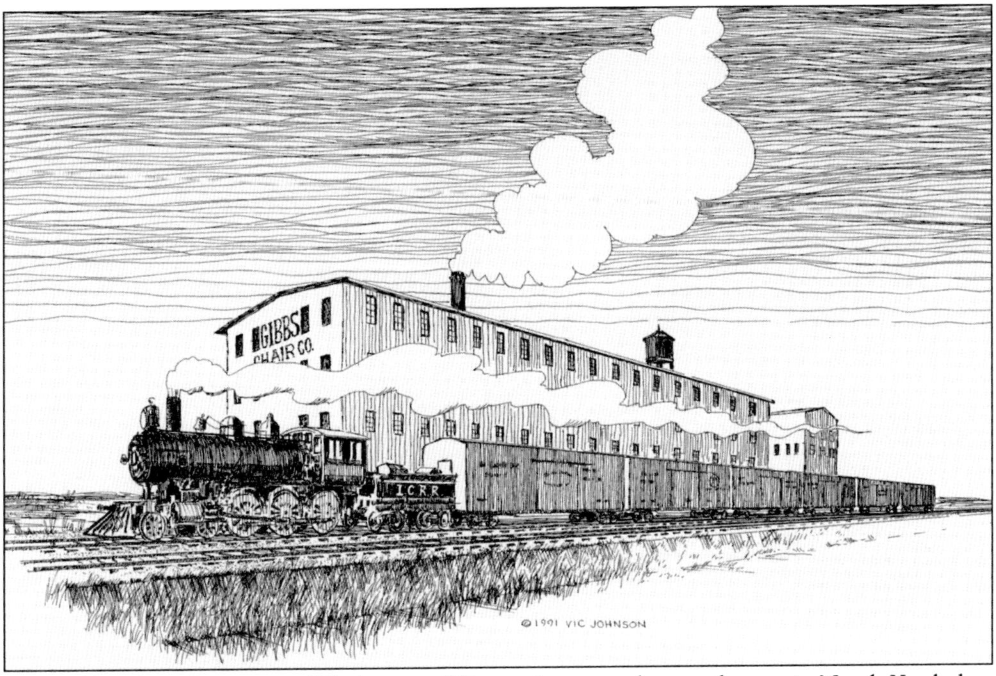

The Gibbs Chair Company of Sheboygan, Wisconsin, opened a new factory in North Kankakee in 1892. It operated out of two buildings on the west side of the Illinois Central Railroad tracks. The Gibbs Chair Company did not survive the financial depression in 1893. Two days after Christmas that year, the *Kankakee Gazette* announced that the Wakefield Rattan Company of Massachusetts had bought the Gibbs factory. Manufacturing in the factory ended in 1896. (Author's collection.)

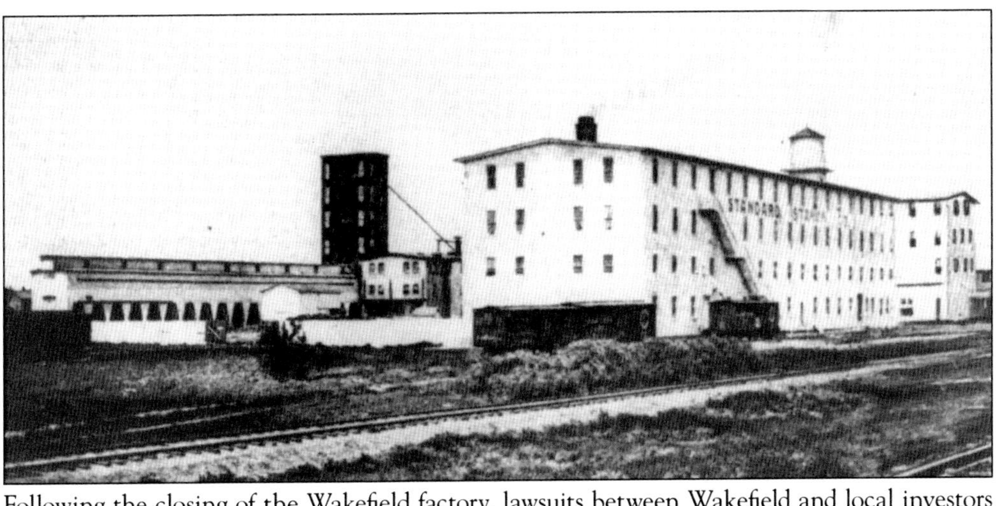

Following the closing of the Wakefield factory, lawsuits between Wakefield and local investors put the future of the company buildings in doubt. Investors managed to gain control of the site and plans were made to bring in new companies. By March 1900, the Standard Starch Company had added other buildings and began making cornstarch. On March 11, 1901, an explosion and fire destroyed what was believed to be the world's largest starch factory. (Thomas J. Lindsay.)

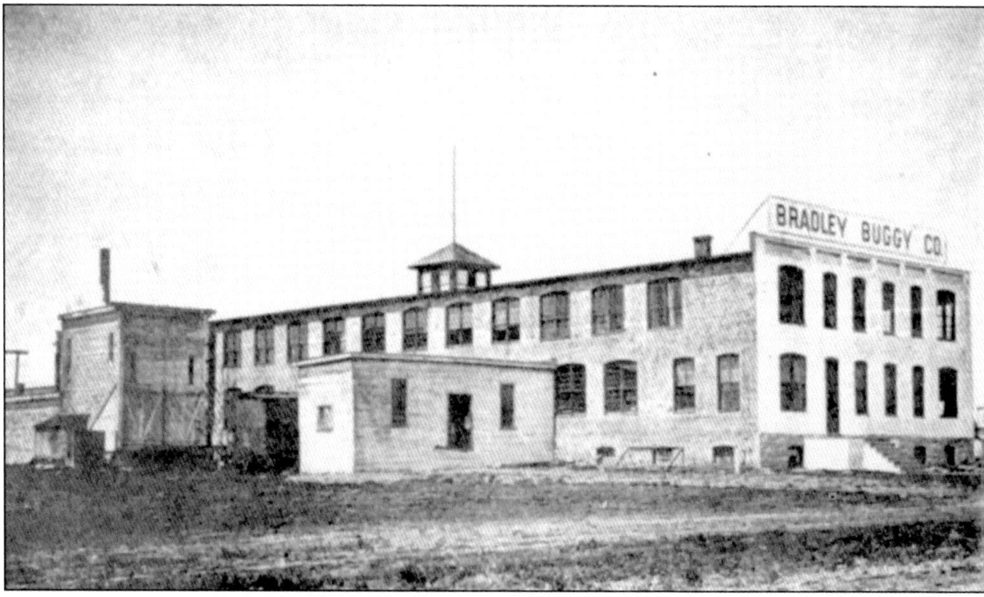

The buildings occupied by the Bradley Buggy Company (established by Grogan Carriage Works of Ohio) were built in the winter of 1891–1892 for the Ideal Folding Bed Company. In April 1892, Ideal was in operation. Later that year, the *Kankakee Gazette* said the factory was producing folding beds and toilet tables. The company employed 50 workers. A year later, it became the first casualty of the 1893 panic. The next occupant of the site was the Bradley Buggy Company. Sometime in the early 1900s, it passed into history. The James H. Watson Company, maker of water tanks, eaves, troughs, and metal ceilings, is the last known manufacturer to hold title to the buildings. (Above, BHS; below, KCM.)

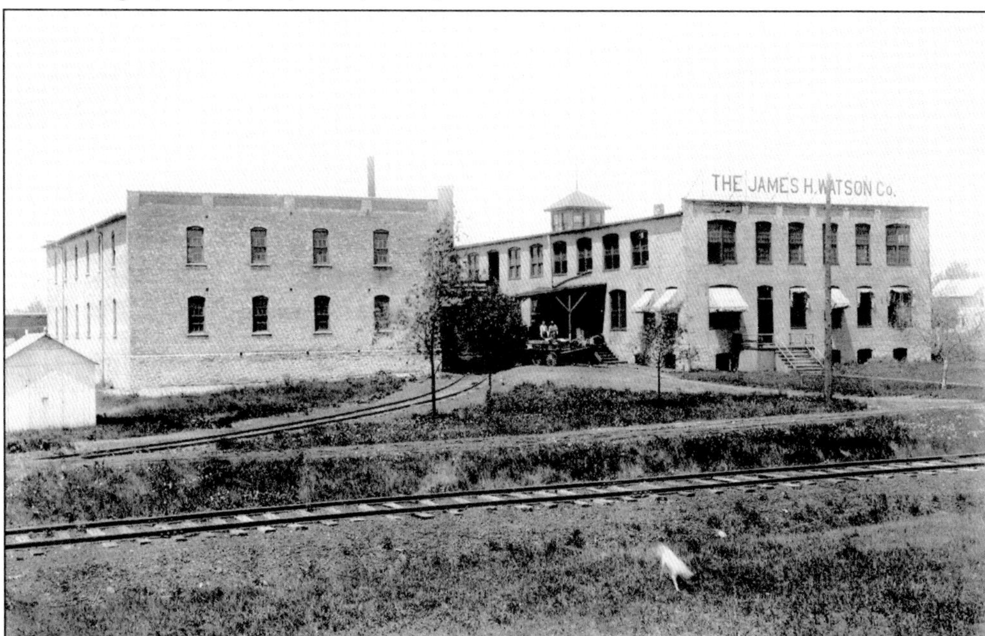

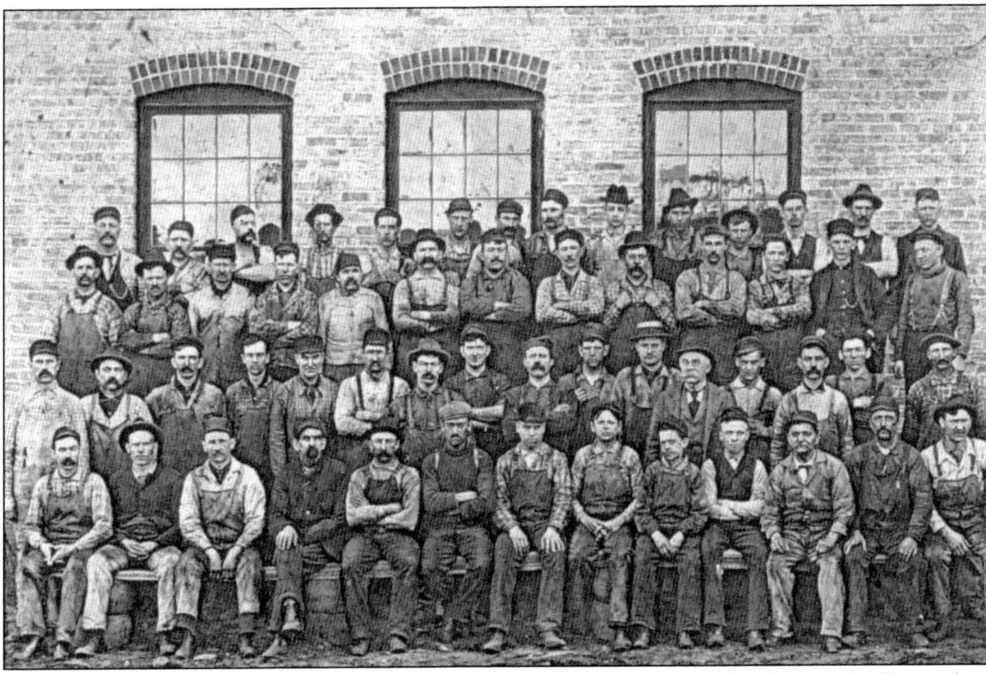

These factory workers (above) are unidentified, as is the factory in the background. The workers are typical of those who came to work in the North Kankakee factories. The managers and office workers of the James H. Watson Company (below) stand in front of the factory on a winter's day. The men are wearing hats and coats, but the ladies, curiously, are only in shirtwaist. Perhaps it was a last-minute invitation? (BHS.)

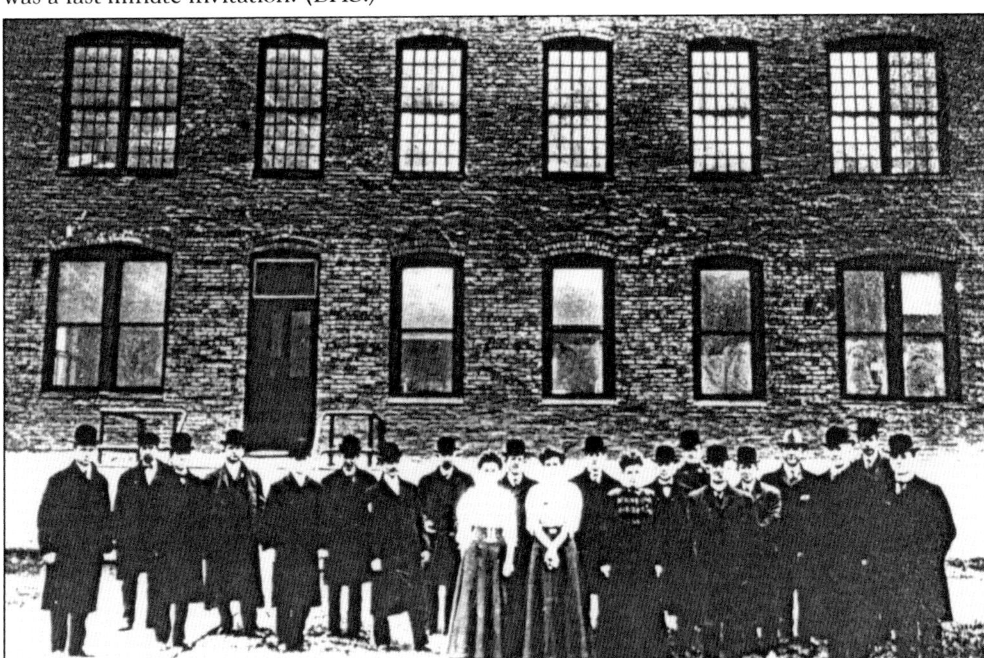

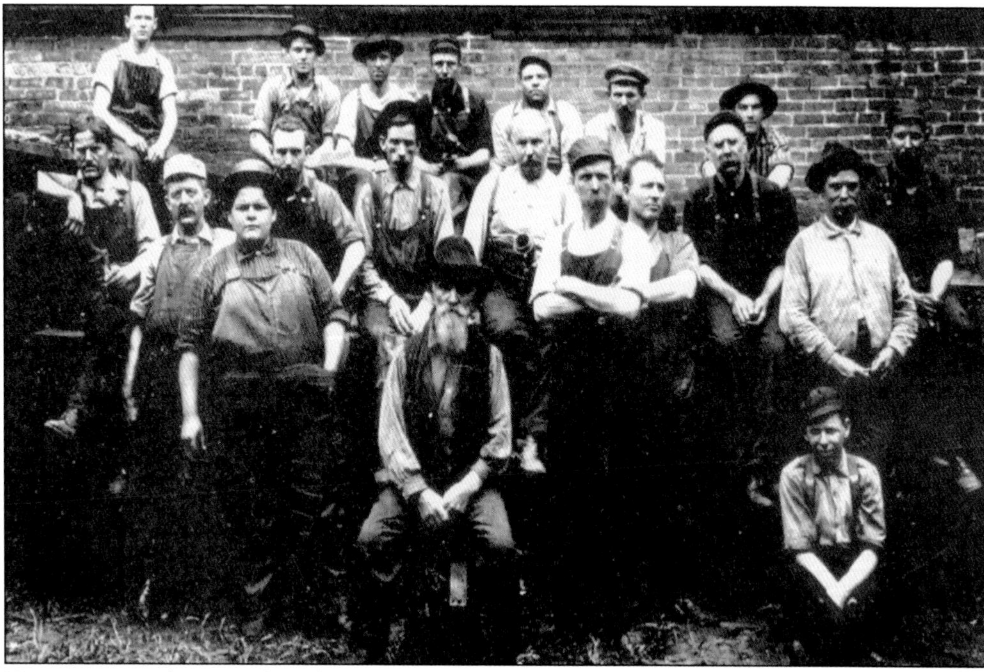

Here is a second group of unidentified laborers. The old gentleman in the foreground has been given a seat of honor. (BHS.)

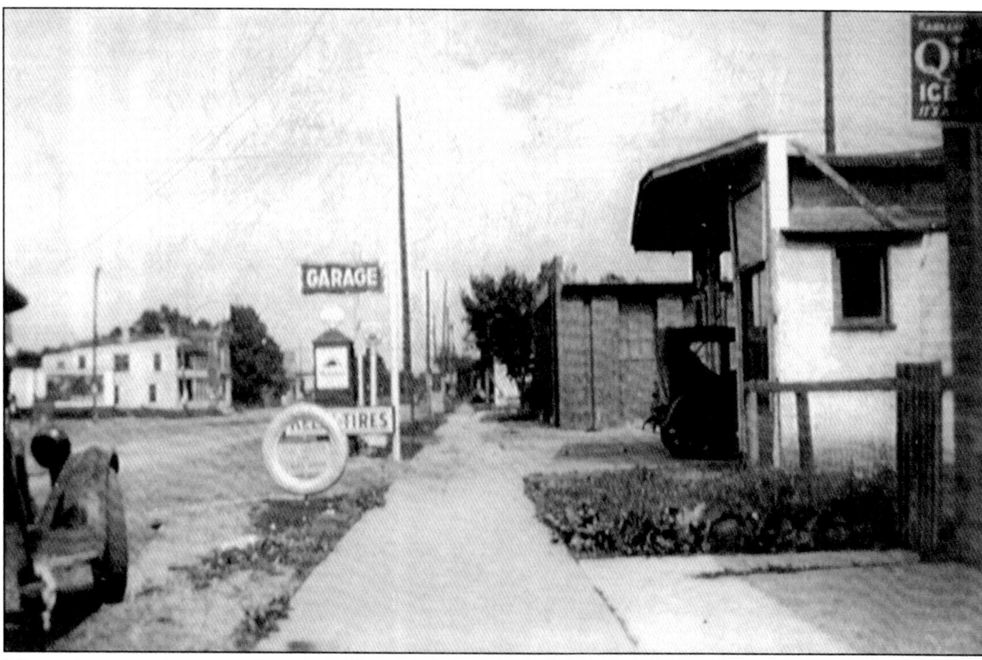

This photograph was taken on the south side of the 300 block of West Broadway, looking east, in the early 1920s. A corner of the old Bear Brand building is near the center of the picture. (RB.)

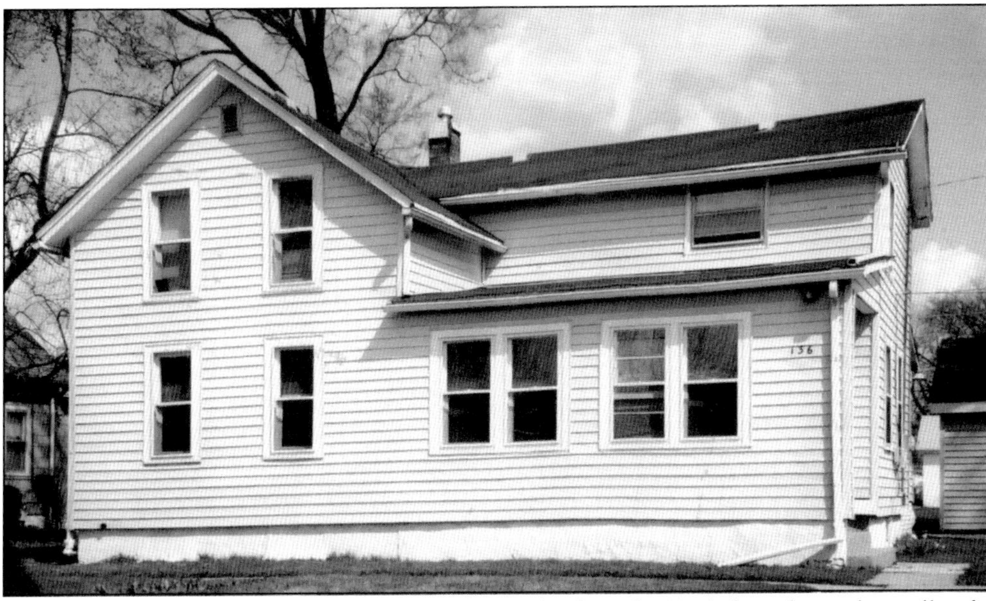

In Burt E. Burroughs's *Legends and Tales of Homeland on the Kankakee*, the author tells of a notable wartime oyster supper at the home of Gurdon Durham. The dinner was held during the dark days of the Civil War. The host, named by his father after his friend Gurdon S. Hubbard, the noted frontier trader and Chicago land developer, lived in a house that stood, according to Burroughs, near "the big front door of the east building of the Bradley factory." Today that house (above), moved and much renovated, is on North Fulton Avenue. An even older house (below) on North Clinton Avenue once belonged to Thomas Durham's son-in-law John Worrel. It survived until a recent encounter with a bulldozer. Worrel came to Illinois from North Carolina and married Durham's daughter Arabella. In September 1892, the *Kankakee Gazette* noted that the "old Worrel homestead on the east side is in the hands of carpenters and plasterers, when thoroughly renovated, Mr. Johnson, the engineer of the Demme and Dierkes factory will move into it." (Author's collection.)

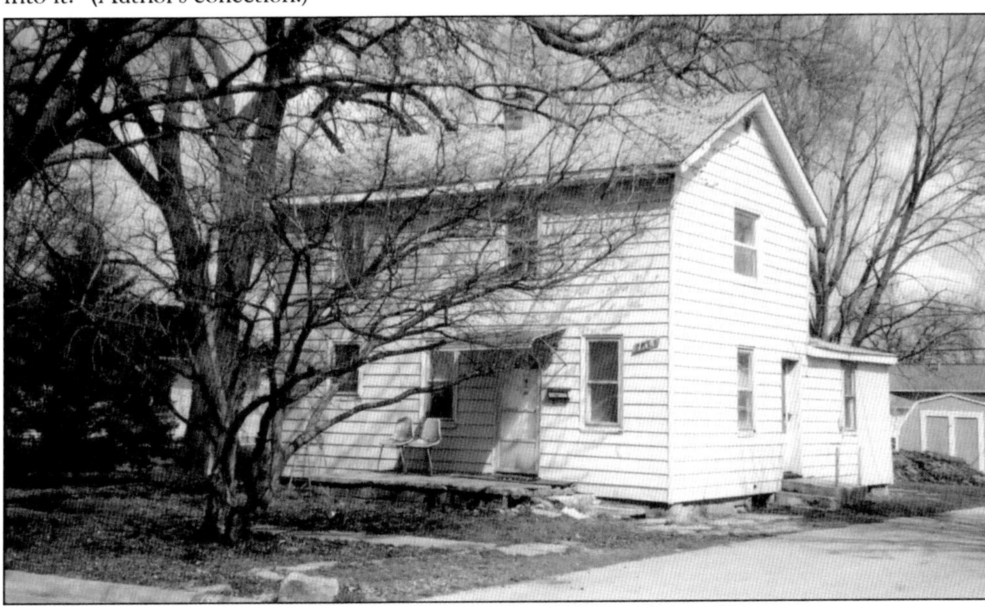

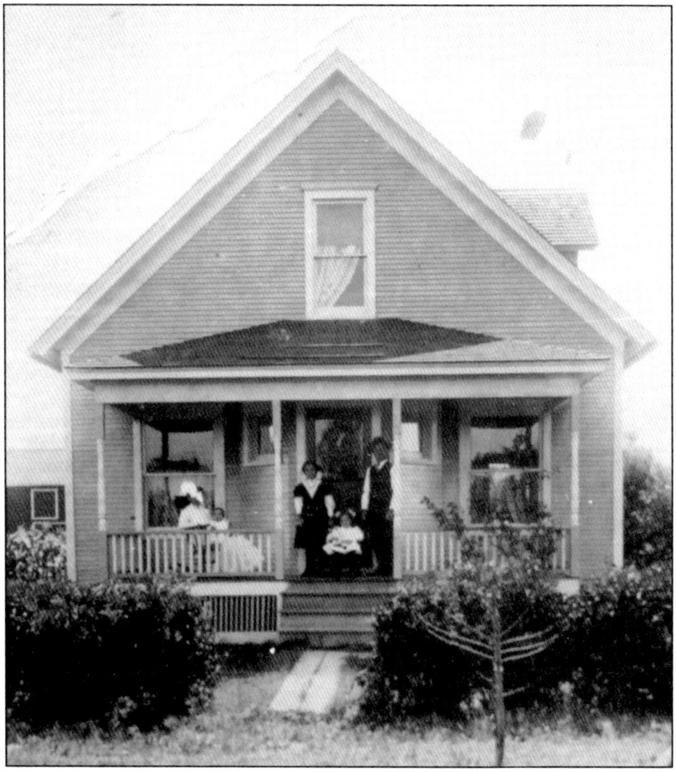

The Mathilda and John Ott house stood at 422 North Center Avenue. Pictured, from left to right, is Mathilda holding baby Herald, Anna (standing), Mildred in the rocking chair, and John. This is the second house in Bradley to have electricity. The wiring was installed by Ed Stelter, who first wired his own house. (Shirley Manley.)

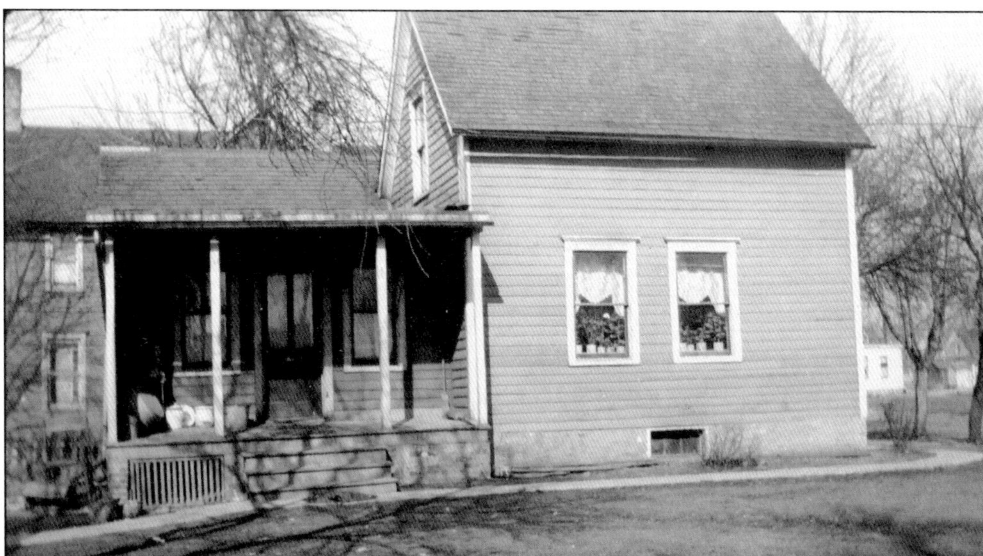

Because of its cherry orchard, this home, built in 1903, became known as Cherry Hill. First it was the home of Soren Rasmussen, and later, Ray Rasmussen. Most of the homes built during the late 1890s and early 1900s were small, simple one or one-and-a-half story houses. (Beverly Rasmussen.)

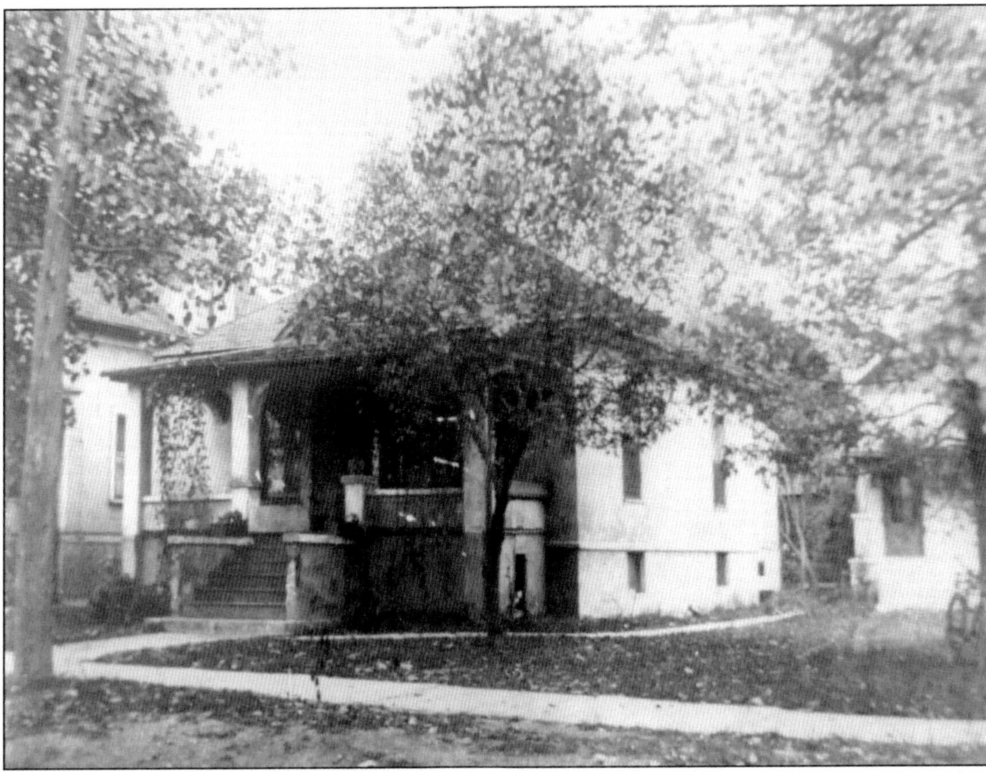

By the 1920s, larger houses dotted the neighborhoods. James Vaughn built this stucco bungalow at 288 South Schuyler Avenue in the 1920s. It is one of a handful of similar houses built at about the same time on South Schuyler Avenue. (Beverly Rasmussen.)

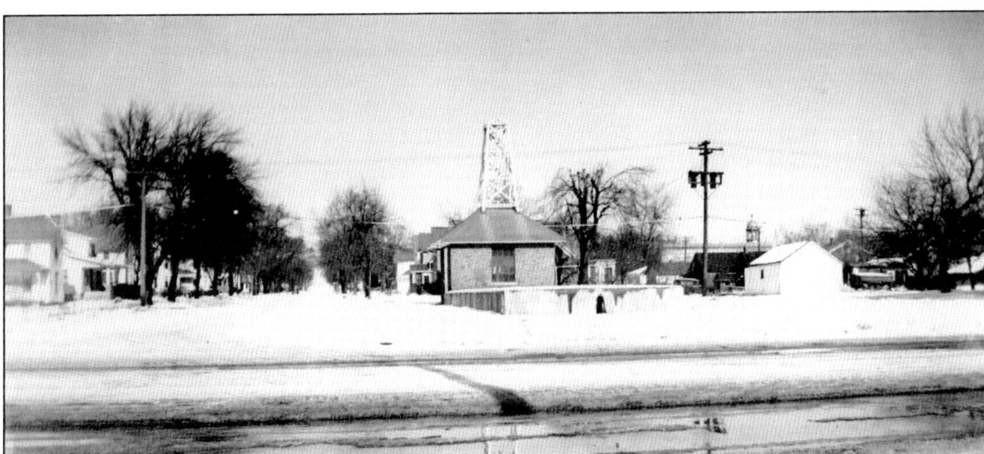

Looking north in the 1940s across Broadway and down a snow-covered Prairie Avenue, the bell tower of St. Joseph church is seen to the right of the telephone pole. In the center of the picture is a pump house for one of the village wells and the cement cover of a large water storage tank. (CE.)

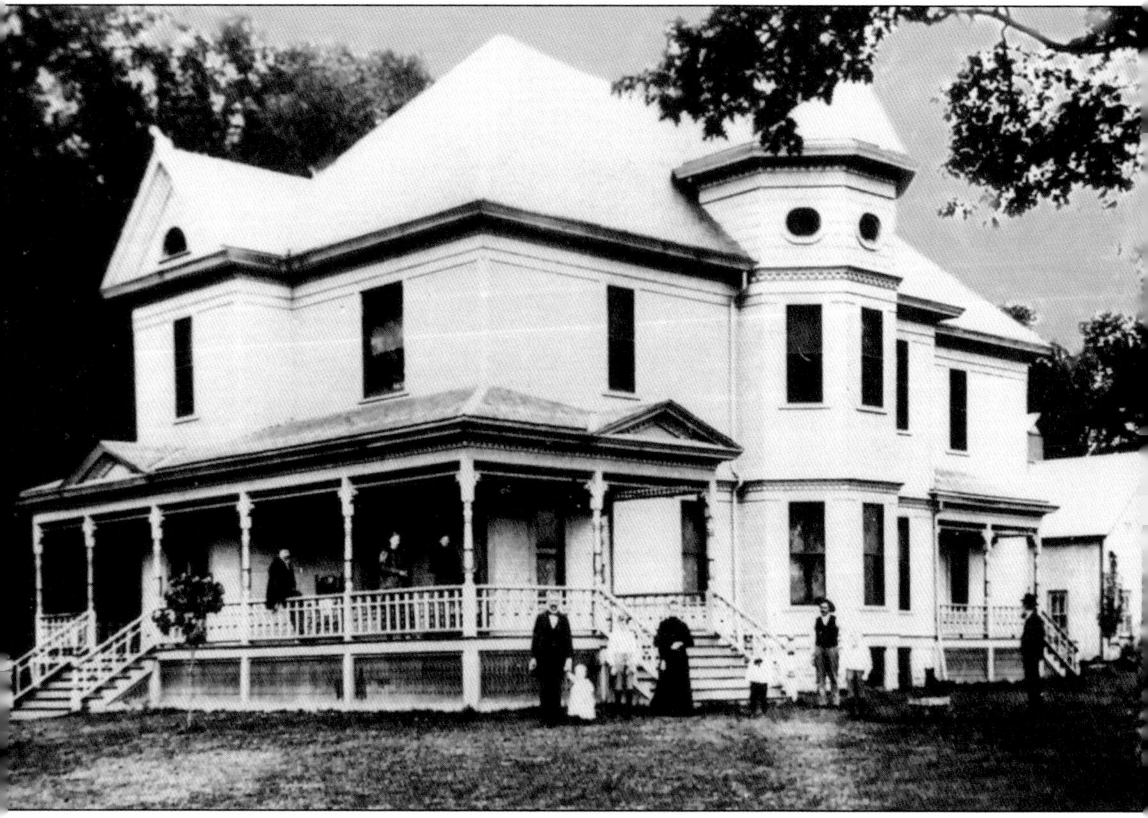

J. Herman Hardebeck planned an exclusive development on 20 wooded acres of the Durham-Perry Farmstead west of what had been the old Bourbonnais Trace (renamed Vasseur Avenue; now known as Kennedy Drive). The plant managers, merchants, and professional people were to live there. No house costing less than $2,000 would be allowed on the 50-by-200-foot lots. Hardebeck built his two-story, 16-room Victorian mansion on the corner of Vasseur Avenue and Herman Place as a model for others. A divided parkway lead west for a mile to a river bridge Hardebeck planned to build. But the managers and people of wealth were lured away to the Riverview district of Kankakee, where another visionary capitalist, Emory Cobb, had established his subdivision along the river's shore and among the ancient oaks of Cobb's Woods. The Hardebeck house was razed in August 1988 to make way for a shopping complex. (BHS.)

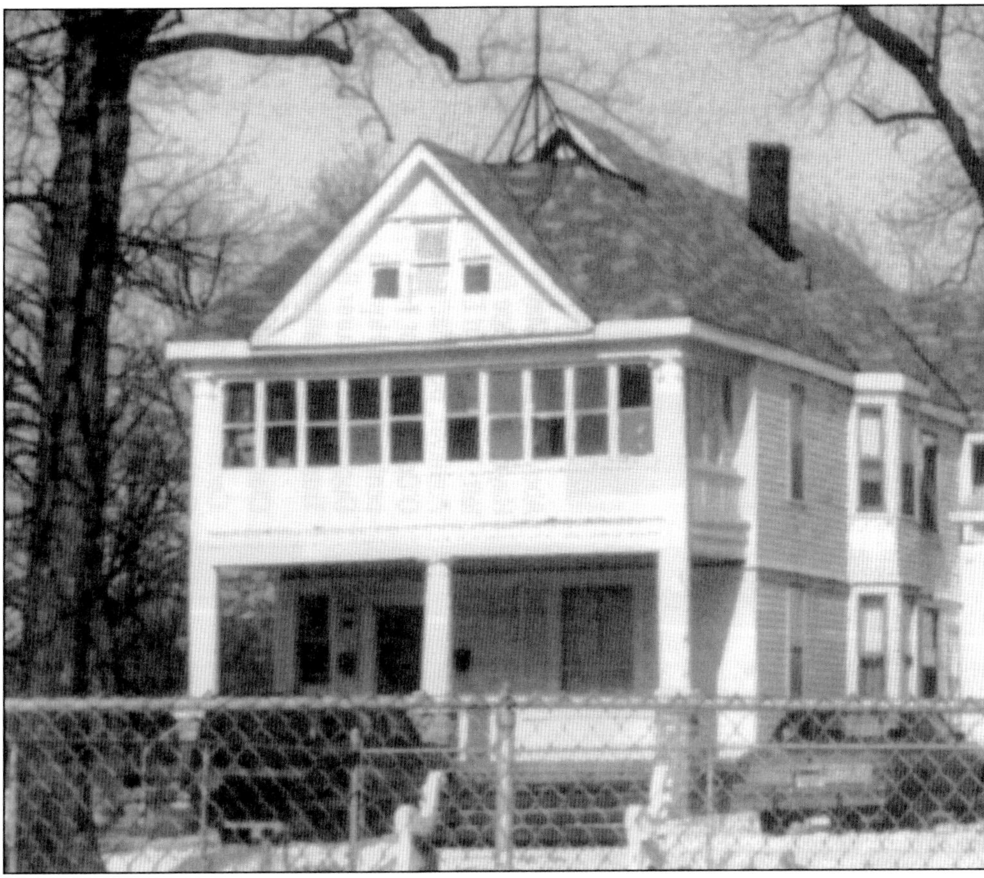

The only 1890s house still standing on Herman Place is this one, now divided into apartments. J. Herman Hardebeck sold the lot to the superintendent of construction for David Bradley, William Brunnemer, on October 7, 1895. Because Brunnemer's name and the names of Cora, Minnie, and Wang Brunnemer appear in the 1895 city directory, it is possible that he built this house shortly after buying the lot for $1,400. Over the years, the house passed through several hands. At one time, it had the unsavory reputation as being a "sporting" house. (BHS.)

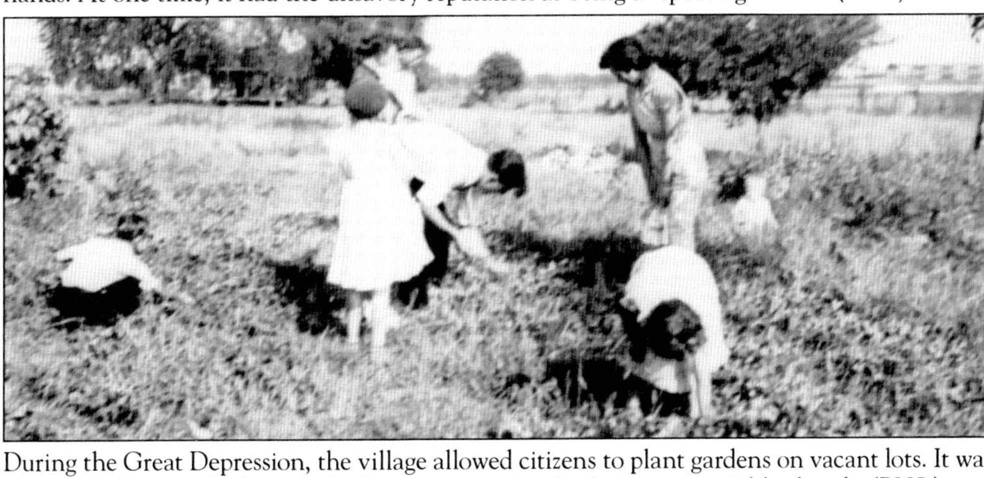

During the Great Depression, the village allowed citizens to plant gardens on vacant lots. It was not unusual to see chickens and a few cows roaming freely in some neighborhoods. (BHS.)

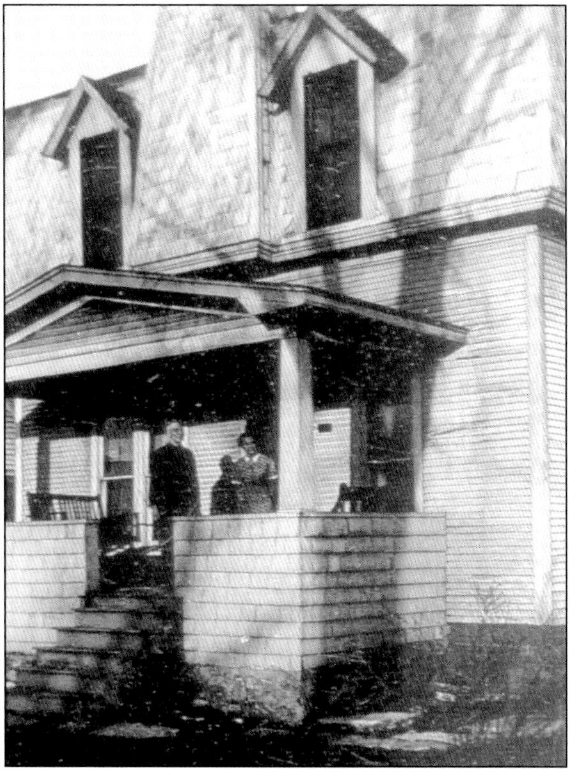

The Fred and Nelda Brosseau home at 148 North Cleveland Avenue has a distinctive Mansard roof and other touches, such as the window pediments, which reflect a Victorian Second Empire design. The styling is unusual for an era (1885–1930) when more decorative Beaux-Arts ornamentation was favored. (Janice Brosseau Sims.)

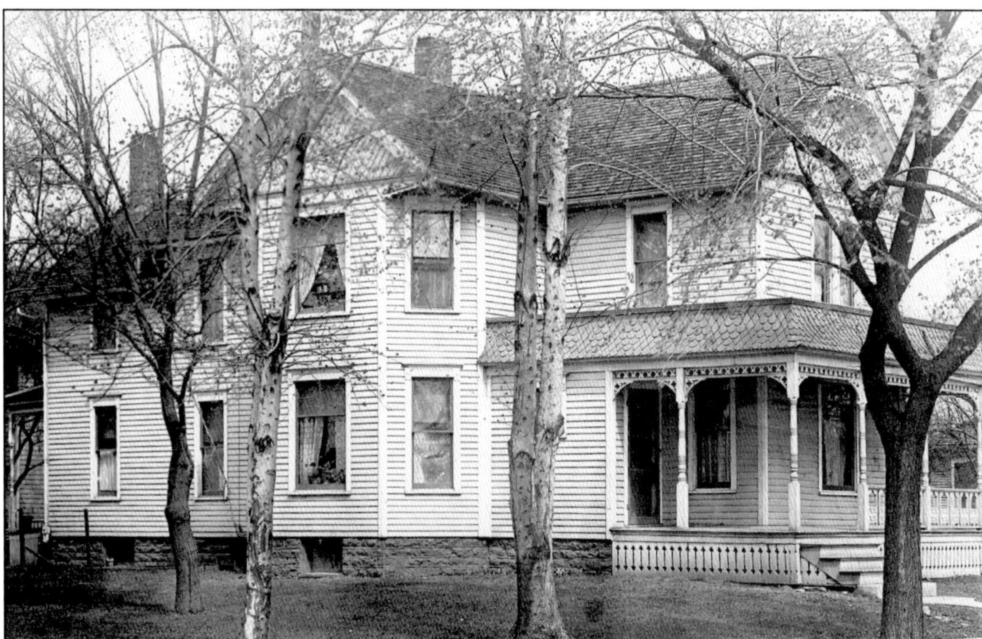

The Emil and Emma Gonderman house is one of the larger homes built in Bradley. It remains, without the front porch, at 211 North Grand Avenue. Emil, a native of Neunkhaugen, Germany, operated a successful farm implement business in both Kankakee and Bradley. (Marietta Tanner.)

Three

The Sun of Opportunity

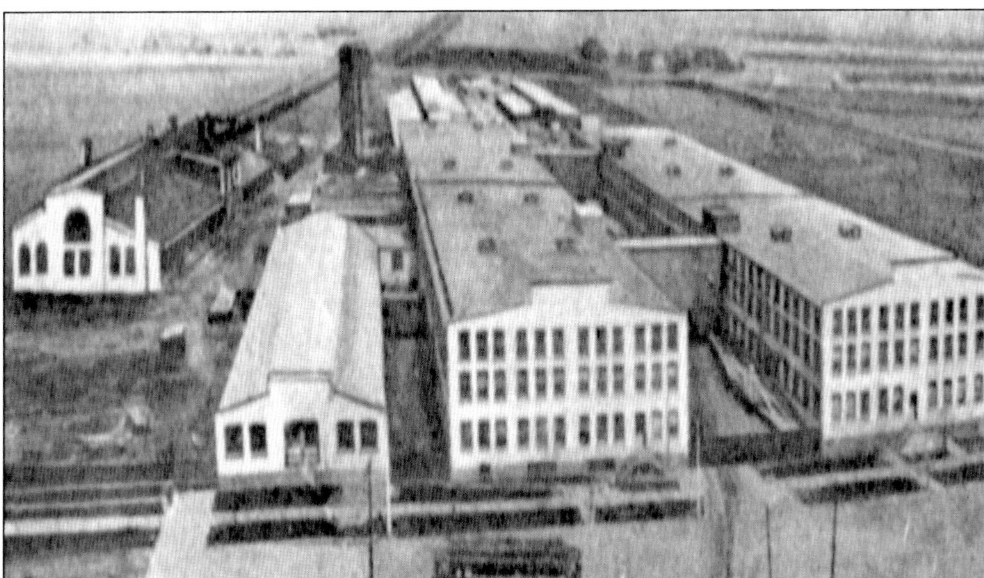

The Demme and Dierkes Furniture Company main office was on Blue Island Avenue in Chicago. J. Herman Hardebeck sold the company's management on the idea of moving their factory to North Kankakee. The new factory would occupy six buildings. Construction began in May 1892. On October 6, 1892, the *Kankakee Gazette* said, "The great Demme and Dierkes factory, the largest furniture factory in the world, is nearly completed. Six hundred hands will be employed on the start, and a number is expected to be 10,000 within a year after commencing work." (BHS.)

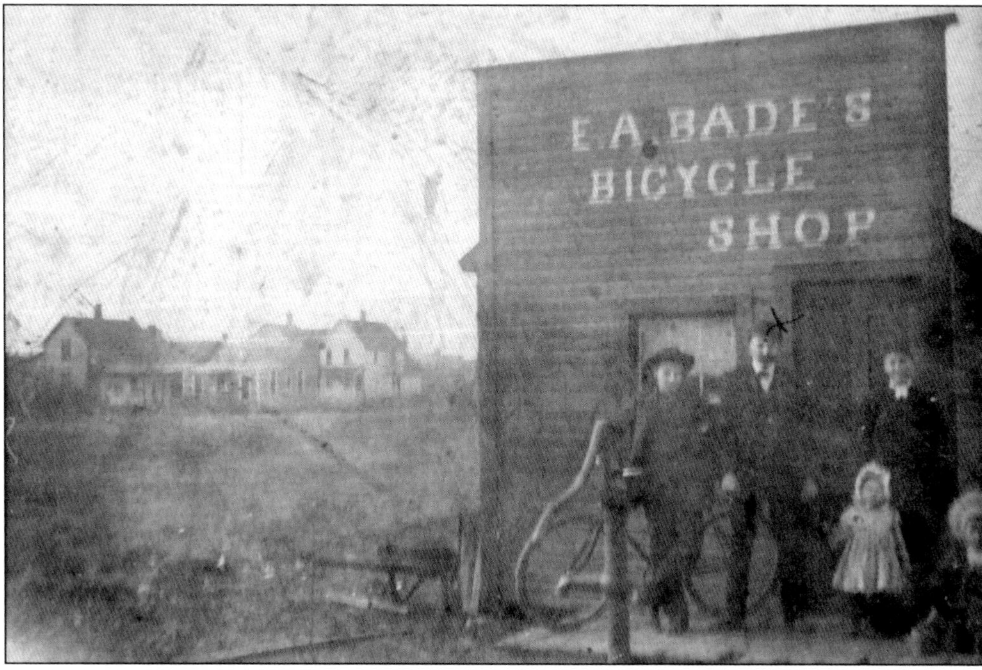

E. A. Bade's Bicycle Shop is one of Bradley's pioneer businesses. Bade family members pictured here, from left to right, are Albert, E. A., unidetified, Irene, Bud, and a baby. (Sue Forgue Bainter.)

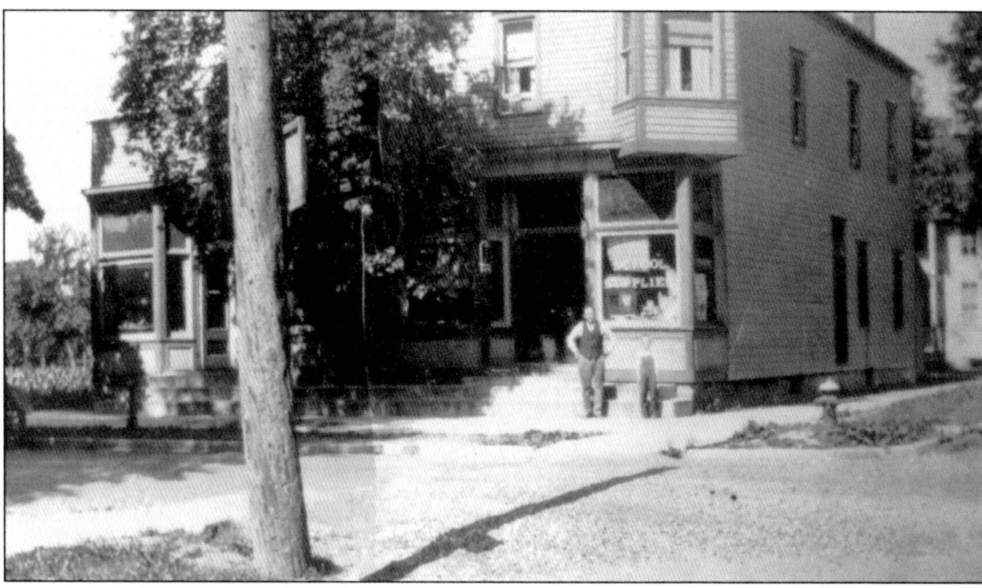

Emil Gonderman and his grandson Robert Tanner stand in front of the Mullenberg grocery store on June 15, 1930. Gonderman's International Implement parts shop is on the left. The building was located on the southwest corner of Wabash Avenue and Perry Street. Cromwell Cleaners later occupied the implement shop, and the Tanners were the last proprietors of the grocery store in the early 1950s. (Marietta Tanner.)

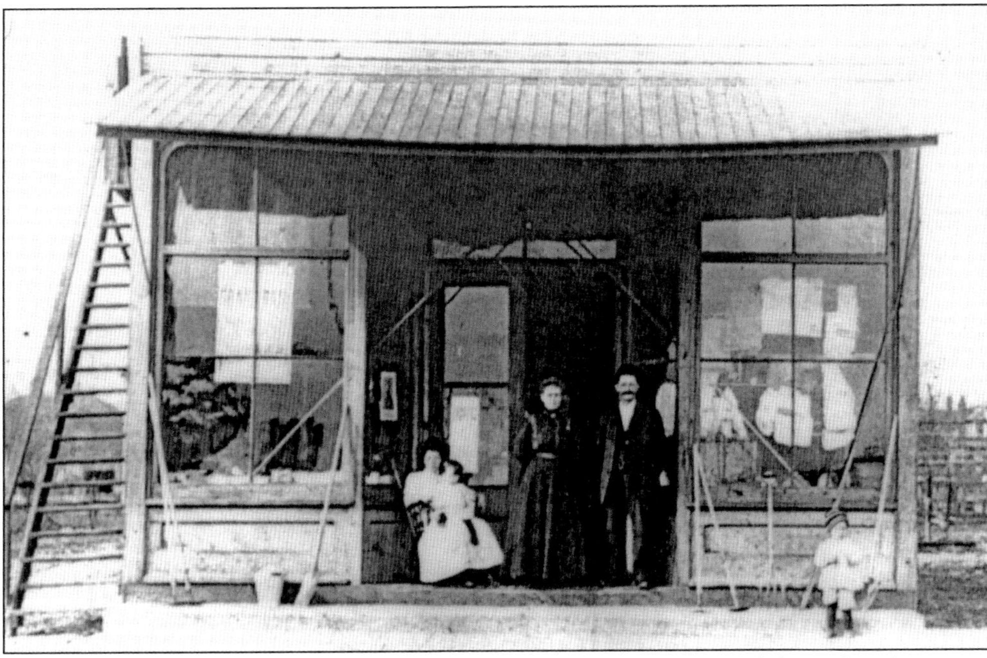

No information is available about this building, except that it was one of the earliest businesses on Broadway. (BHS.)

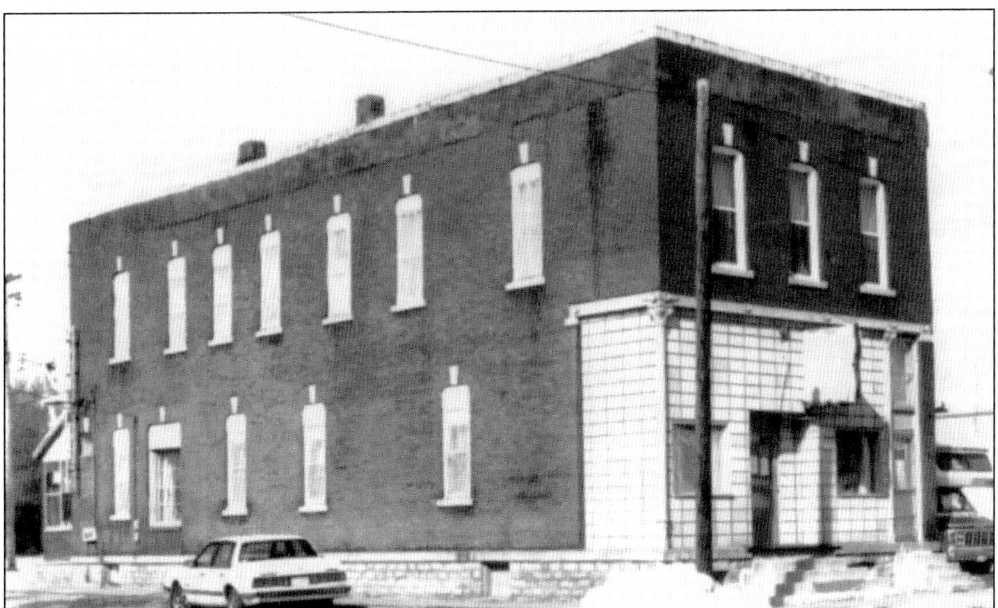

Joseph Legris built this building for North Kankakee's first bank. Hardebeck moved his office here from Kankakee's Arcade in August 1893. Later the bank became a hotel, and it is now an apartment building. (Author's collection.)

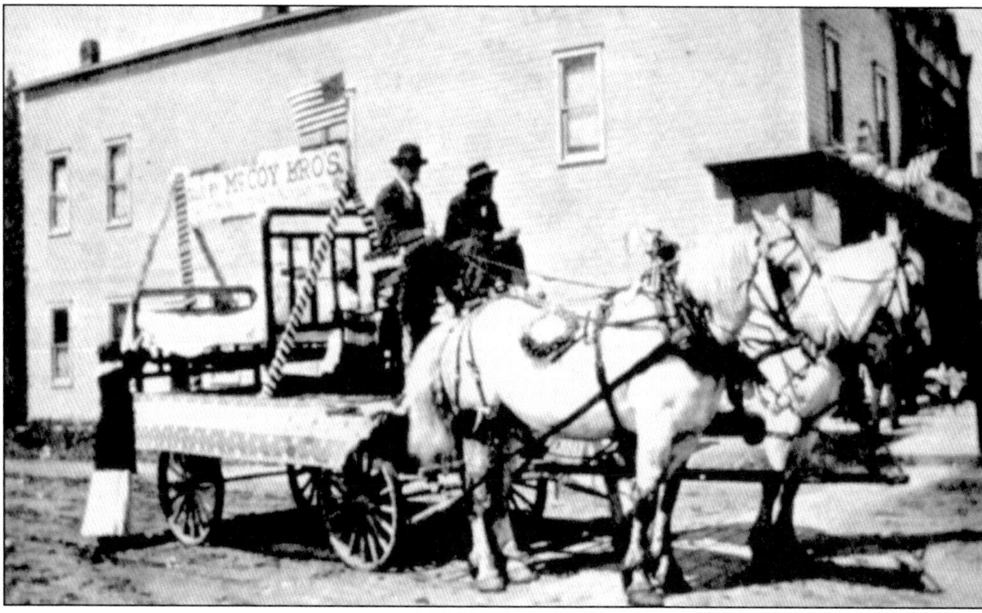

McCoy Brothers entered this advertising float in the Fourth of July parade at the dawn of the 20th century. Their stock in trade appears to be metal bedsteads made by the Turk Furniture Company. The building in the background is the Independent Order of Odd Fellows hall on the southwest corner of West Broadway and South Wabash Avenue. (BHS.)

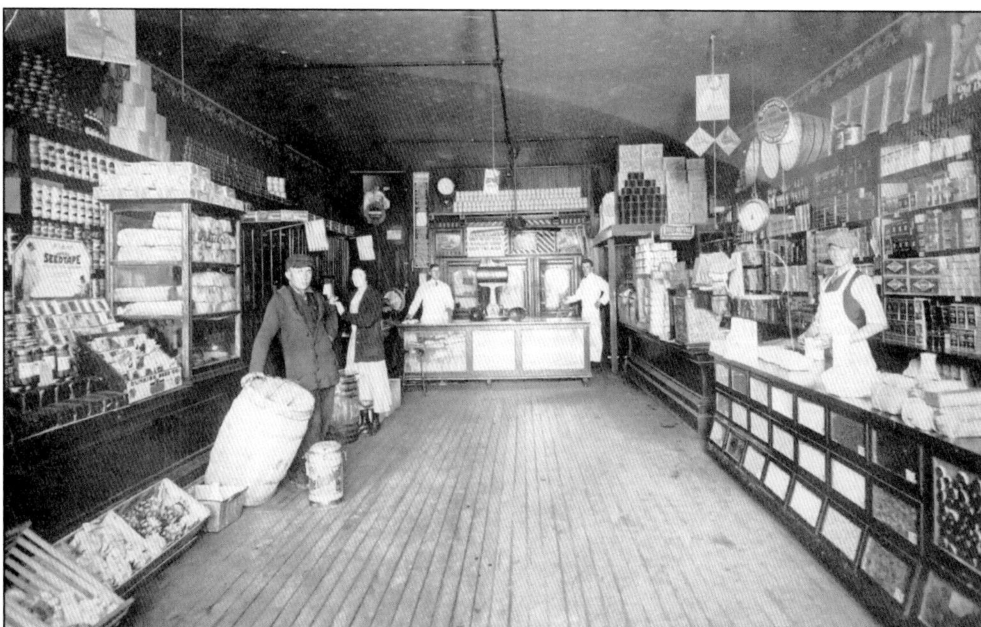

This is the interior of Obie Magruder's general store about 1909. There is everything one needs, from garden seed, canned goods, and bread on the left to meat in the ice locker at the back, and canning jars, wash tubs, wash boards, soap, "new" Post Tosties corn flakes, coffee, and tea on the right. (DM.)

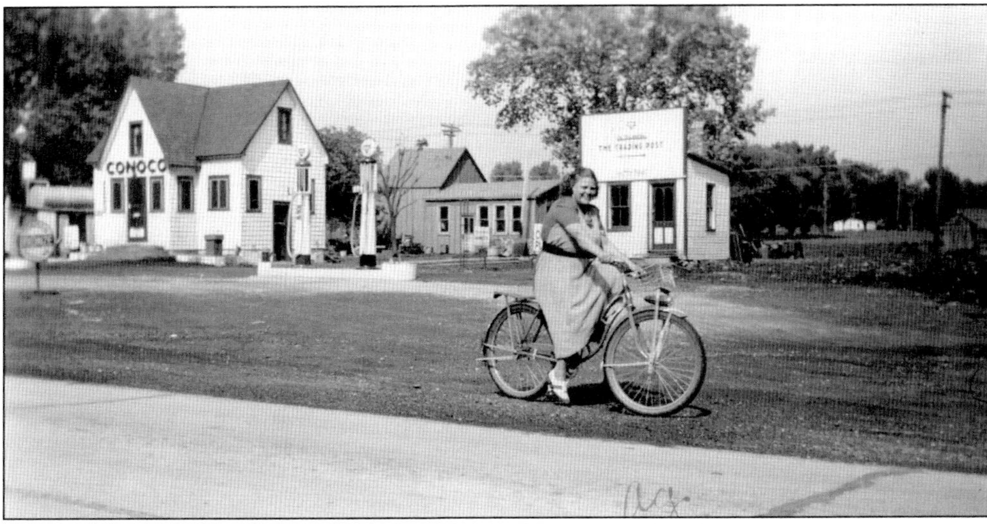

The Trading Post owned by C. B. Chambers was a Bradley landmark for decades. It stood on the east side of Vasseur Avenue (now Kennedy Drive), across from the Perry farm. The young lady on the bicycle in this early 1940s photograph is Agnes Spivey. (Francis Brais.)

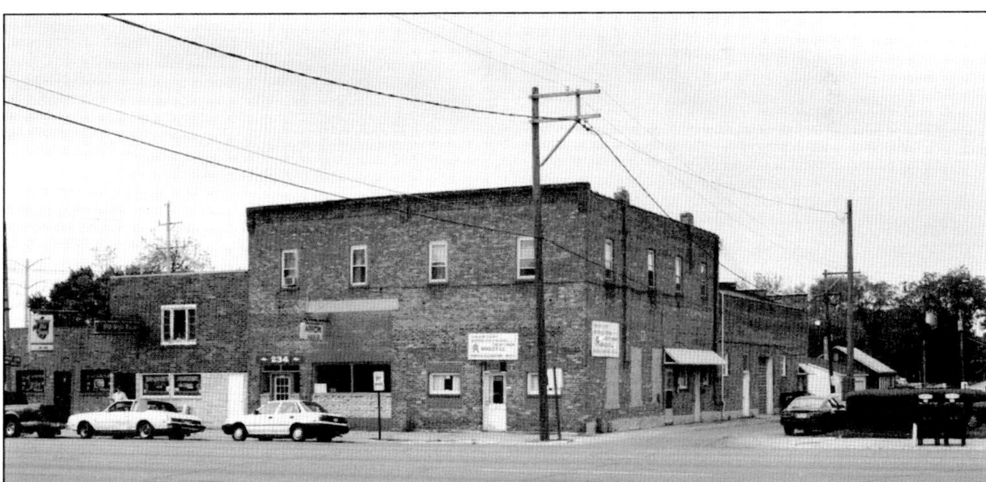
Edward LaBounty built this building in March 1893 in the 200 block on the south side of West Broadway (see page 66). It was first used as a hotel. Flat roofs replaced gabled roofs on commercial buildings in the 1890s. Rolls of asphalt-saturated felt paper were laid over the roof deck then coated with hot asphalt and a layer of gravel. (Author's collection.)

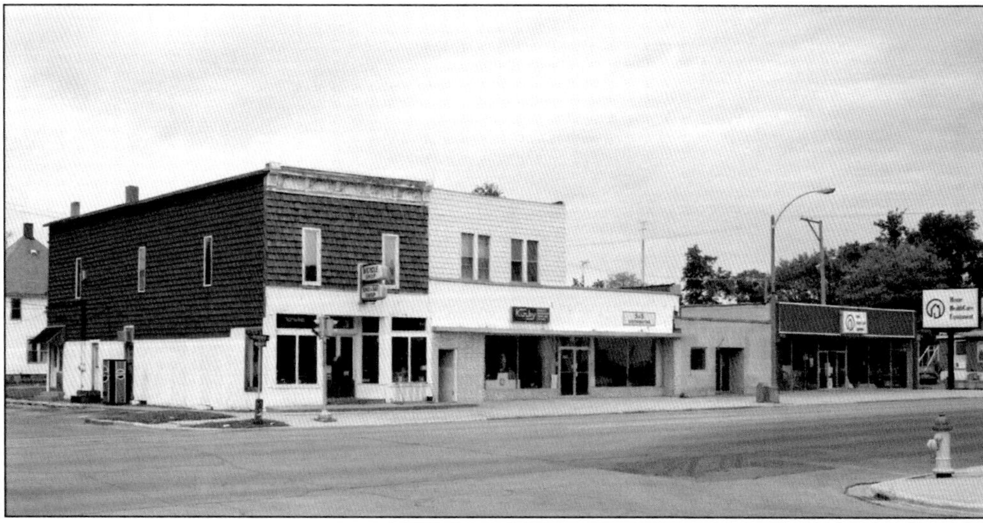

The Bradley Independent Order of Odd Fellows met on the second floor of the corner building in the 1890s. In 1898 and 1899, the Francis X. Crevier general store occupied the first floor. Years later in the 1920s, the George C. Schnider Rexall pharmacy was located there. In the 1920s, the National Tea Company store occupied the building immediately to the right. (Author's collection.)

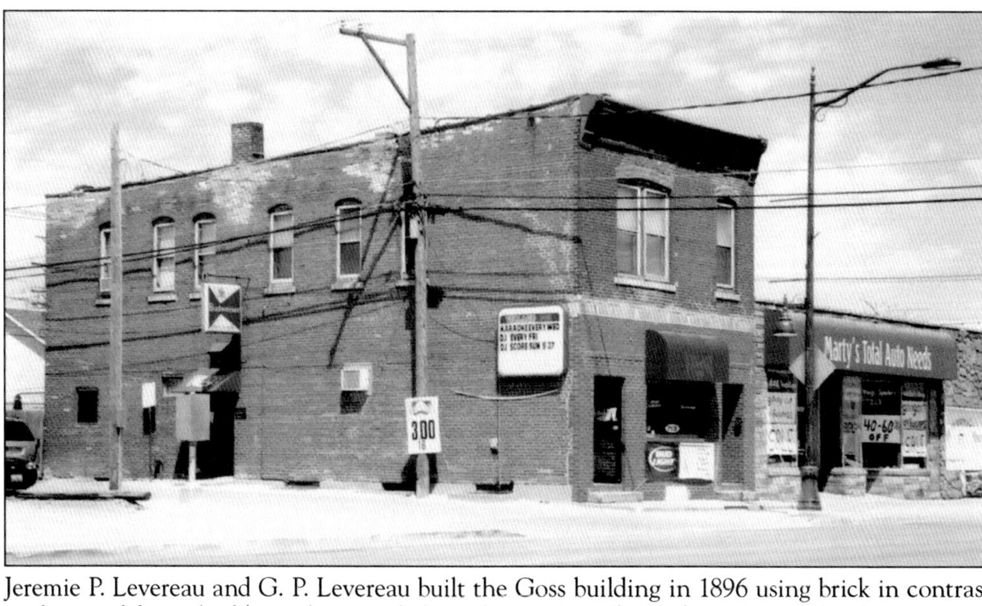

Jeremie P. Levereau and G. P. Levereau built the Goss building in 1896 using brick in contrast to the wood-frame buildings that stood along this section of Broadway. First utilized as a general store by grocer J. F. Goss and clerks Peter L. and Louis Goss, the building later became a saloon. (Author's collection.)

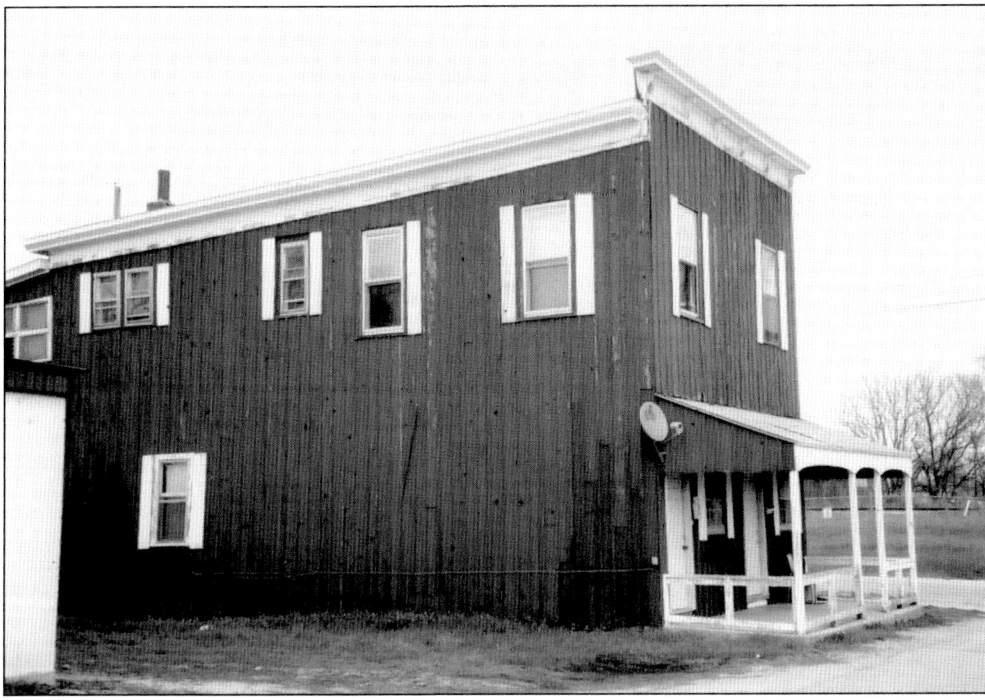

Barney Burns opened the first saloon licensed by the village of North Kankakee on November 9, 1892, on lot 17 in the 100 block of West Broadway. The saloon later was then owned by a Mr. LaPlante in 1896 and later that same year by Joseph Surprenant. (Author's collection.)

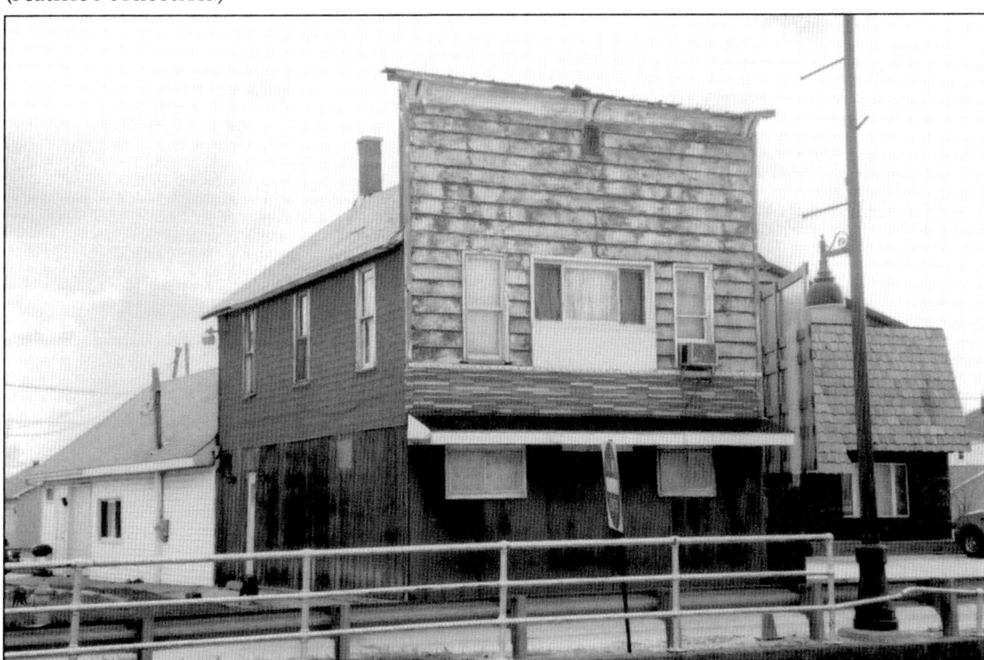

Also in 1892, Albert Bentz kept a saloon across Broadway from the Burns tavern. Bentz and his family lived on the second floor. (Author's collection.)

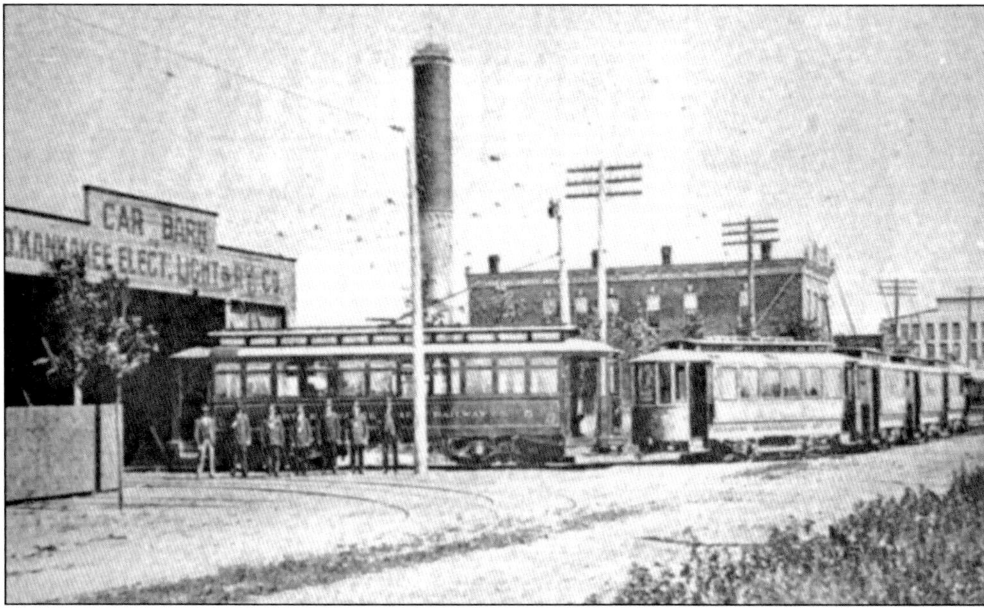

The North Kankakee Electric Light and Railway car barn on North Schuyler Avenue was used to service the streetcars. For a short time, the company generated electricity for North Kankakee until the proprietors found that they could buy electricity from Kankakee at a cost lower than the cost of running their own generators. In the background are the Bradley factory water tower and the Legris bank building. (BHS.)

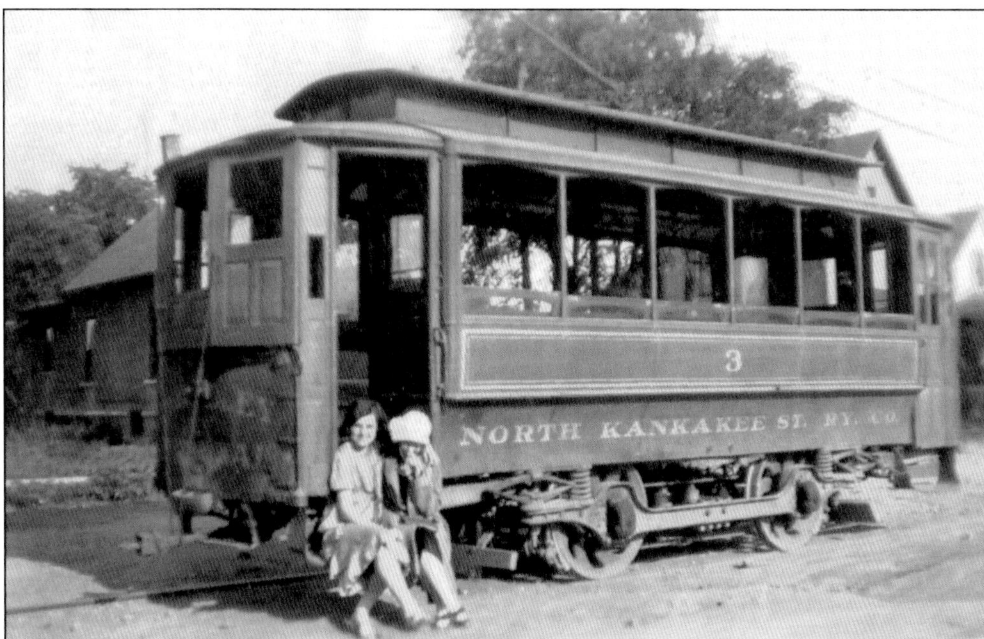

The North Kankakee Electric Railway Company was organized in Kankakee in 1891. It opened a line to North Kankakee and Bourbonnais in 1892. Operations ceased in 1931 or 1932. Kankakee Motor Coach buses took over the routes until 1960, at which time the company went out of business. (RG.)

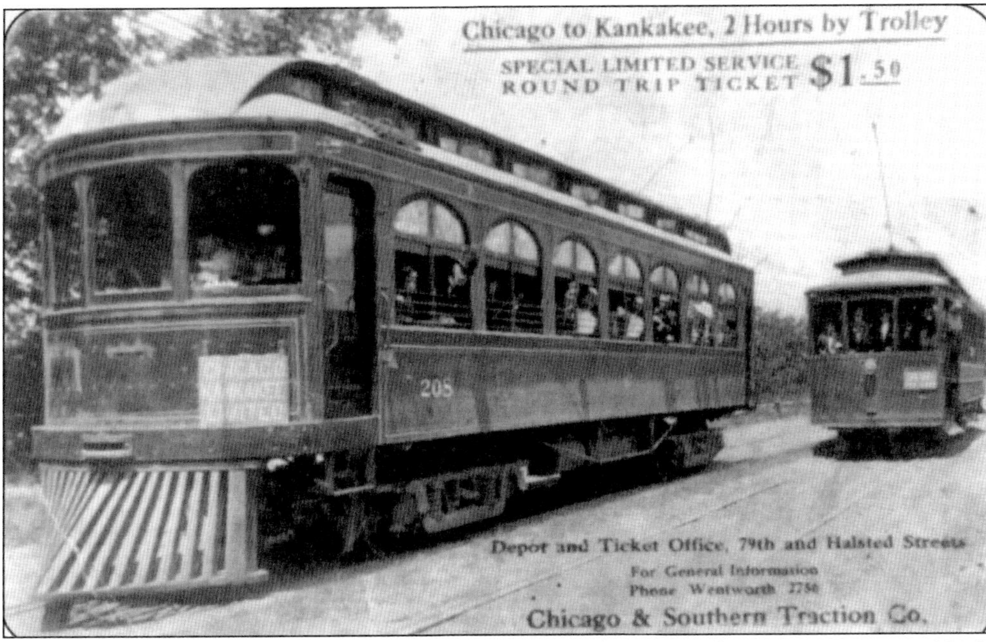

The Chicago Electric Traction Company converted from battery to electric operation in 1901. It became the Chicago and Southern Traction Company in 1904 and built an interurban line to Kankakee in 1907. The first scheduled car arrived in North Kankakee in 1909. Losing passengers to the Illinois Central Railroad, the company ceased operations 20 years later. To the right of the interurban coach is a North Kankakee Electric Railway streetcar. (KCM.)

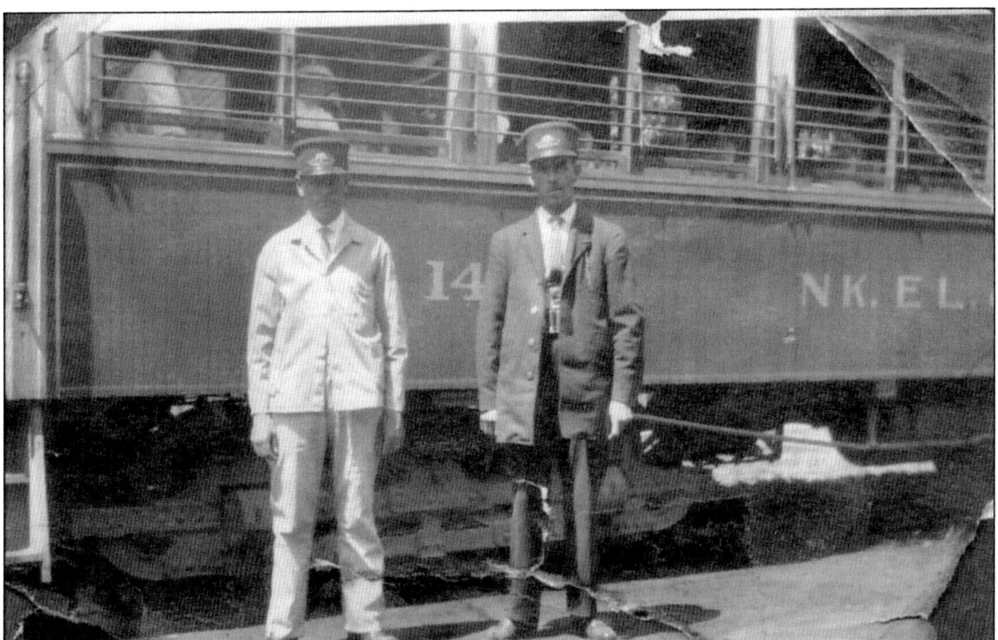

Joseph Nicklas of Bradley, on the right, was a conductor for the North Kankakee Electric Railway. The interurban went out of business in 1927, and the North Kankakee Electric Railway folded in 1932. Nicklas is said to have put the last streetcar in the barn. (Nicklas family.)

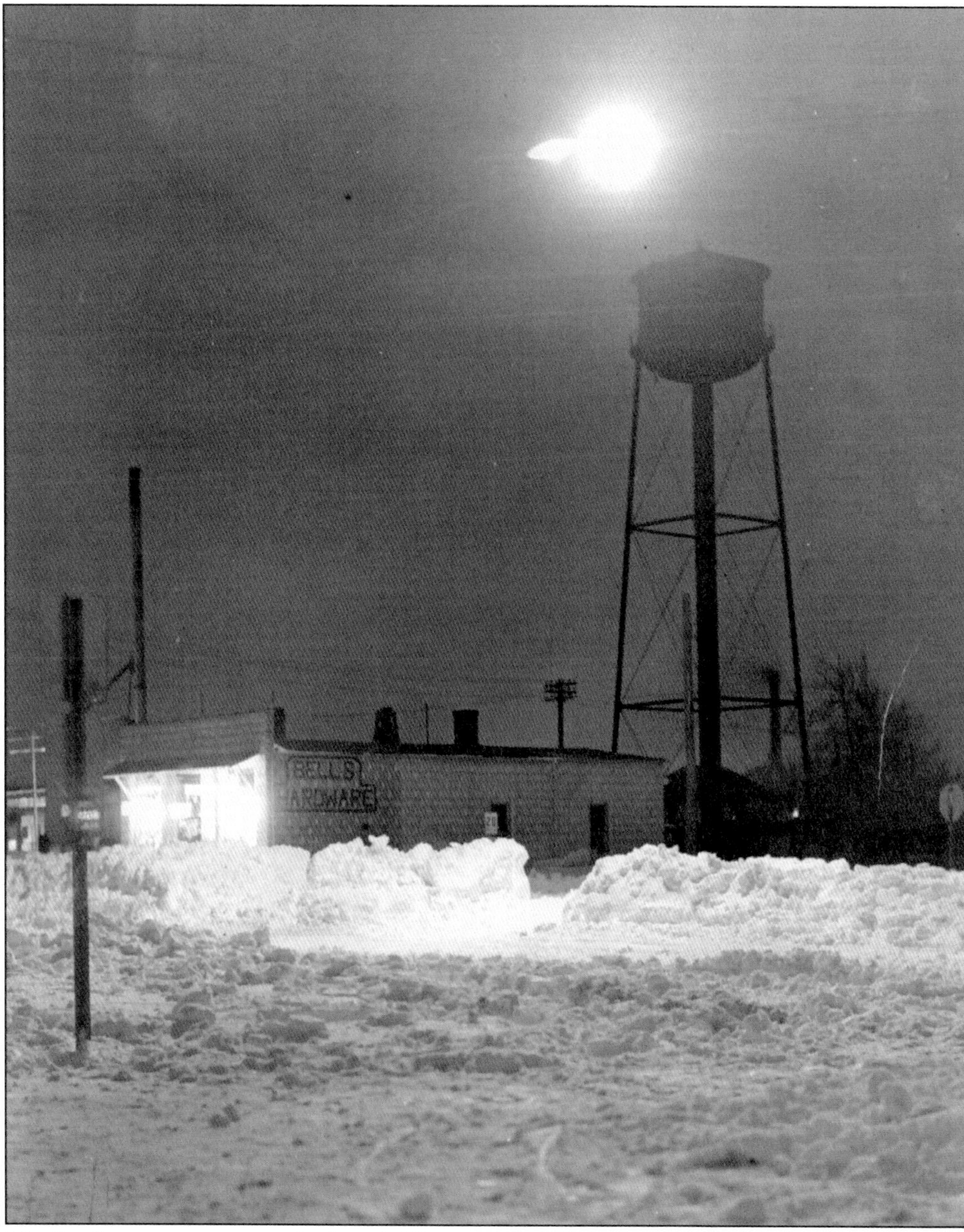

The Bradley water tower was built in 1905 to accommodate the new Bradley water system. It was 114 feet high and held 60,000 gallons. The village opened a sanitary sewer system in 1920, but it was not until 1929 that privies and privy vaults were banned by village ordinance. A major extension of the water system was made in 1927. The original Bell's Hardware store opened in the building to the left of the tower in 1925 (see page 74). (Pug Benoche.)

Four

Snatched Back from Disaster

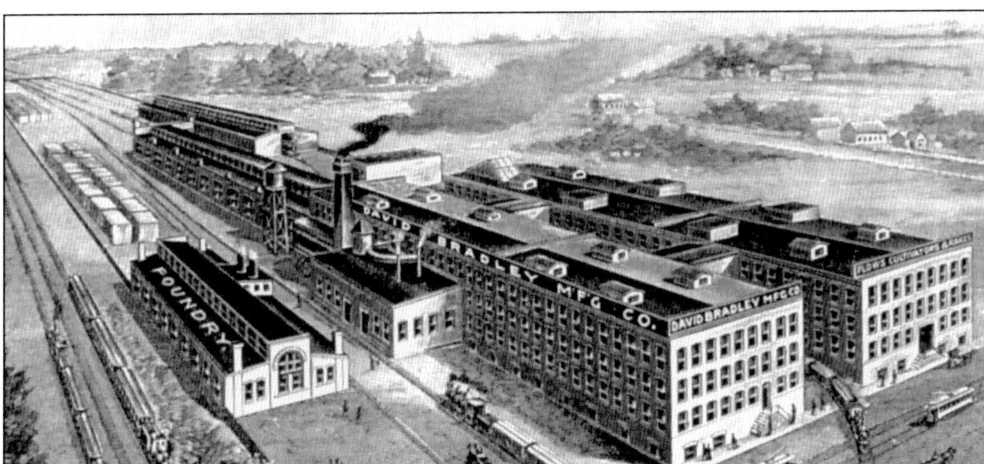

The 1893 financial panic struck North Kankakee in April. While one factory after another closed, J. Herman Hardebeck still believed that the community had a future. On Saturday, January 12, 1895, he rounded up a platoon of Kankakee's influential business men. A train took them to Chicago to the David Bradley Manufacturing Company plant. Hardebeck negotiated a deal that brought the Bradley works to North Kankakee. On April 5, a telegram was put on display in the Kankakee Post Office. It read, "Deal consummated. Bradley's will locate in North Kankakee at once, J. H. Hardebeck." In August 1895, the village name was changed to Bradley City. The next year the name was shortened to Bradley. (RB.)

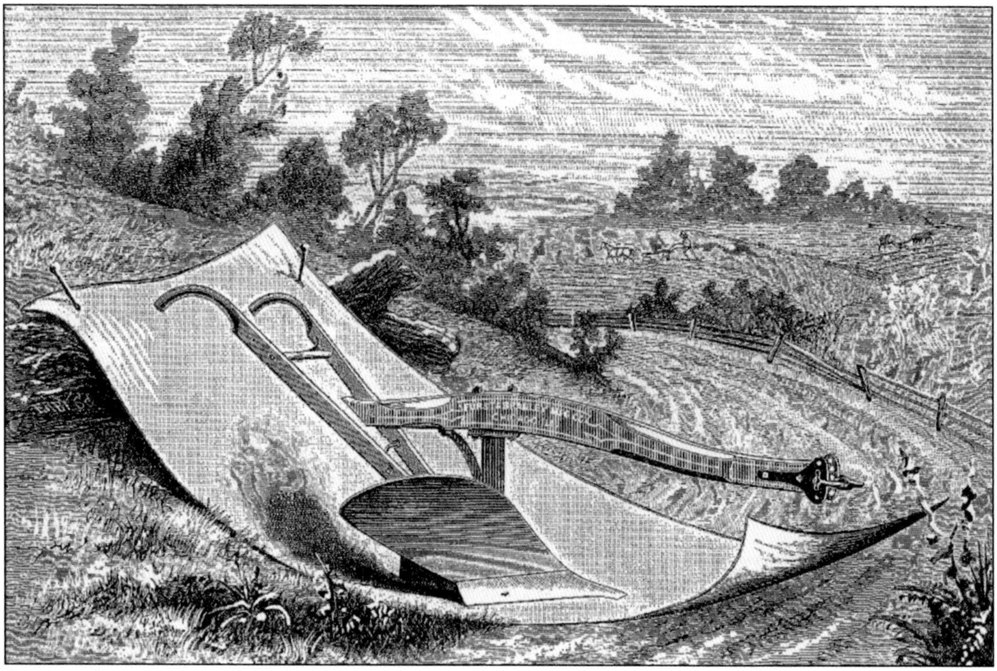

During the 1870s, Furst and Bradley Manufacturing Company of Chicago used this woodcut to advertise their plows. Conrad Furst and David Bradley were in partnership from 1872 to 1884. In 1884, Bradley and his son J. Harley bought Furst's interest in the company. (RB.)

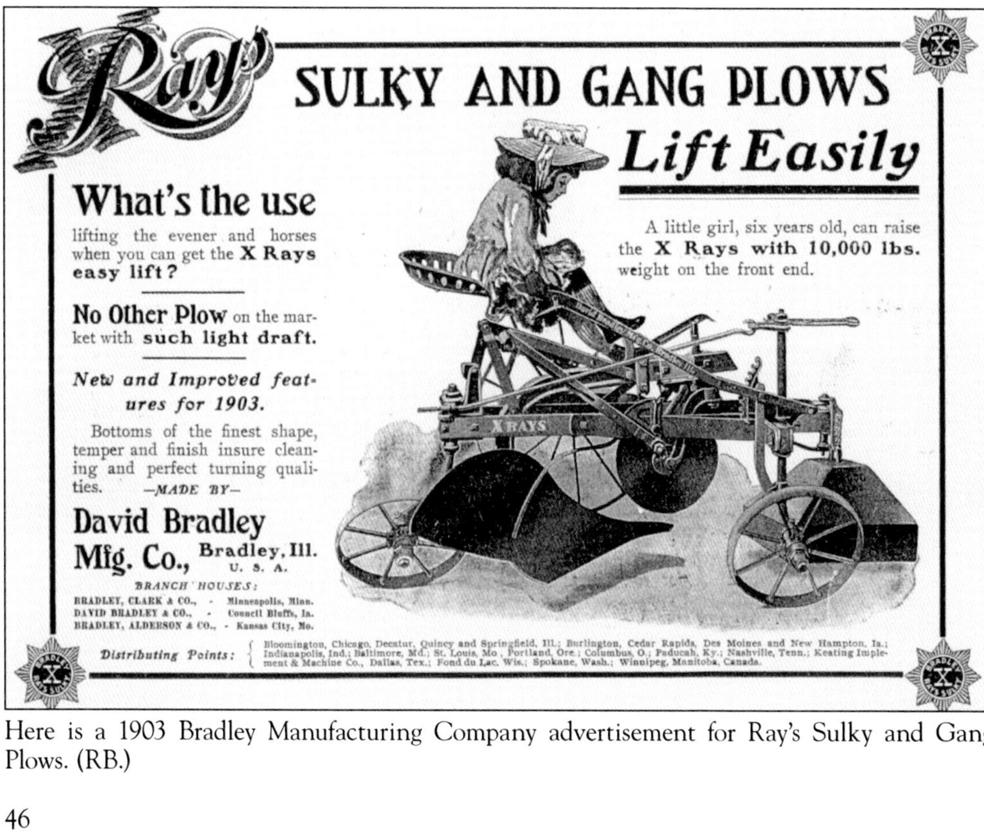

Here is a 1903 Bradley Manufacturing Company advertisement for Ray's Sulky and Gang Plows. (RB.)

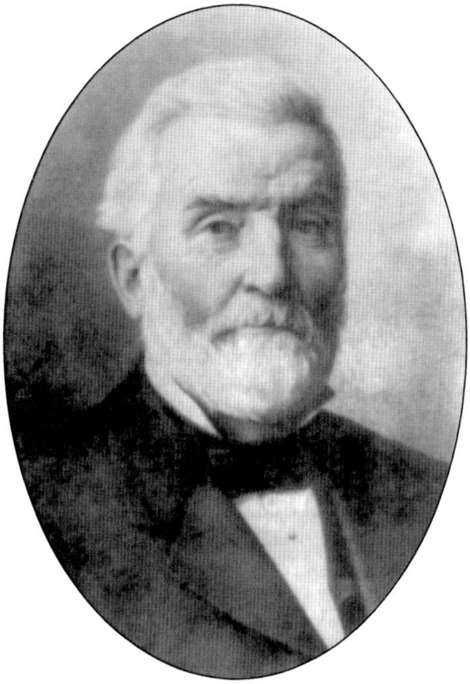 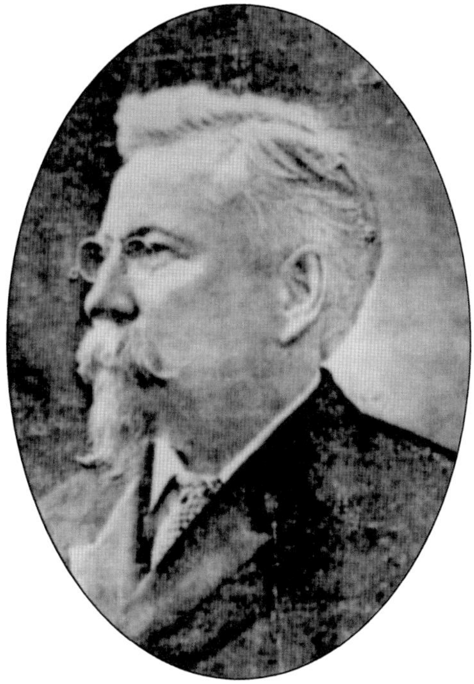

David (on the left) was born at Groten, New York, on November 8, 1811, to Daniel and Patience (Cooper) Bradley. He went to Chicago in 1835. In 1854, he joined Furst in manufacturing wagons and buggies. A stock company, Furst and Bradley Manufacturing Company was formed in 1872. In 1884, David and his son J. Harley (on the right), bought out the interest of Furst. J. Harley was born in Racine, Wisconsin, in 1844. He joined his father's company in 1872. David died in 1899. J. Harley became vice president and treasurer of the David Bradley Manufacturing Company of North Kankakee. His brother Byron was plant superintendent. Below is a 1910 postcard of the David Bradley Manufacturing Company at the time that it was bought by Sears, Roebuck and Company. The cylindrical water tower had a crown of lights at the top that illuminated the surrounding park at night. (Above, RS; below, John J. Tofari.)

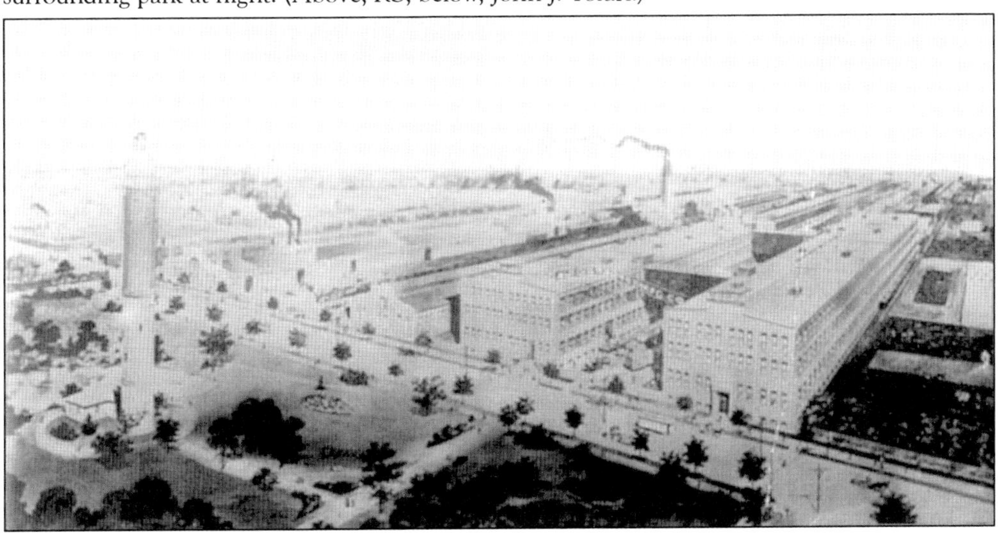

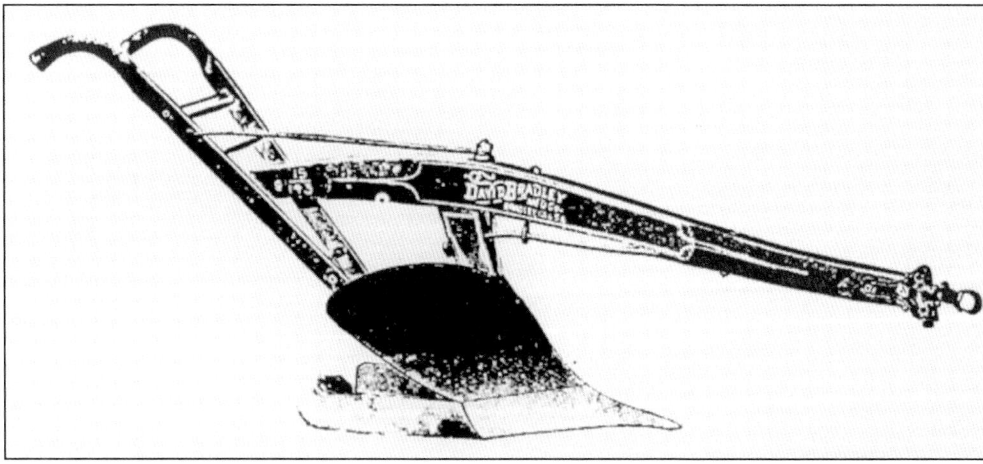

Two standard David Bradley Manufacturing Company products, the Diamond Breaker plow (above) and the horse-drawn manure spreader (below), were typical of the company's skill in designing durable farm equipment. The Diamond Breaker plow was developed by David Bradley, and it is a forerunner of today's modern plows. The Diamond Breaker won major prizes at the 1893 World's Columbian Exposition. The manure spreader was only one of several Bradley-made buggies, carriages, surreys, driving wagons, and planters. (RS.)

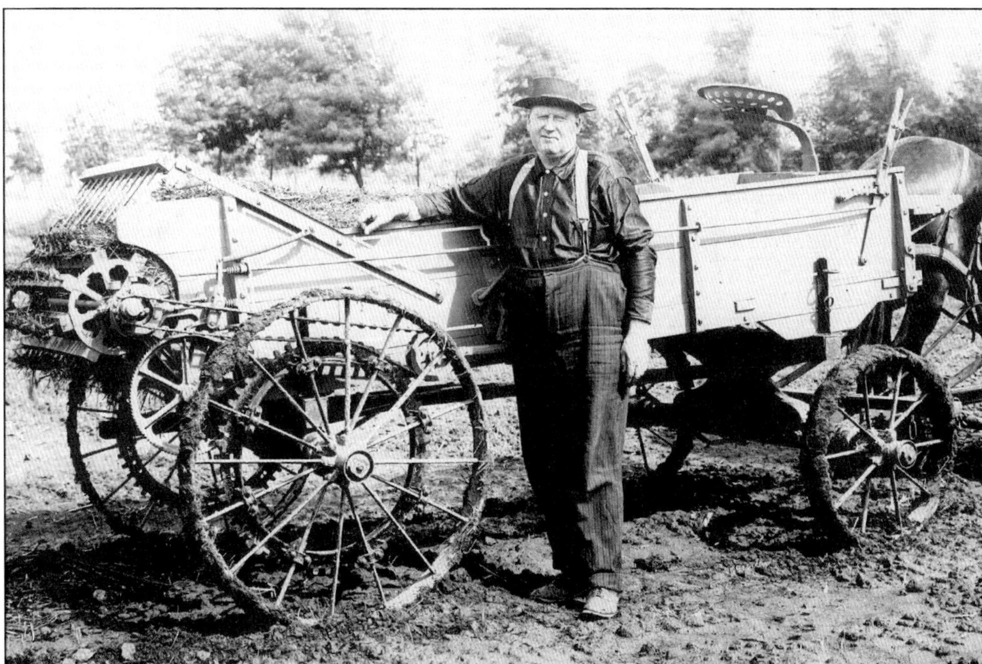

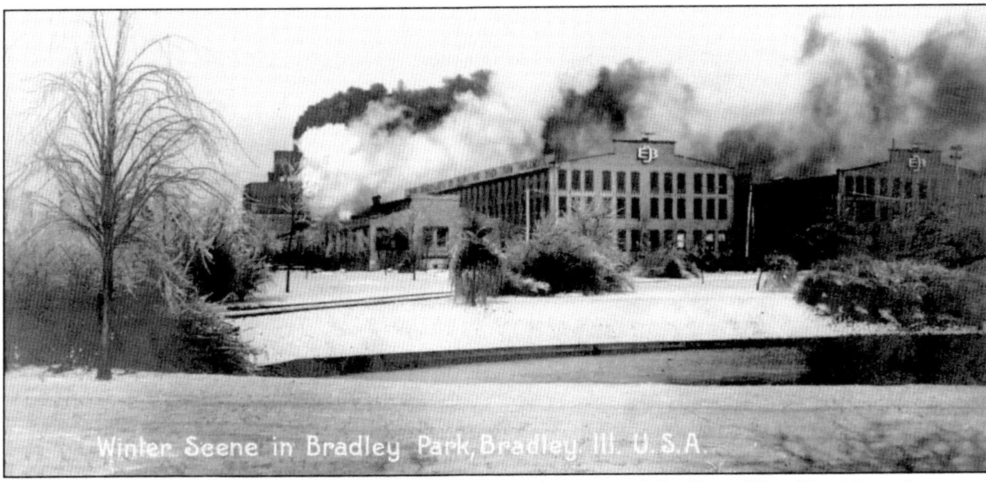

A snowy winter day offered an opportunity to make this view of the David Bradley Manufacturing Company for use on a postcard. (KCM-KDJ.)

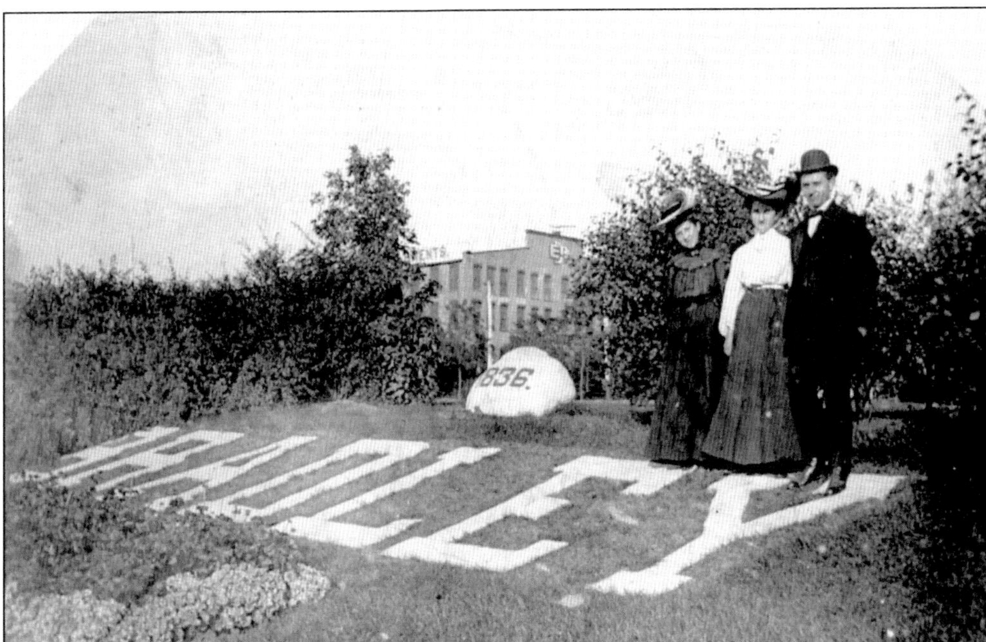

What was known as Bradley Park in the early years of the 20th century occupied land across East Broadway from the David Bradley factory. The word "Bradley" appears to have been on each side of a small landscaped mound. "Bradley" in this photograph faced the Illinois Central tracks. The young David Bradley had arrived in Chicago in October 1835. He and William H. Stow built an iron foundry for Jones, King and Company on the south bank of the Chicago River at Polk Street. The year 1836 (partially visible on the whitewashed boulder) is possibly a reference to the year David Bradley either imported the first load of pig iron into Chicago, or when he began working on farm implements in the foundry. (KCM-KDJ.)

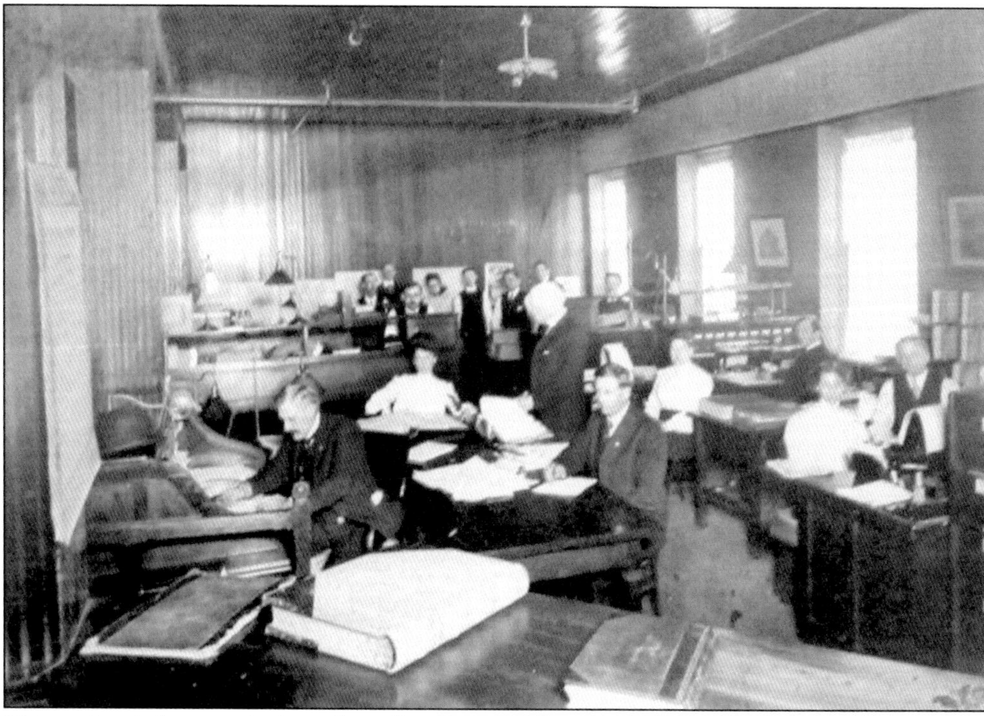

This undated photograph, from the collection of William R. and Martha Dickinson Bond, shows the interior of the David Bradley Manufacturing Company office. (Elizabeth A. Keithcart.)

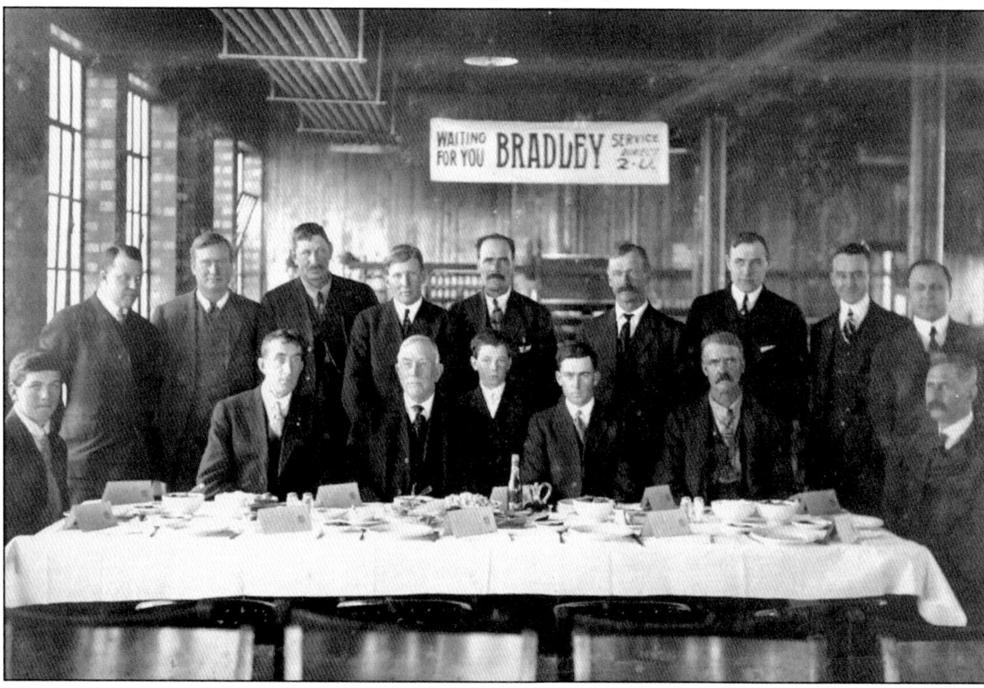

The variety of farm products sold by David Bradley Manufacturing Company and the Sears, Roebuck and Company required a group of sales service representatives. Some of them are pictured here. (RB.)

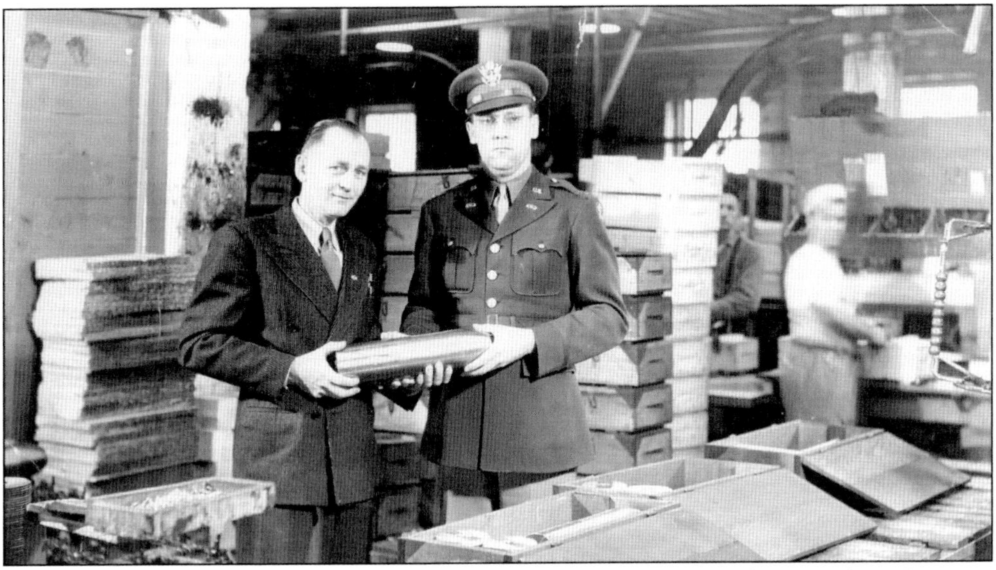

During World War II, the David Bradley Manufacturing Company, Defense Products Division, received a government contract to make several types of military ordnance including 4.2 chemical mortar shells. The one millionth shell produced (above) is displayed by Edward Keller, superintendent of the shell division, and 1st Lt. Ernest Ruddes on January 16, 1945. The shell casings are featured along with ploughshares and other farm implements in the photograph below. The Bradley factory received the coveted Army-Navy E award for its wartime contributions. (Above, KCM-KDJ; below, BHS.)

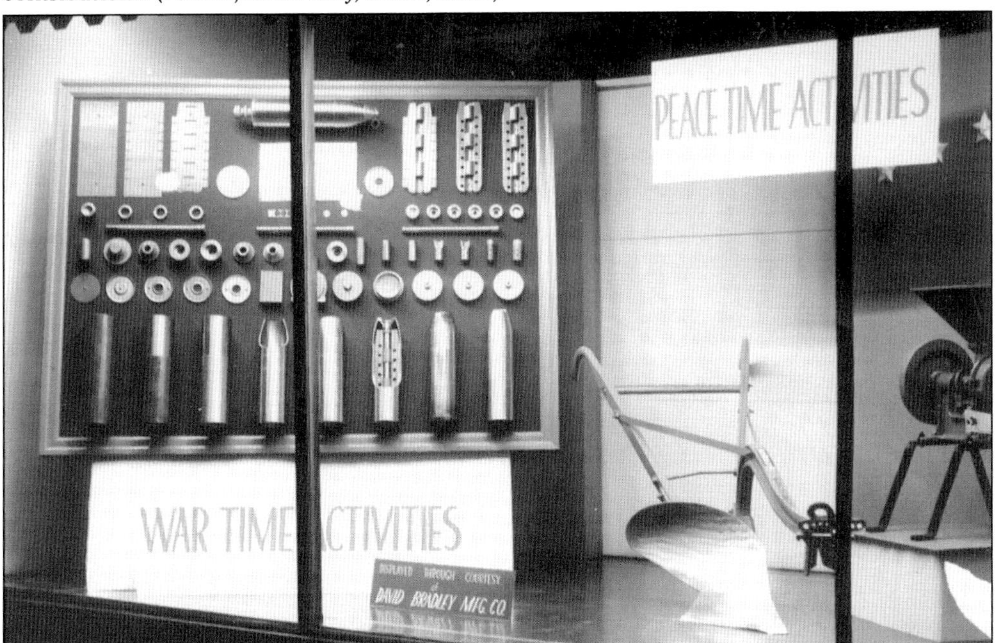

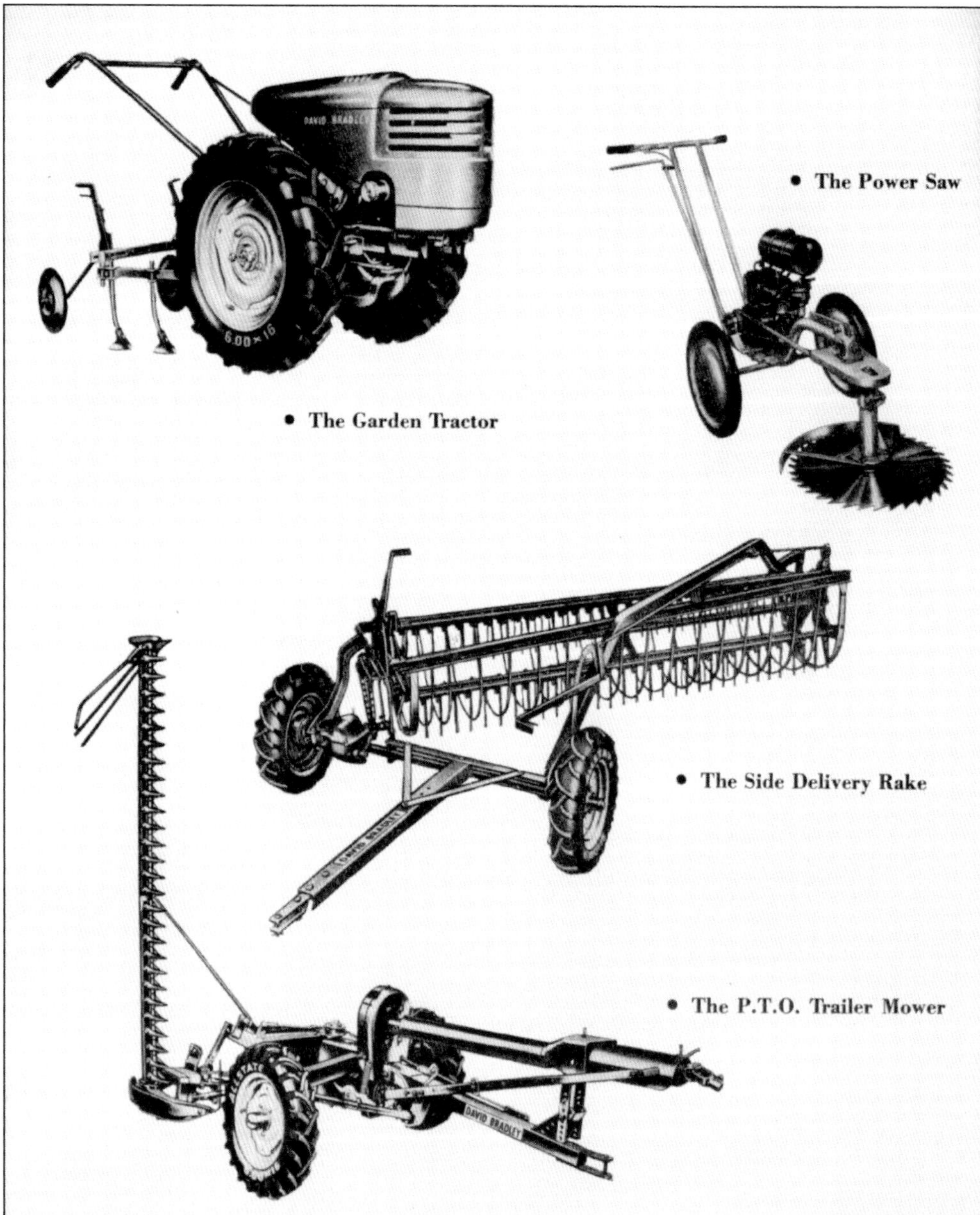

The David Bradley Manufacturing Company during the late 1940s produced many products for gardens and farms. They were sold worldwide by Sears, Roebuck and Company. (RS.)

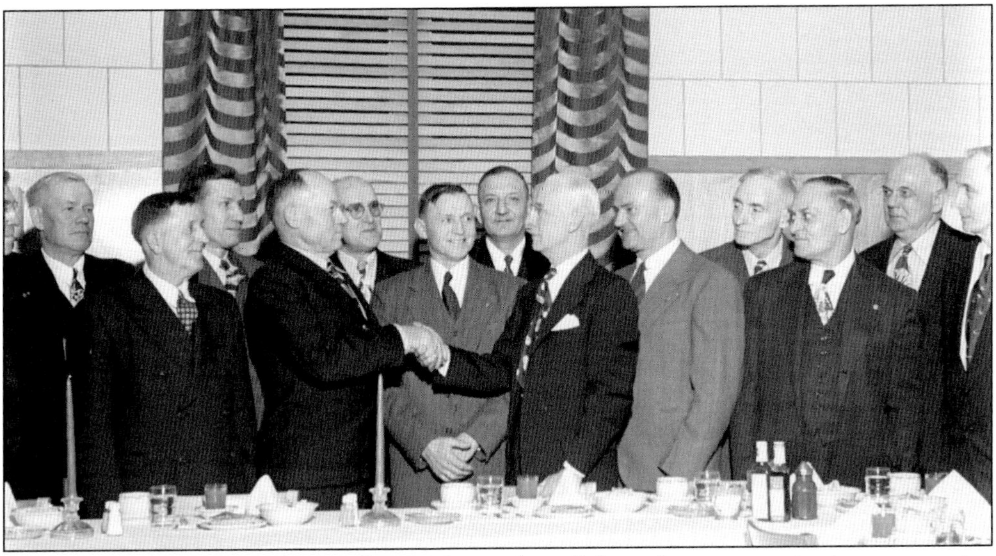

On April 15, 1949, a total of 15 Bradley employees (not all shown) were recognized as representing 542 years of continuous service in the company. Awards were made during a dinner at Pete's Steak House. All of the men had at least 30 years with the company. James C. Hagearty, shaking hands (right) with Frank Marawski, started working at the David Bradley Manufacturing Company factory in 1901. (KCM-KDJ.)

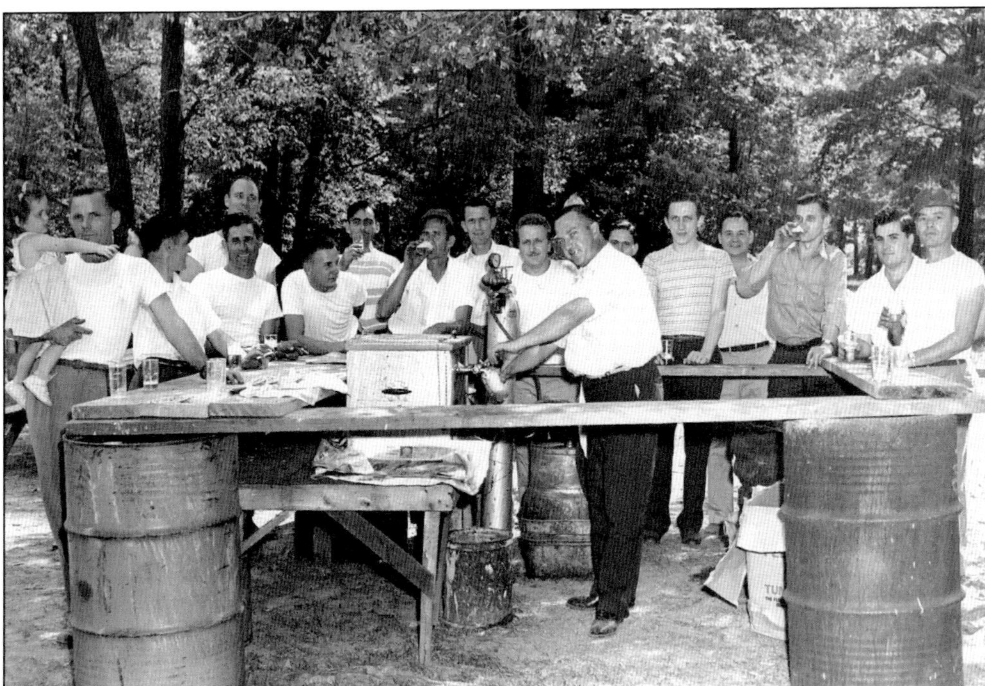

Summer picnics were an annual event for employees of the David Bradley Manufacturing Company. (RS.)

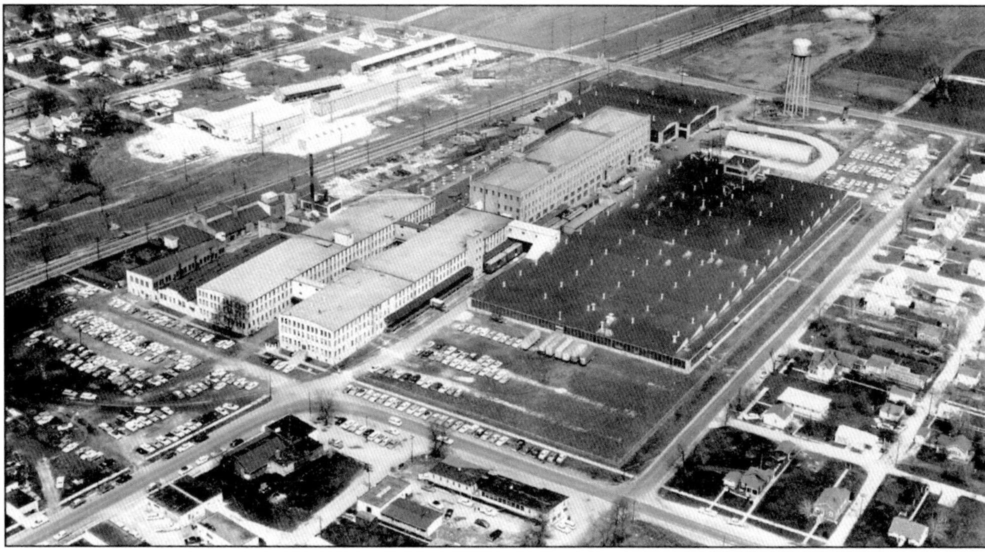

The Newark Ohio Company bought the David Bradley Manufacturing Company from Sears, Roebuck and Company in 1962. A few years later, Newark merged with the Roper Corporation. This aerial view of the Bradley factory complex was taken in the 1960s. (Adrien M. Richard.)

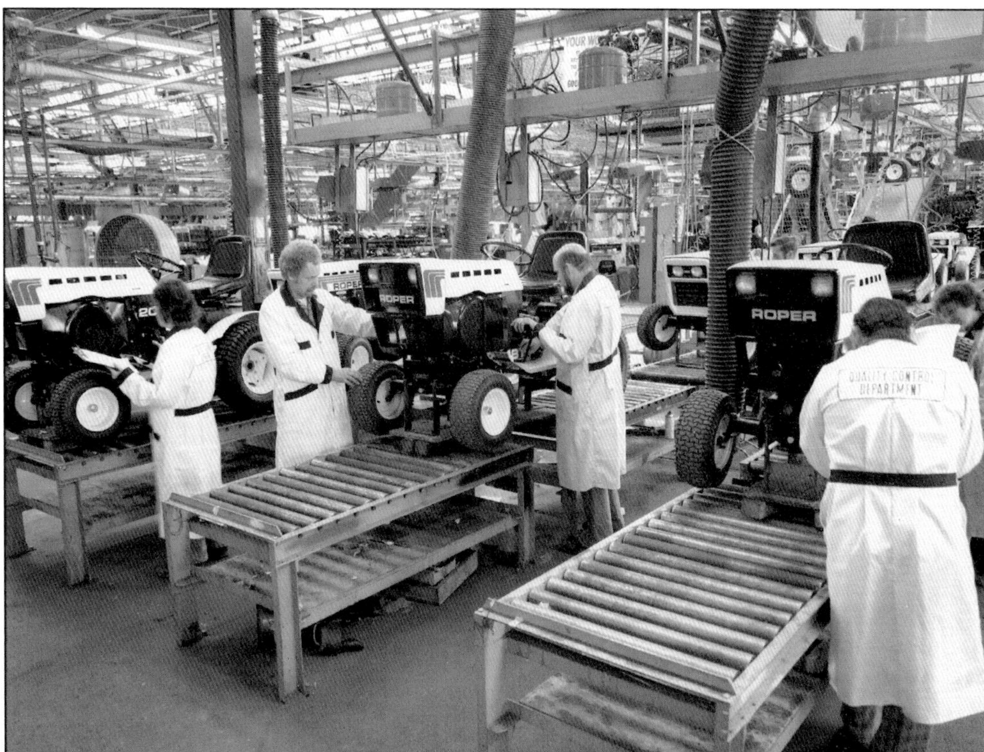

Roper Corporation garden tractors were assembled in the old Bradley factory during the 1970s. (RS.)

Peter Edward Kroehler was born April 3, 1872, at Mound Prairie, Houston County, Minnesota. He is one of 13 children born to Jacob and Anna (Eberhardt) Kroehler. Peter went to work at the Naperville Lounge Company in 1893. In 1896 he became a partner in the company. The Archer Starch Company buildings had occupied a block on the west side of the Illinois Central Railroad tracks in North Kankakee until they burned in 1901 (see page 25). In 1910, the Naperville Lounge Company bought the old Archer site and built the P. E. Kroehler Manufacturing Company plant. The original building was named Plant No. 3. On April 1,1915, the name of four existing factories became "Kroehler Manufacturing Company." By the 1930s, the Kroehler company had added Plant No. 4 to the Bradley site (below). The engraving shows the complex as it appeared at that time. The Kroehler company and its 10 factories in the United States and Canada, became the world's largest furniture manufacturer. But the company gradually faded from the scene in the 1970s. In the summer of 1989, fire destroyed the abandoned Plant No. 3. (DM)

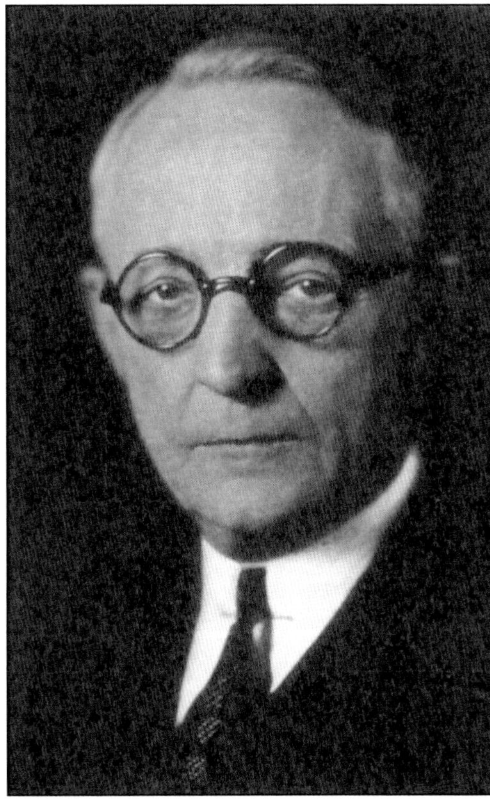

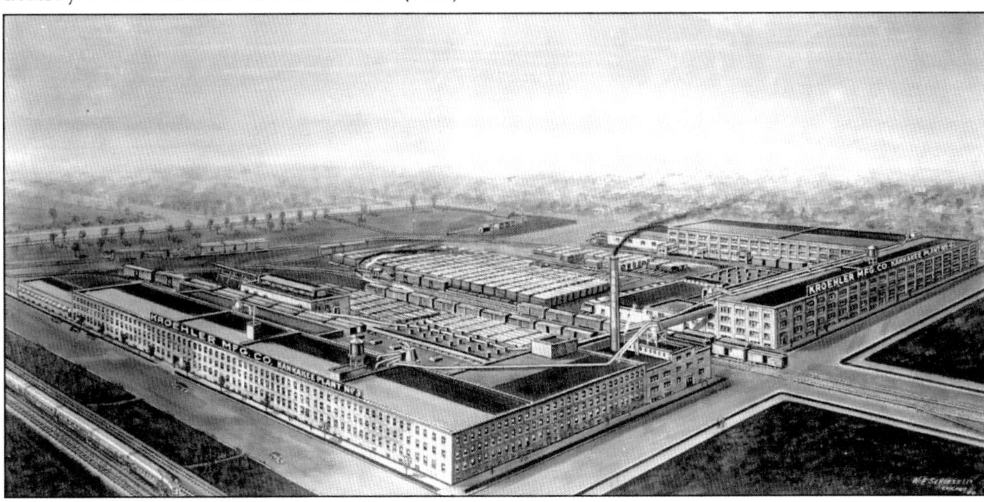

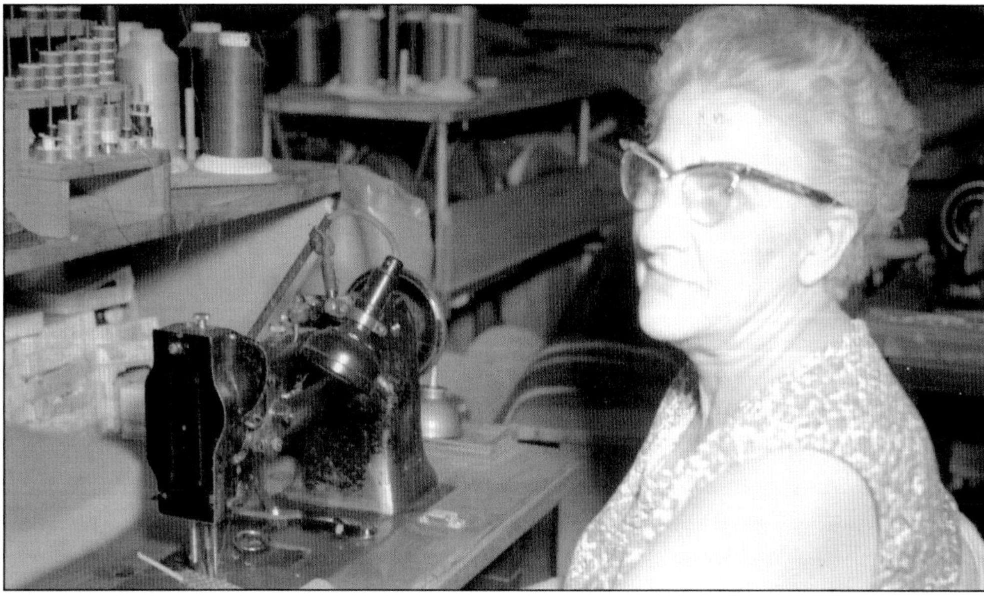

The Kroehler Manufacturing Company produced upholstered living room suites and bedroom and kitchen furniture. People with many different skills were employed. The woodworking plant used various machine operators, who ran saws, lathes, and planing and sanding equipment. Wood finishers were needed to apply stains, lacquers, and varnishes. The upholstery department needed people to cut, fit, and sew fabrics. Seen here is Gladys (Boudreau) St. Peter, who was an upholstery sewer. (Nelda Ravens.)

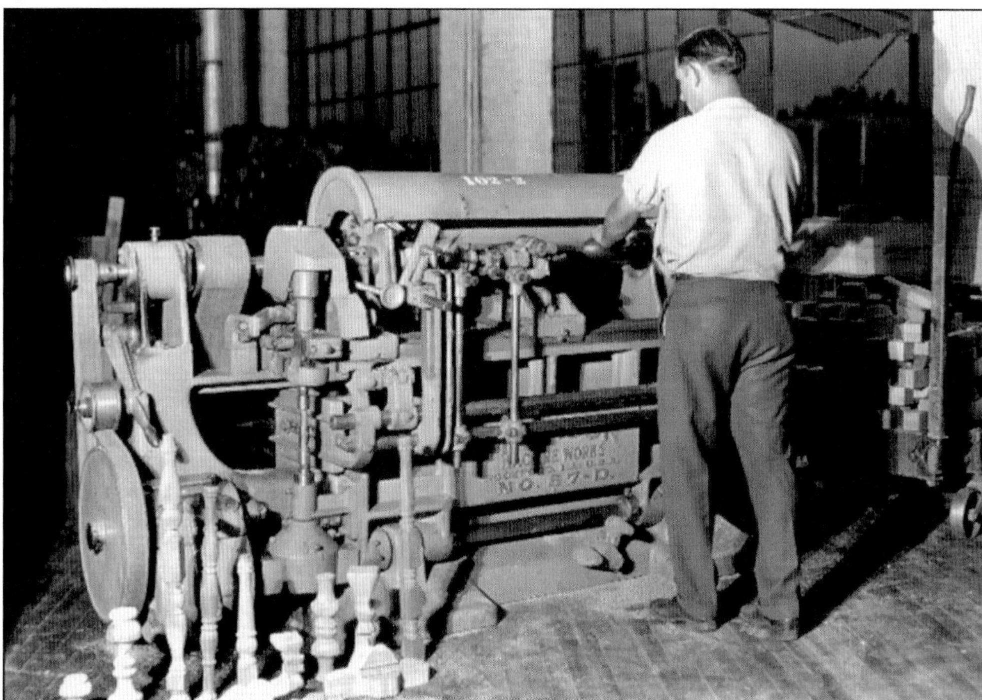

Anthony Rittmanic worked for the Kroehler Manufacturing Company for 36 years. He was photographed in the 1940s operating a wood-shaping machine in the Kroehler plant. (DM.)

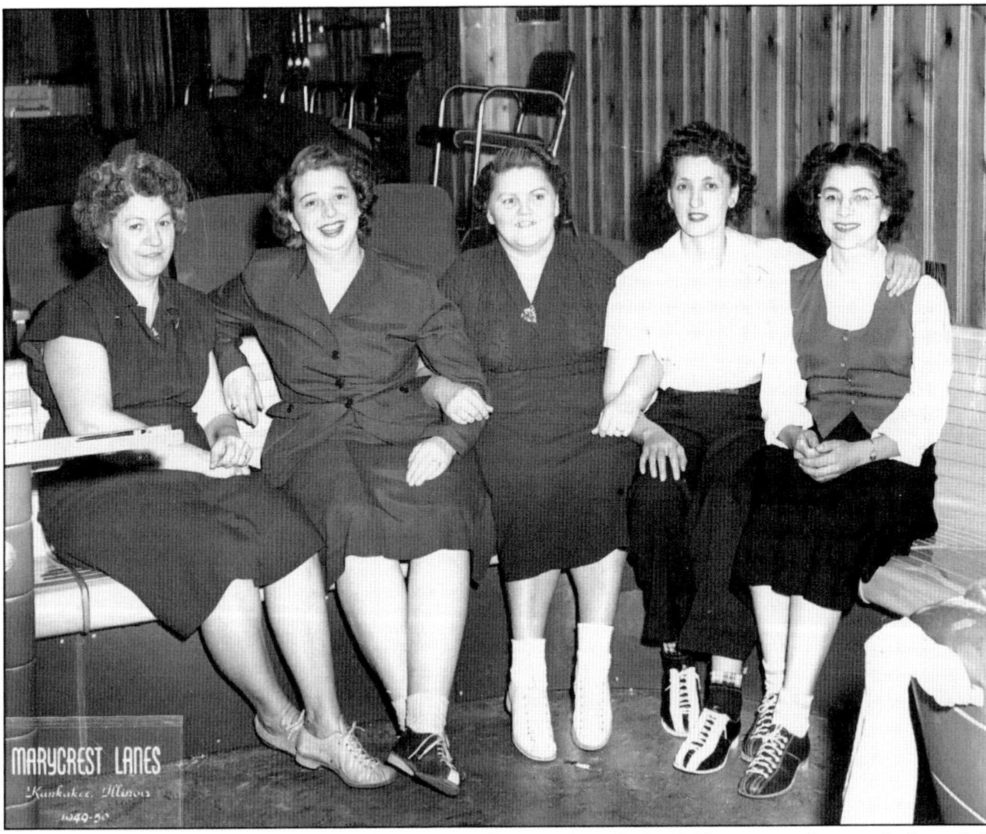

Kroehler sponsored this ladies bowling team during the 1949–1950 season. Pictured, from left to right, are Marguerite Strahl, Marjorie Waselewski, Leona Larkins, Elvie Surprenant, and Marjorie Kanoski. (Thomas J. Lindsay.)

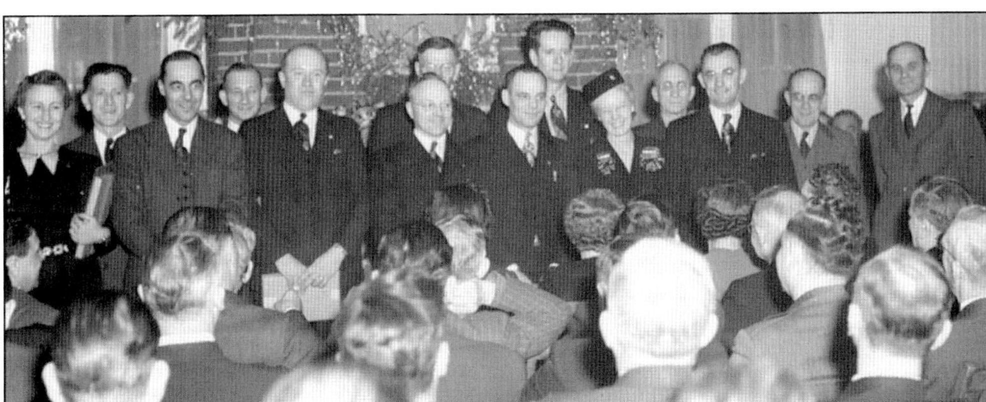

Kroehler employees assembled at the Kankakee Country Club in late December 1945 to celebrate Christmas and to give recognition to 33 people who had worked for the company for 20 years. (KCM-KDJ.)

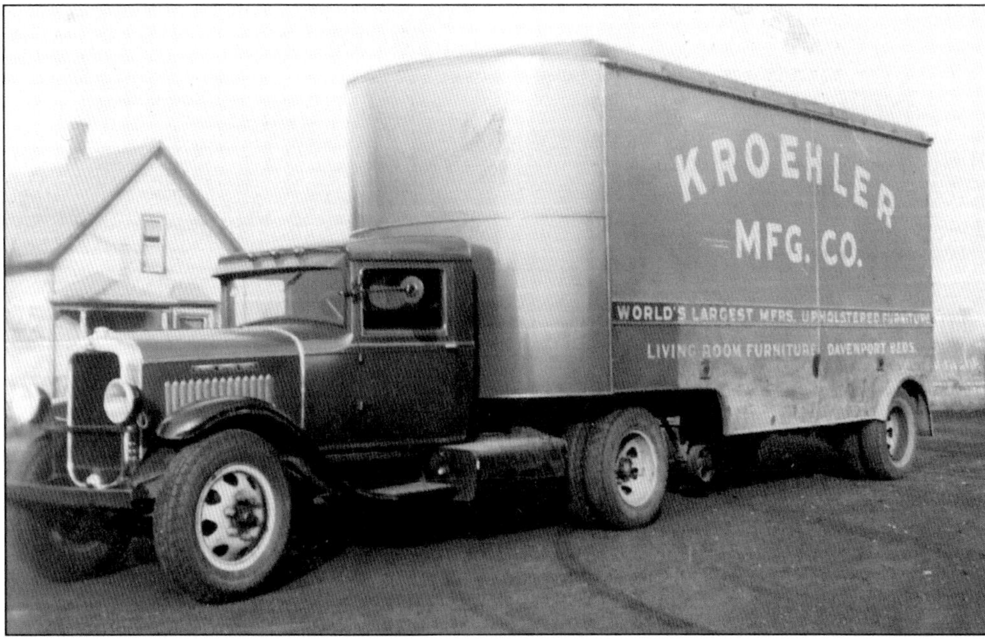

A large fleet of trucks was maintained by the Kroehler Manufacturing Company. This is a photograph of one of the early ones. (RS.)

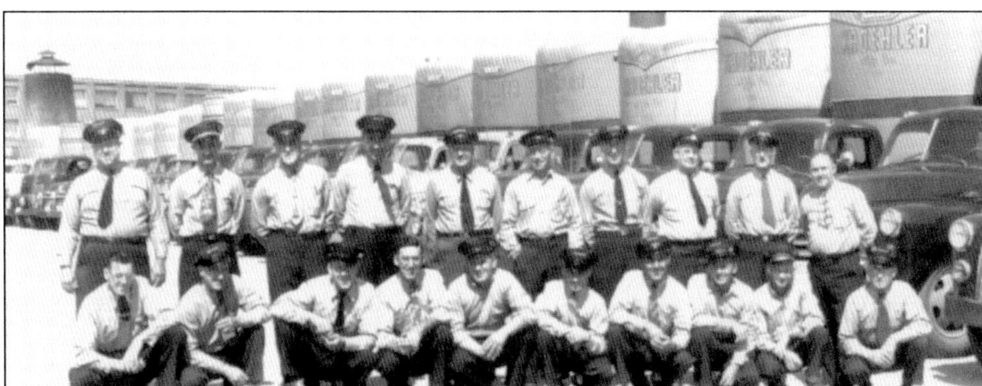

Truck drivers, from left to right, are (first row) Ray Doud, Louis Lenfelt, Richard Doud, Viator Hammende, Stanley Zajc, Clayton McQuillen, Verl Johnson, James Elliot, Everette Imhauser, and Jesse McElroy; (standing) Joseph Surprenant, Cifford Robins, Aaron Compton, Ted Martin, Pete Guimond, Harry Patterson, unidentified, Homer McElroy, Stafford Dusenbury, Emil Robbins. (BHS.)

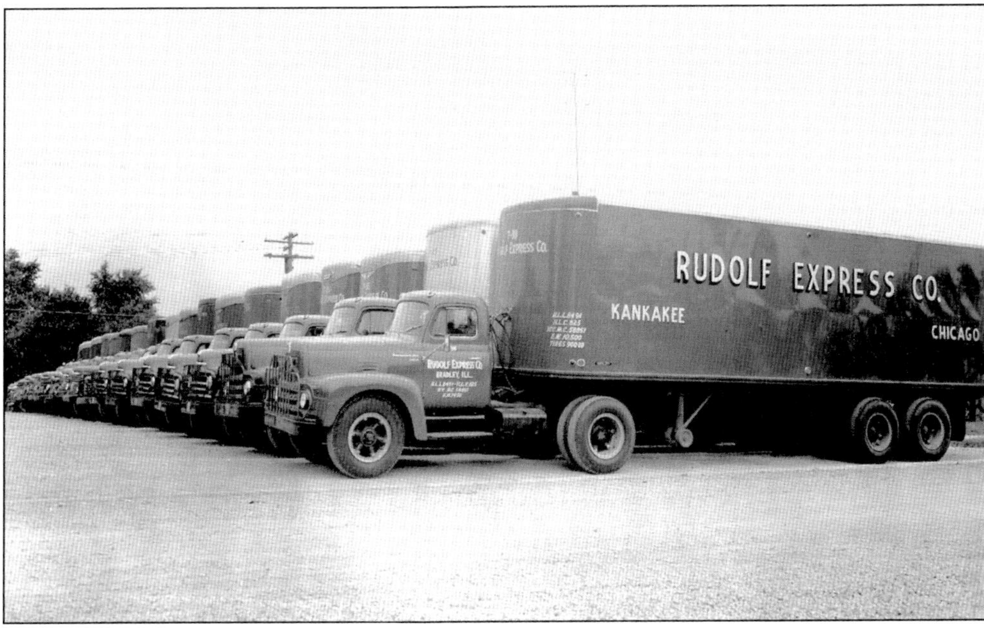

The several manufacturers in the Bradley are created opportunities for enterprising transportation companies. Rudolph Express Company was established in Bradley by Anton Rudolph. The Rudolph Express Company maintained a large number of over-the-road trucks. Rudolph was born in Hochberg, Germany, in 1896. He came to America in 1926, and for a time worked for Roosevelt Cartage in Chicago. (Rudolph family.)

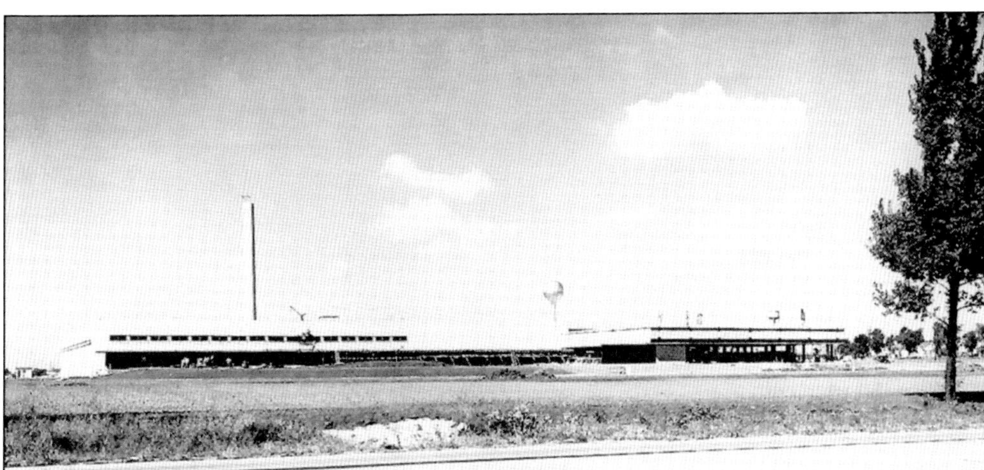

A new era began for Bradley when Armour Pharmaceutical Corporation opened a new $5 million plant on the eastern edge of the village in 1952. (BHS.)

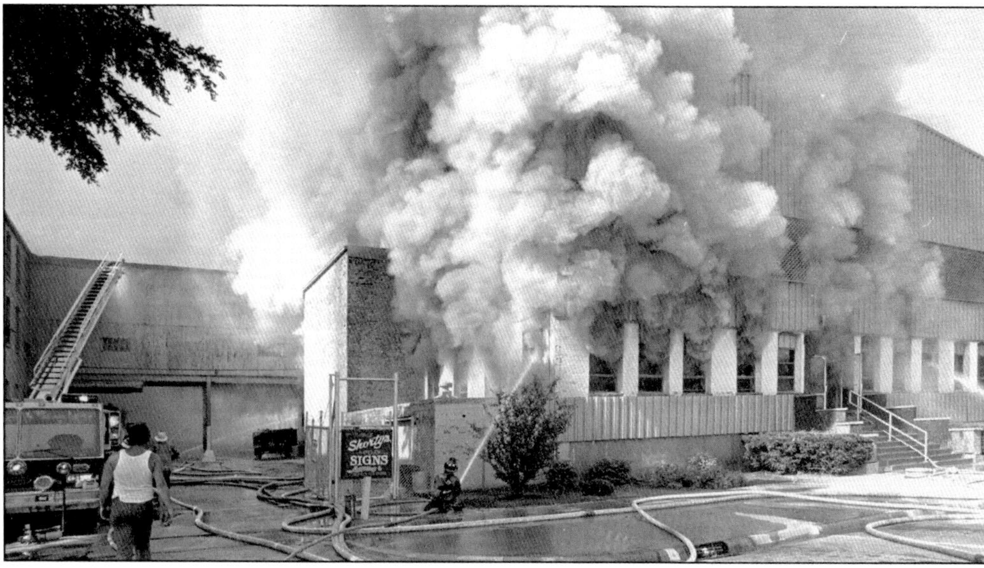

By October 1982, the Bradley Roper Corporation factory closed, and the property was given to the village of Bradley. Kankakee County unemployment reached 21.4 percent in February 1983. Plans were made to convert the plant site into a model of economic recovery. On July 14, 1986, fire destroyed six of the factory buildings. Only a part of the Sears, Roebuck and Company warehouse remained. (KCM-KDJ.)

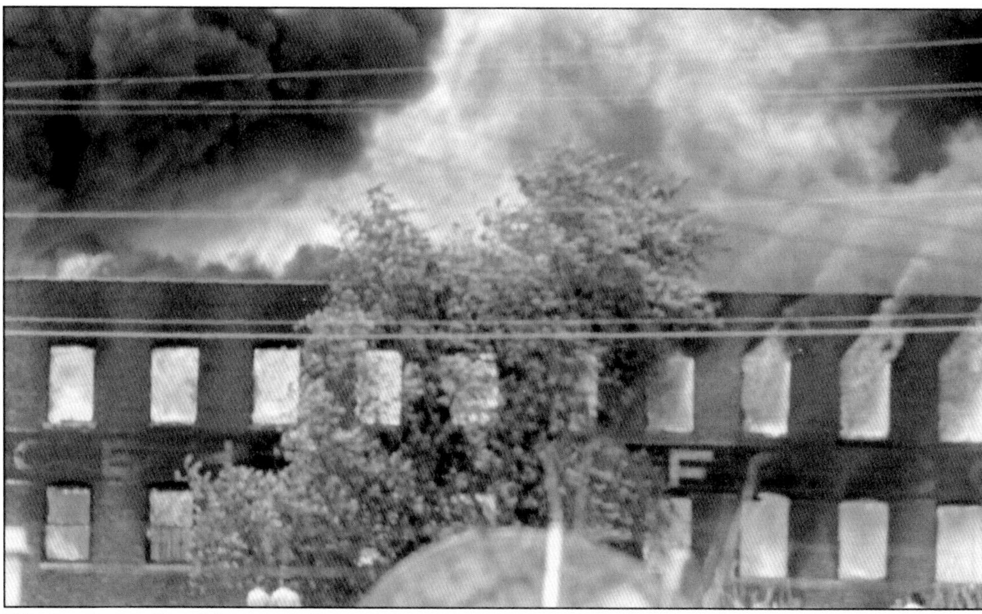

The bankrupt Kroehler Manufacturing Company passed into the hands of a Chicago investment company by 1981. All but the Kroehler plant in Bradley and three others were sold. In April 1982, the Luxor Spring Company of Chicago bought the Bradley plant and became licensed to sell furniture under the Kroehler name. Four years later, Luxor declared bankruptcy. The View Fan company set up shop in Plant No. 3 in 1987. The west building was rented by Quality Pallet Company. Plant No. 3 and the View Fan operation were consumed by fire on June 3, 1989. (KCM-KDJ.)

Five

BROADWAY

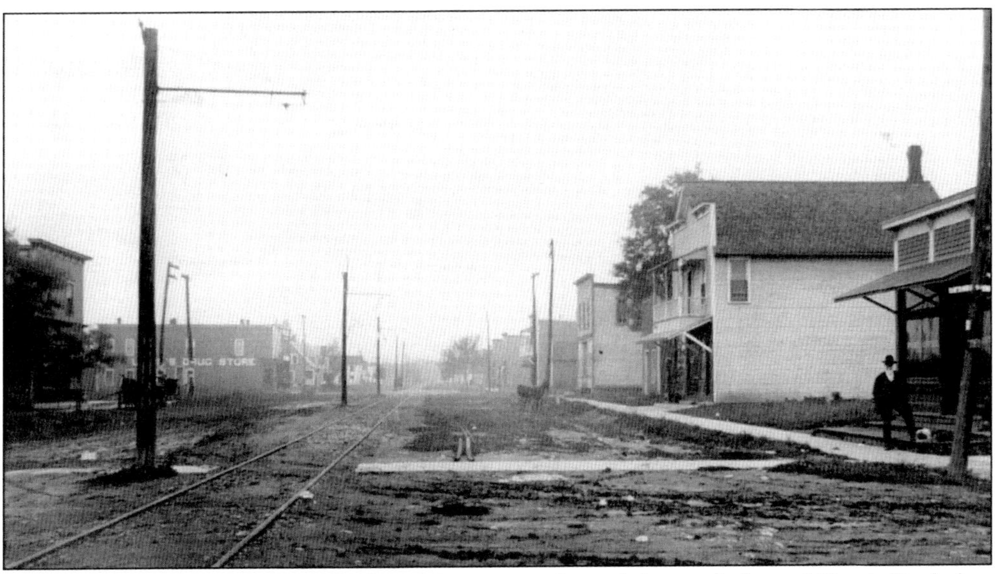

On June 4, 1892, Dr. Benjamin F. Uran became president of the newly-formed North Kankakee Electric Light and Railway Company. West Broadway, 100 feet wide and approximately a mile long, became North Kankakee's main street. On January 12, 1893, wires for the North Kankakee electric lights were being strung. On June 5, 1894, an electric light and water committee was appointed by board president Robert L. Cox. Stores and offices occupied the first floor of these buildings, with living quarters on the second floor and meeting halls for Woodsmen of the World and Independent Order of Odd Fellows. (SC.)

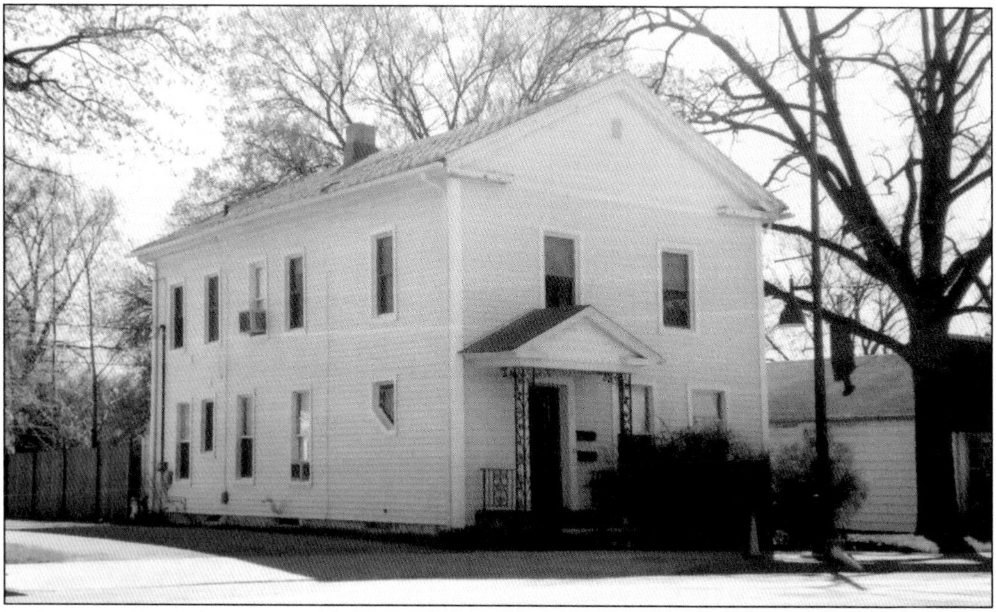

In August 1892, Celestin Graveline moved this building from South Main Street in Bourbonnais to a lot between Grand and Center Avenues on the south side of West Broadway. Possibly built in the 1860s, it is the oldest structure remaining in Bradley. The Worrel house (see page 29) might have been older, but it no longer exists. The front gable, side entrance design reflects a Greek Revival influence in architecture that was popular around 1860. (Author's collection.)

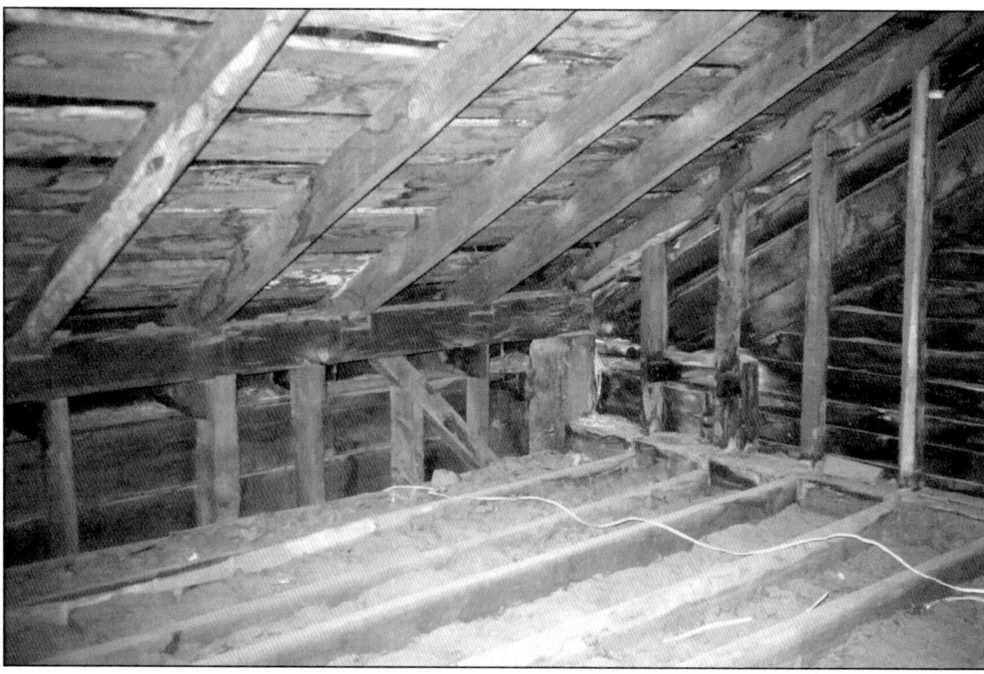

Even though the house has been renovated several times, traces of its original timber-frame construction remain. (Author's collection.)

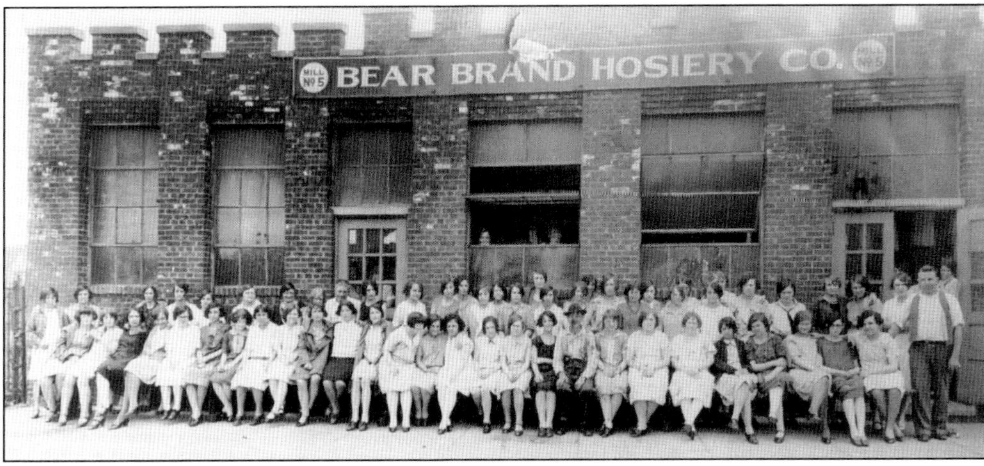

The Bear Brand Hosiery Company building stood in the 300 block on the south side of West Broadway. The photograph was taken in 1927 or 1928. (Flossie Gulzynski.)

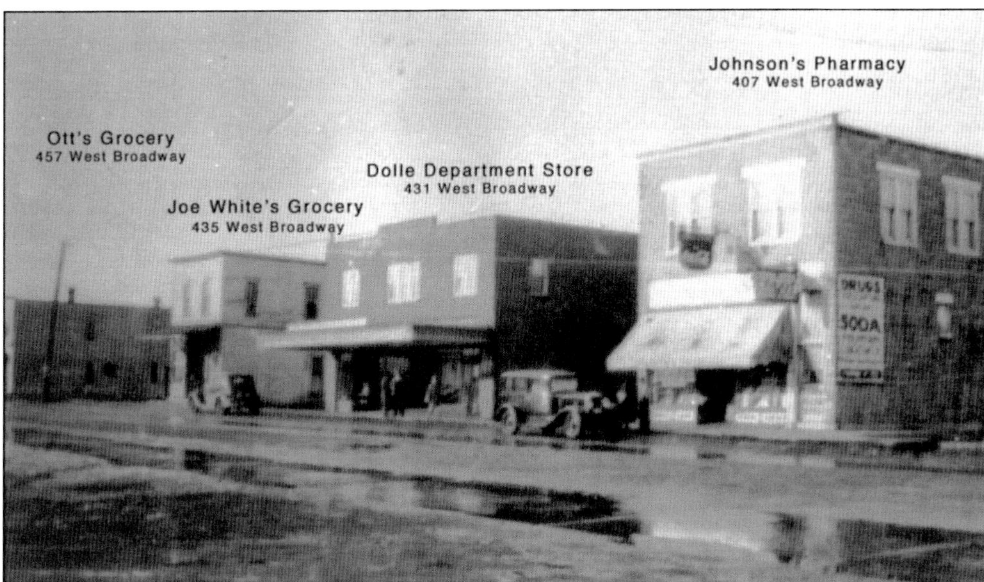

There are nine blocks on West Broadway between the Illinois Central Railroad tracks on the east and Vasseur Avenue (now Kennedy Drive) on the west. Most of the first buildings on this street, with a few exceptions, were frame, two-story flats. The building to the left of the center is a good representation. By 1898, West Broadway would have had 27 or so buildings. Emory Souligne opened the first general store at 341 West Broadway in May 1892, and later this store also housed the post office. (BHS.)

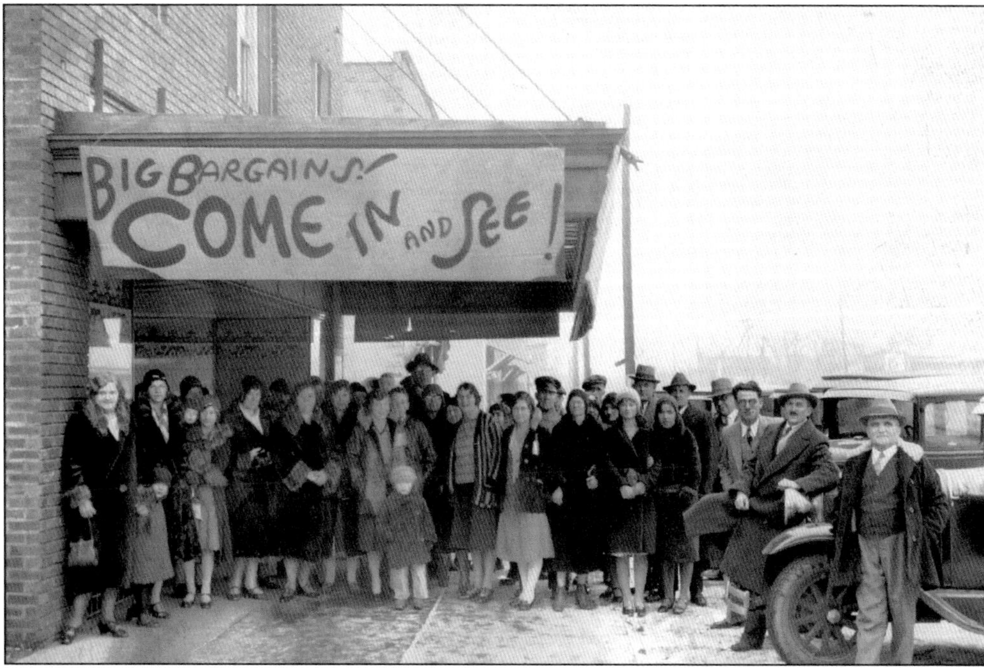

The group of people in this photograph appear to be anticipating the opening of Dolle's Department Store. The building was built by Alphonse Dolle in 1930 at 423 West Broadway. (James Guiss.)

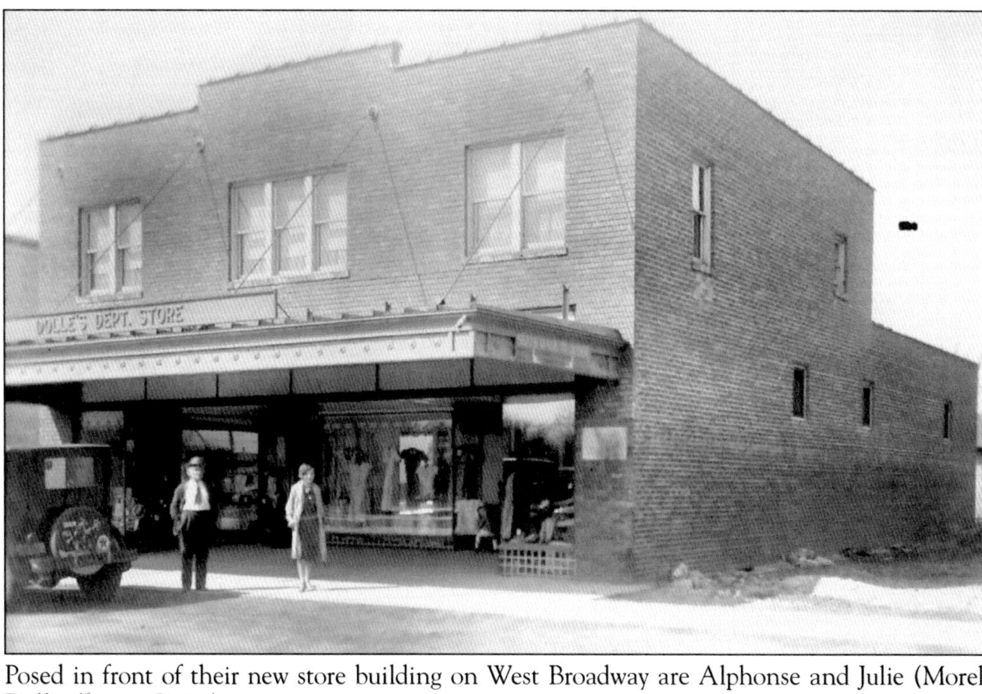

Posed in front of their new store building on West Broadway are Alphonse and Julie (Morel) Dolle. (James Guiss.)

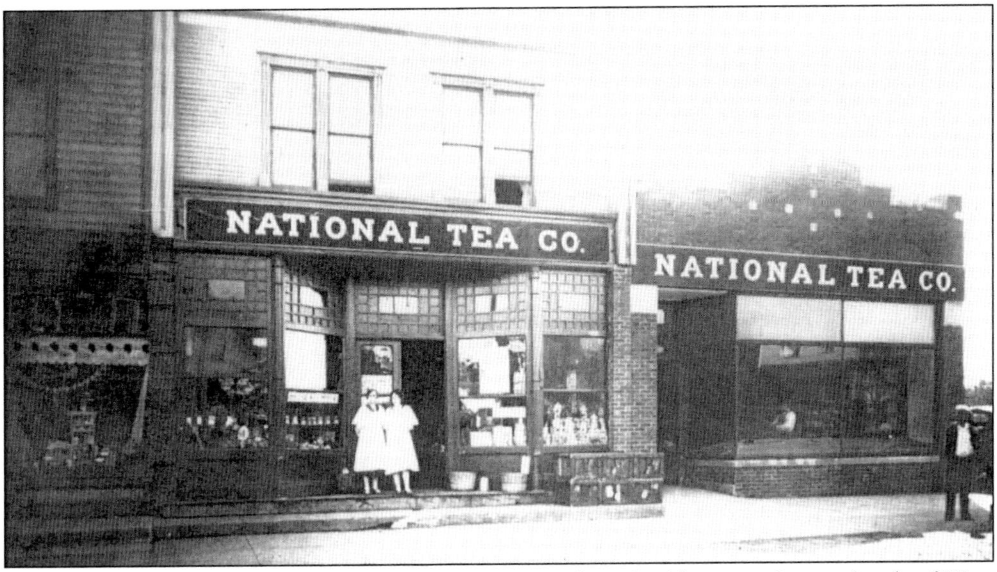

The National Tea Store, a chain grocery store, occupied two buildings on the south side of West Broadway during the 1940s. Frank W. Hoehn (village trustee in 1909 and village board president in 1913) had been the proprietor of a grocery store (below) in this same location. At far left in the above photograph is the International Order of Odd Fellows building (southwest corner of West Broadway and South Wabash Avenue). Francis X. Crevier kept a store on the first floor in 1898. A later occupant was George C. Schneider's Rexall Pharmacy. and during the late 1950s, the Erickson Cafe. (Above, BHS; below, DM.)

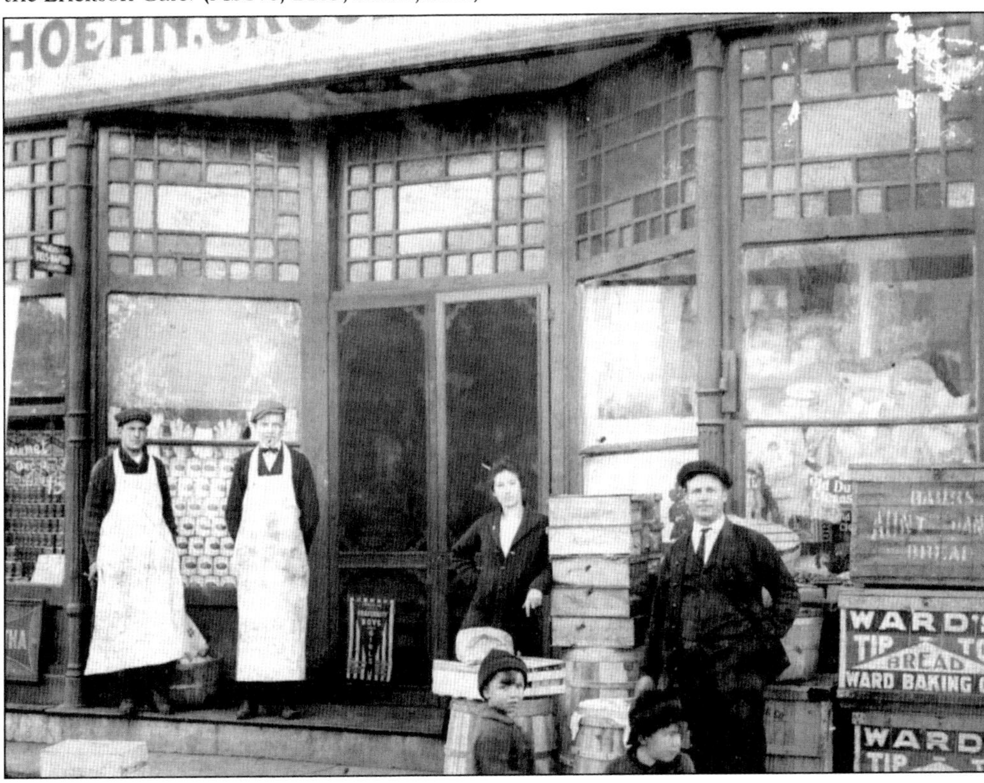

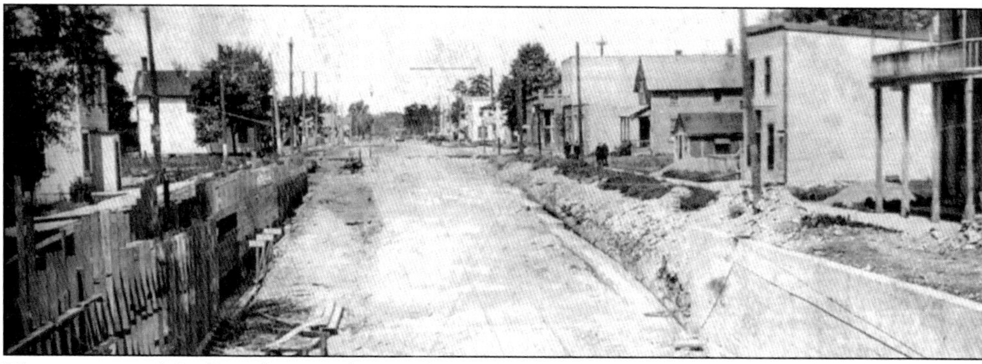

The opening of the Broadway underpass beneath the Illinois Central Railroad and the laying of concrete strips on either side of the streetcar tracks on West Broadway in 1926 was a major event. It called for a celebration with dancing, a parade, and other festivities. This photograph, taken during construction in 1925, shows new streetcar tracks in the foreground. North Washington Avenue is at the top of the slope. (RG.)

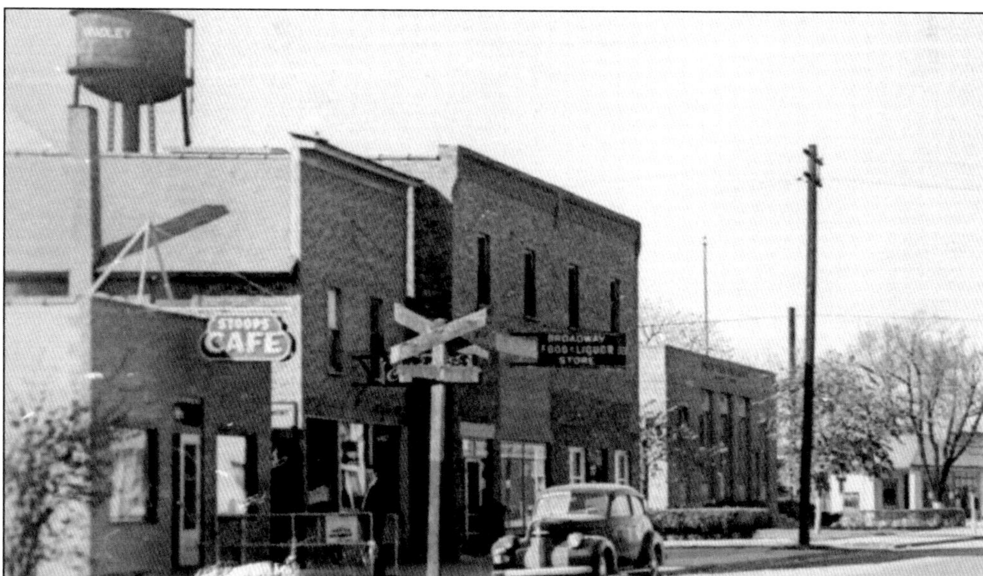

The new Bradley Post Office (1938) is left of center in this early 1940s photograph. The two-story building in the center of the picture was originally a hotel built by Edward LaBounty in March 1893. In the late 1930s, the first floor was occupied by the Broadway Food and Liquor store. Stoops Cafe (left) stands on the southwest corner of West Broadway and South Washington Avenue. The railroad crossing sign warned motorists to observe the railroad spur running down Washington Avenue. A bakery run by Henniche and Stewig was on that corner in 1898. (BHS.)

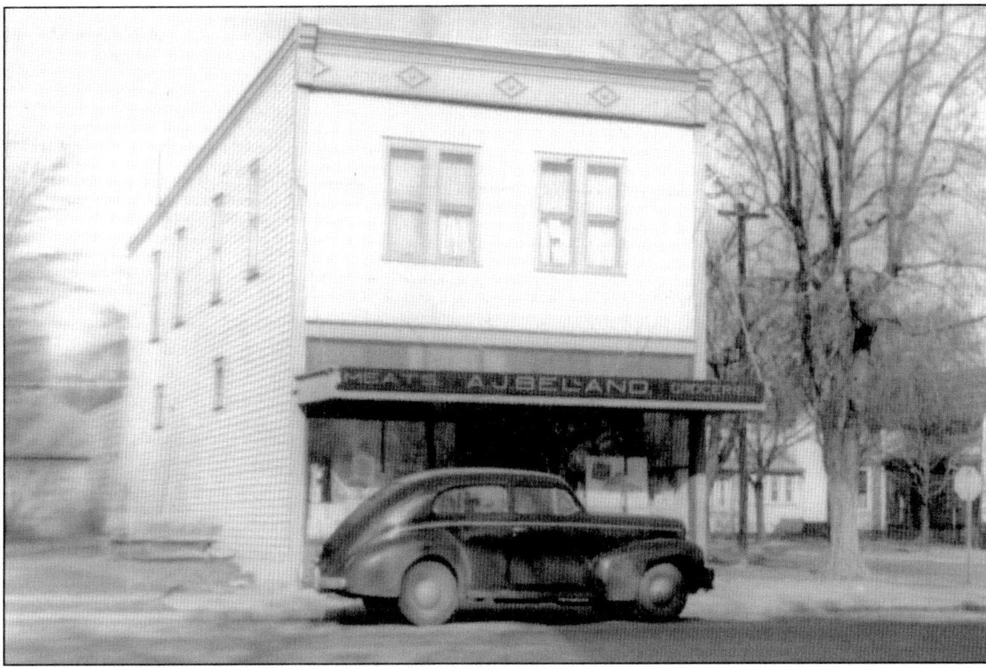

Both photographs are of the same building. It was built by William E. Kennedy as a storeroom in 1892 on the northwest corner of Center Avenue and West Broadway. In that year, in the last week of November, W. O. Umstead of Colfax opened a restaurant on the first floor. This building became known as Umstead Hall (second floor). The first Catholic services in Bradley were held in Umstead Hall in 1904. The Norris Saloon later occupied the first floor, and Arthur J. Beland kept Beland's Meats and Groceries store there in the 1930s and 1940s. Hubert Brothers ran a "self service" food market in the Beland store for a short time in the early 1950s, but by 1956 the store name had reverted back to Beland's Meats and Groceries. (CE.)

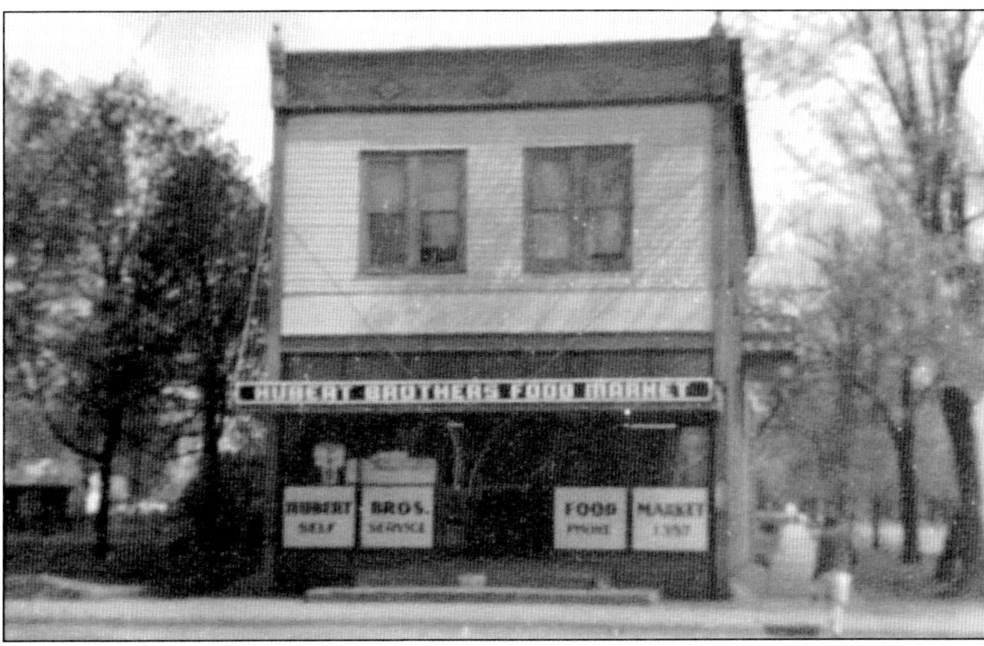

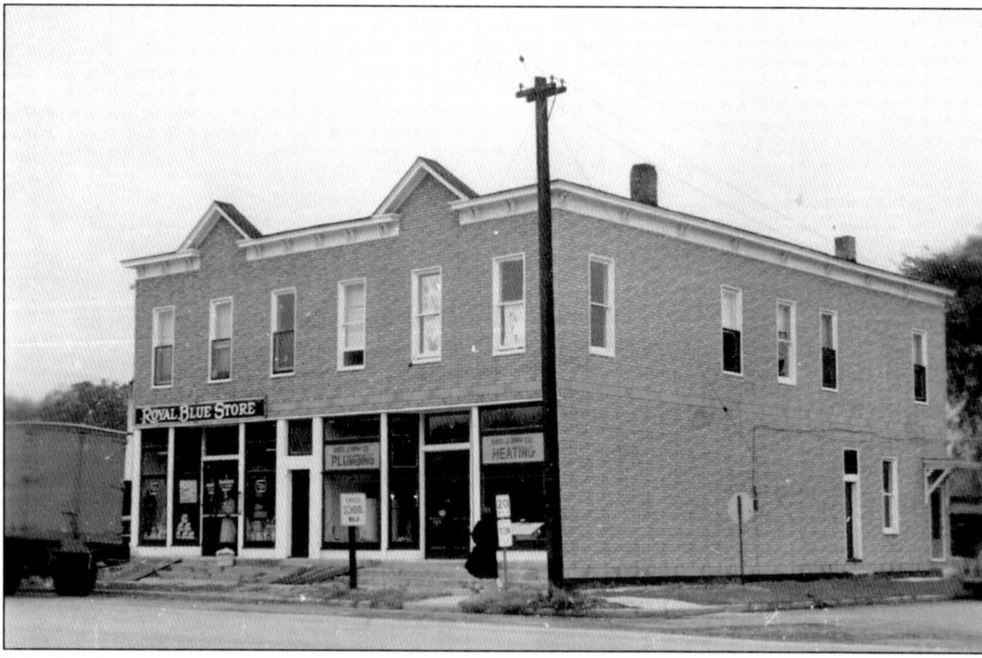

The first known occupants of this building were pharmacist D. G. Kitner and watch and clock maker Ida V. Worth, in 1898. This photograph was taken in the 1940s. At that time, Samuel N. Longtin was the Royal Blue store's proprietor. Next door, on the right, was George Ray's Plumbing and Heating business. (CE.)

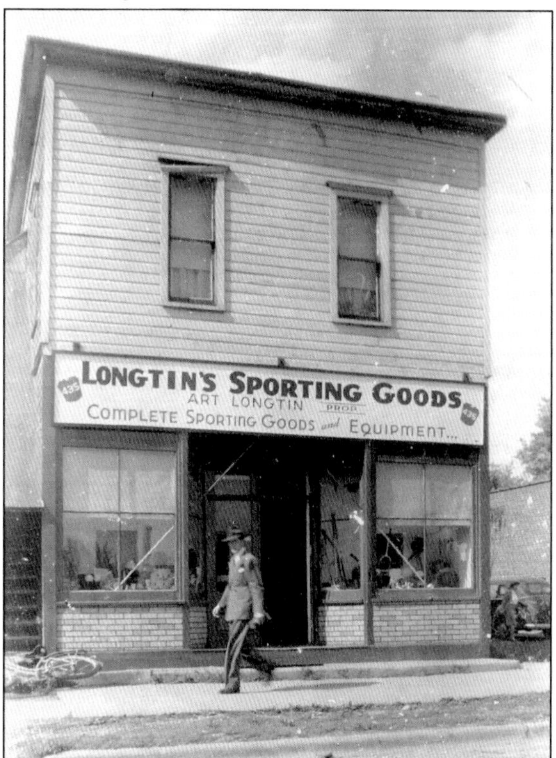

In 1947, one would have found Art Longtin's Sporting Goods Store at 435 West Broadway. It was in this building that Joe White kept a grocery store in the 1930s (see page 63). (CE.)

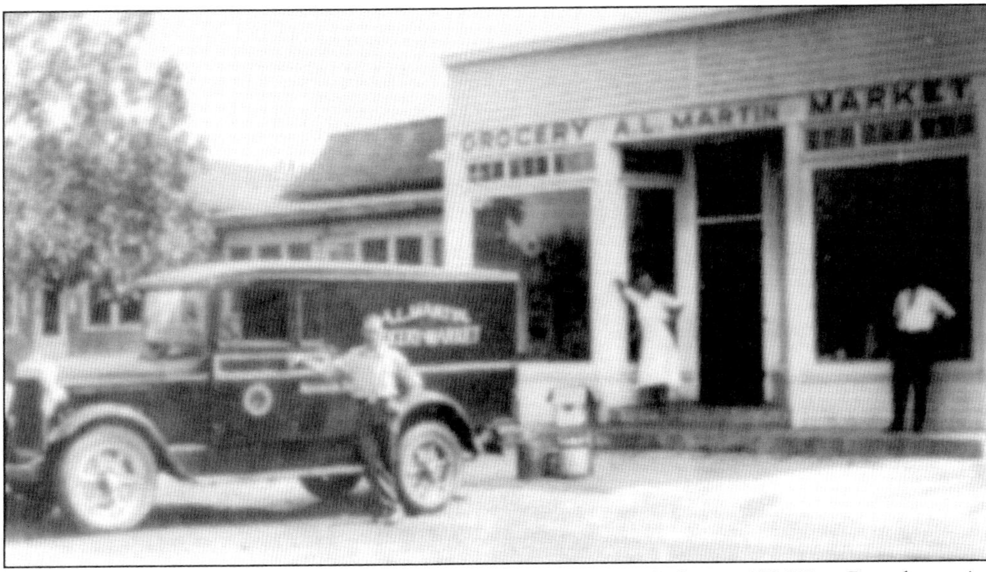

The 1920s photograph above shows A. C. Martin's Grocery Market at 370 West Broadway. An interior view is seen below. Ray Rasmussen is on the right behind the counter. Years later, this building housed the first Rudy's Market in Bradley. (Above, BHS; below, Beverly Rasmussen.)

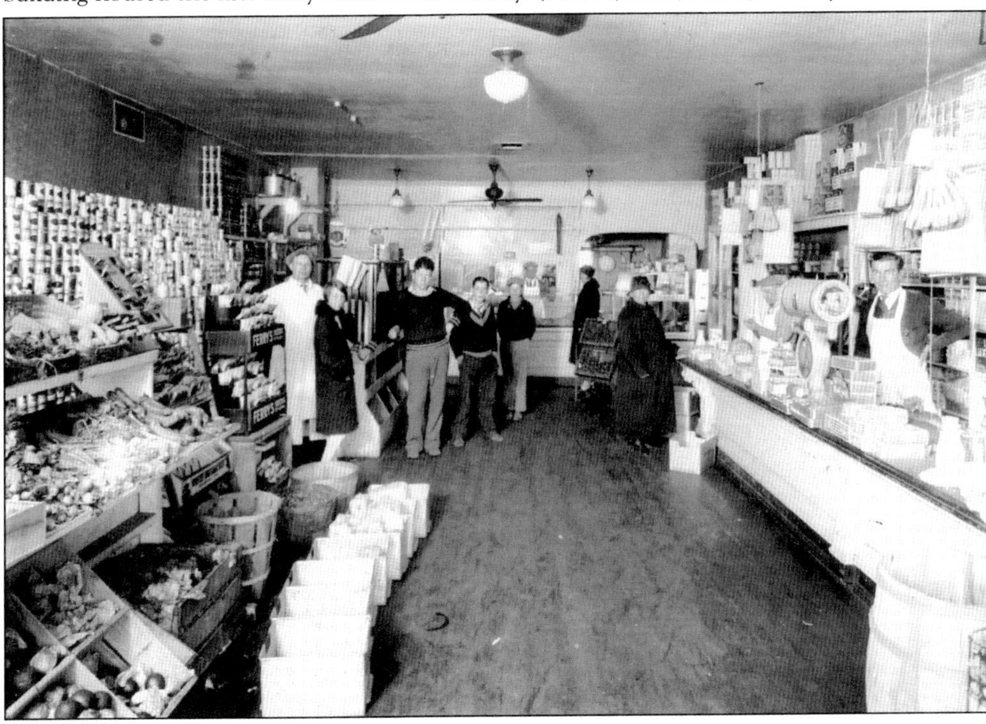

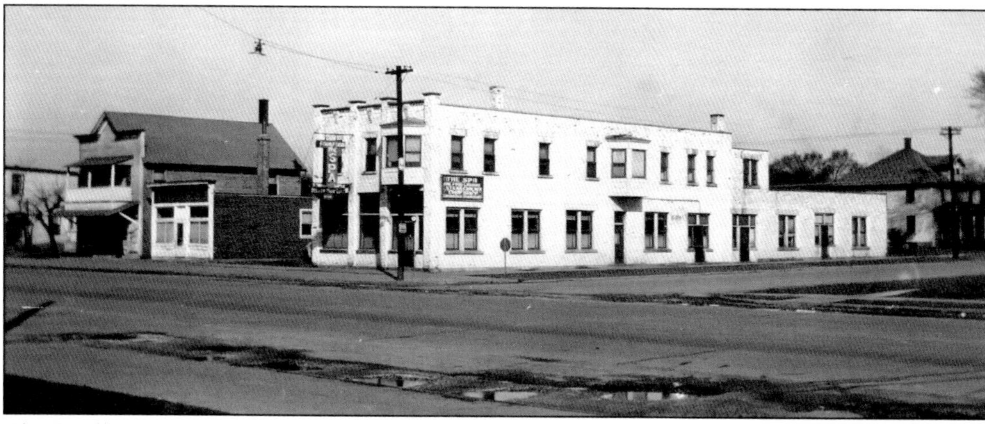

The Bradley Post Office had occupied the original building on this site from 1889 to 1899. The Bradley State and Savings Bank relocated to this building on December 18, 1911. The bank president was Frederic F. Marcotte, the vice president was George M. Dilley, and the treasurer was E. C. Vandagrift. The bank's elected directors included Joseph Peschel, Len Small (the future governor of Illinois), Nathan Block, Marcotte, C. E. Robinson, Joseph Surprenant, C. R. Miller, Dilley, David C. Wikoff, and Vandagrift. At the time this photograph was taken, The SPA, a bar and restaurant serving Chinese and American food, occupied the building. (CE.)

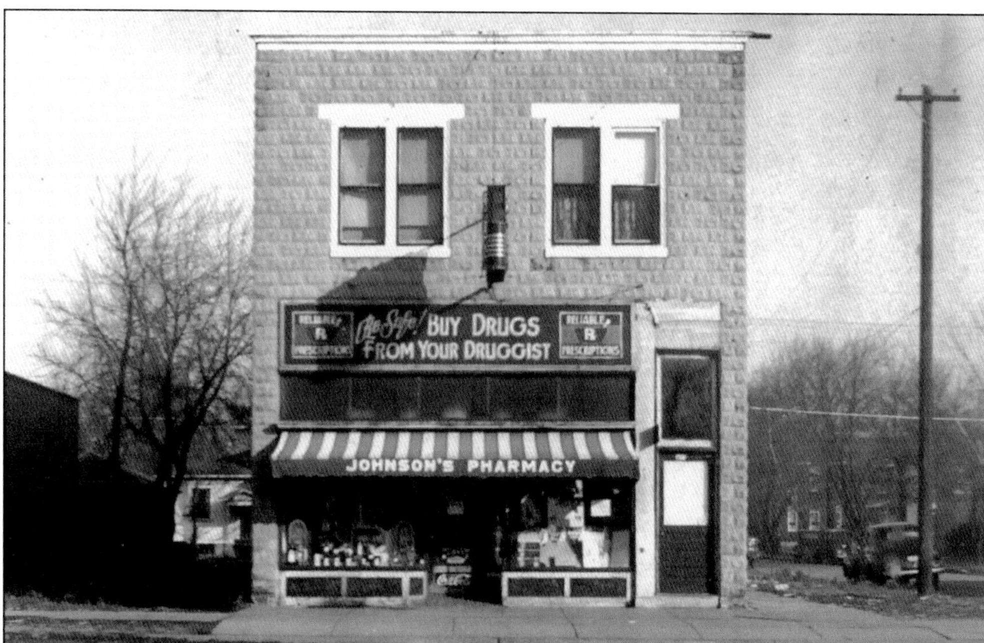

This cement block building was built at 407 West Broadway in 1912. It housed the Orpheum Theater where Art Baldwin operated the projector. Years later, the Orpheum Theater became Johnson's Pharmacy. It is now Westphal Jewelers. The Scenic Theater opened at 457 West Broadway in 1907. The Scenic Theater, which was located in a building later occupied by Ott's Grocery (see page 63), was the first moving-picture house in Bradley to show silent films. (CE.)

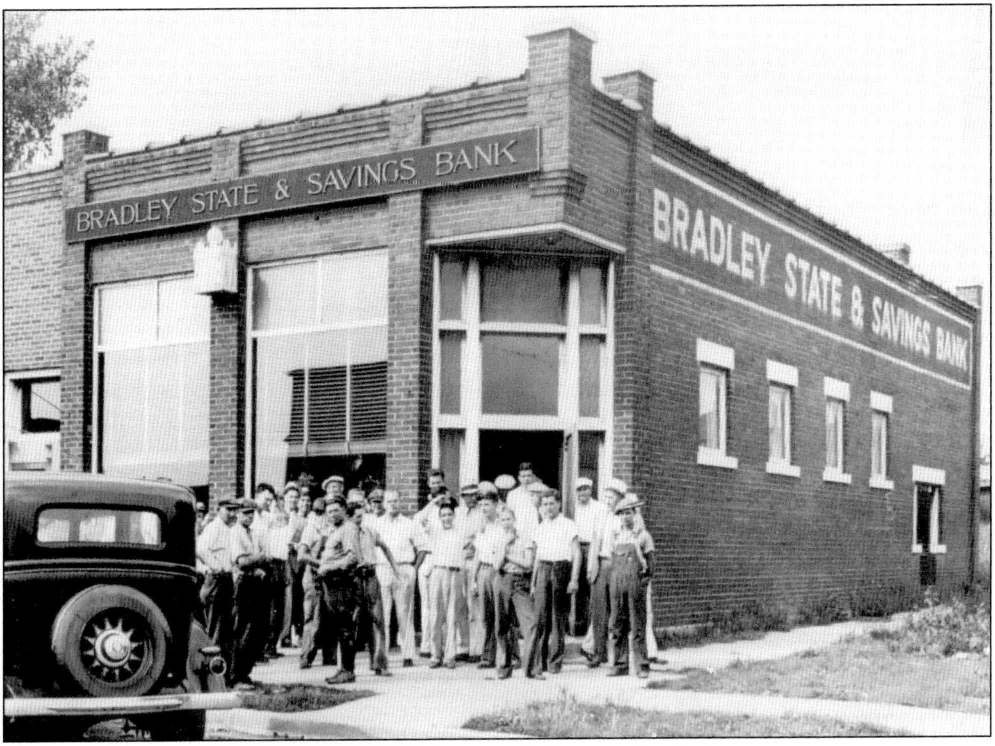

These are photographs of the Bradley State and Savings Bank in its new quarters on the northwest corner of West Broadway and North Washington Avenue in the late 1920s or early 1930s. (KCM.)

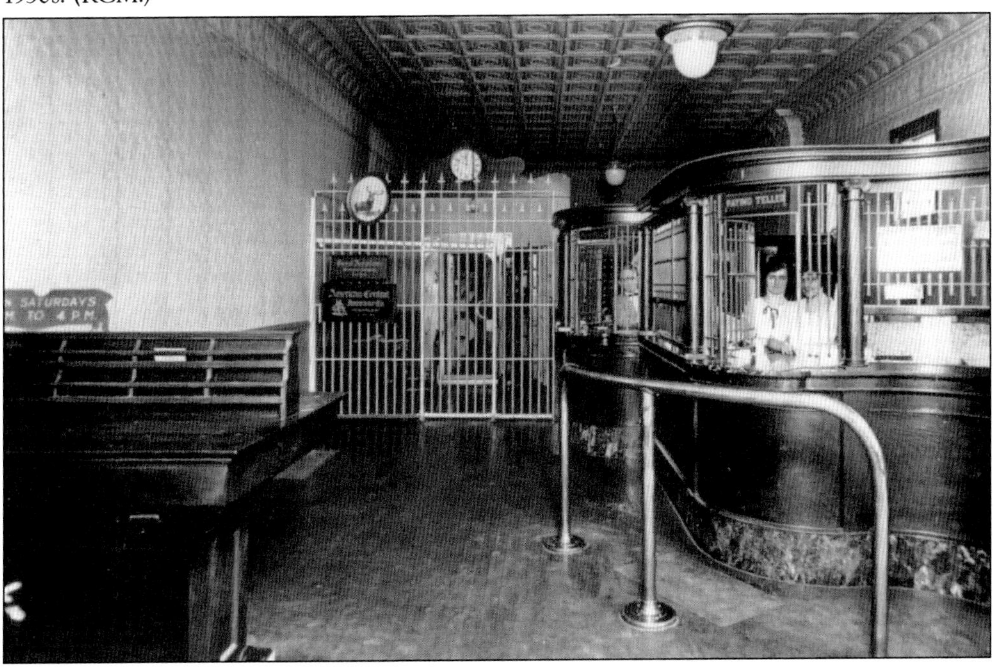

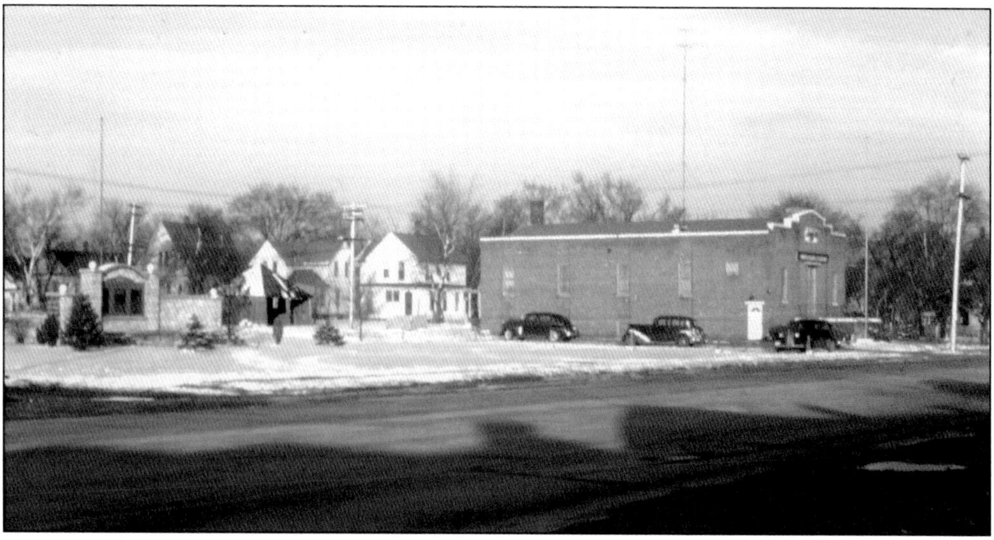

Veterans of World War I organized Bradley's American Legion Post 766 on September 24, 1934. The first commander was Walter Heinz. Meetings were held in the Independent Order of Odd Fellows hall on West Broadway. In November 1934, Ruth Bleaus became the first president of the American Legion Auxiliary. During the early 1940s, the members built the American Legion Post building. (CE.)

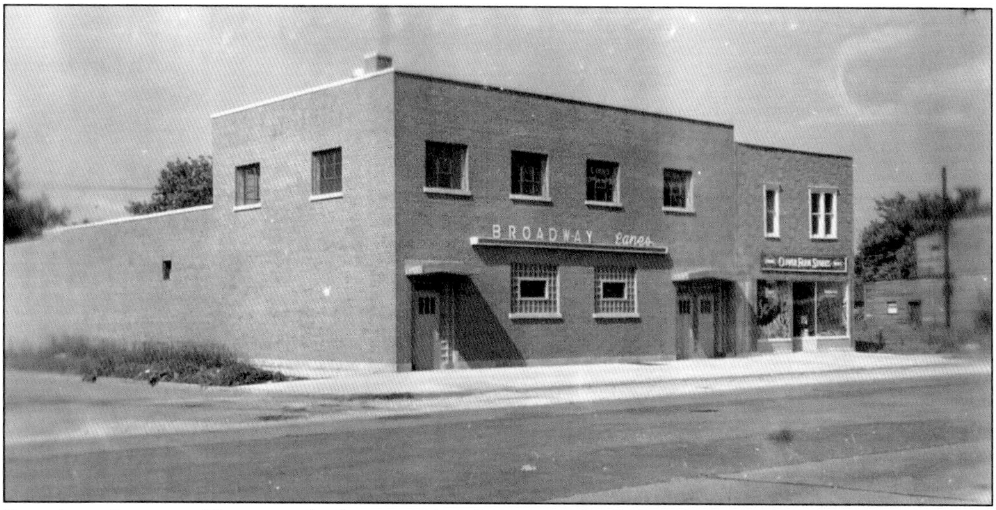

Broadway Lanes, offering eight lanes of bowling, was built by the Dandelles family in 1948. George Dandelles was the proprietor. He was assisted by Ralph and Fritz Legris. This photograph was taken soon after the bowling alley opened. The bowling alley closed in the mid-1950s. The building still stands on the northeast corner of West Broadway and North Grand Avenue, and it is now a martial arts school. In the 1940s, the Clover Farm Store occupied the building on the right. During the early 1900s, it had been the Scenic Theater, and much later, it became Ott's Grocery. (CE.)

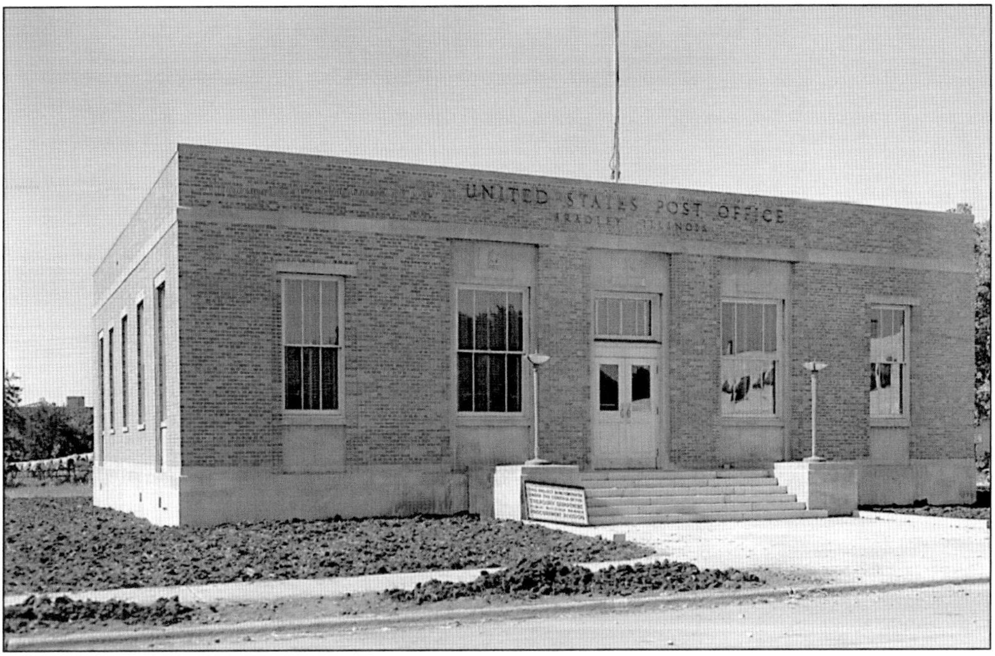

Construction of a new post office building in the 200 block of the south side of West Broadway took place during the first seven months of 1938. It was the first federal building in Bradley. On Monday, August 15, the post office opened for business. Helen S. McCarthy was the acting postmistress, and Edward Mulligan and Theodore Mailloux were employees. (KCM-KDJ.)

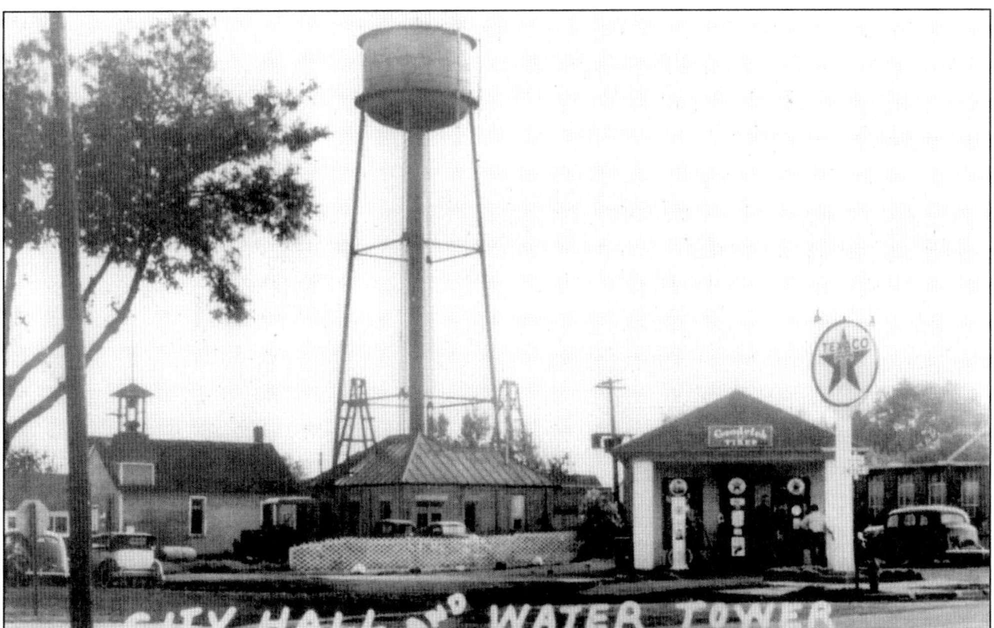

Clifford E. Coash was the proprietor of the Texaco Service Station on the southwest corner of West Broadway and South Michigan Avenue in the 1940s. The village pump house and water tower are in the center of the photograph, and the village hall with the fire bell on top is on the left. (BHS.)

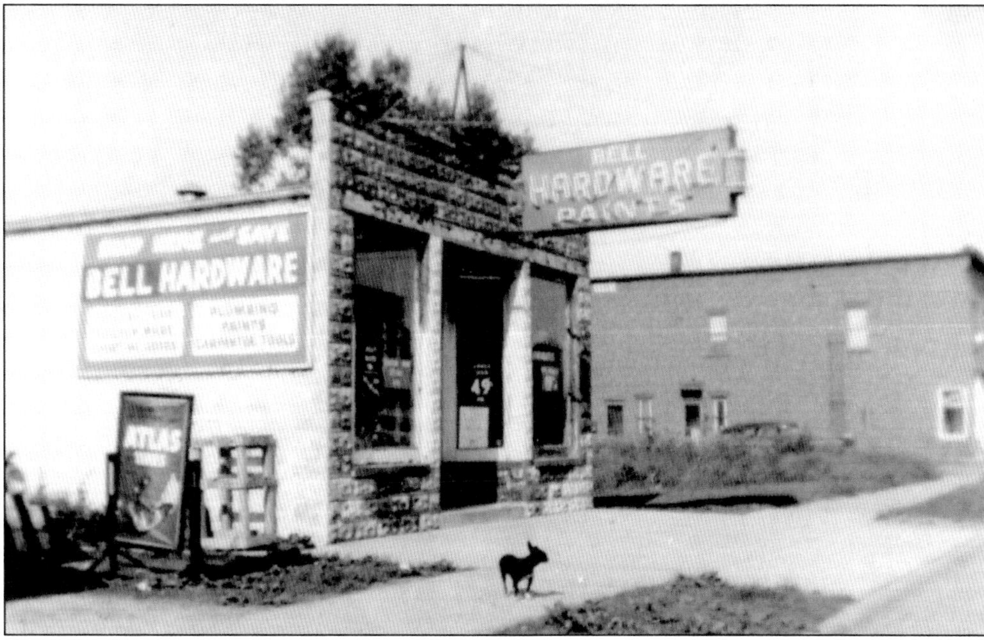

Bell Hardware and Paint store was established in 1925. It was located at 358 West Broadway, just west of the Standard Oil station. The Independent Order of Odd Fellows hall is in the background. (RB.)

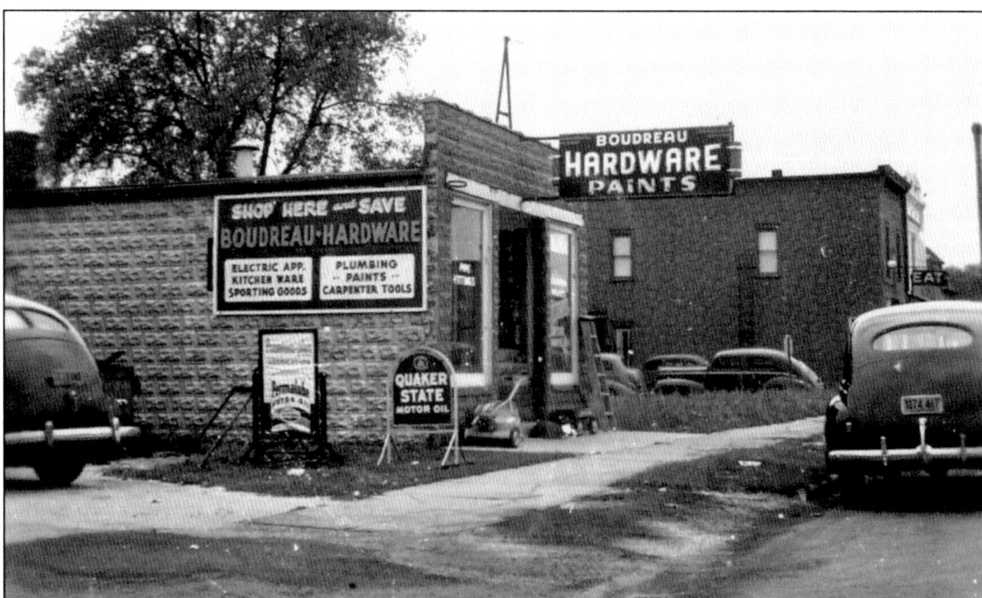

The original Bell Hardware and Paint store was sold to William and Donald Boudreau in 1948. The Boudreaus were sign painters. They maintained the store for two years. Robert Bell bought the store back in 1950 and modernized the front and built an addition for sporting goods and radio service. Bell sold the building in 1960 and moved to a new location (see page 76). (CE.)

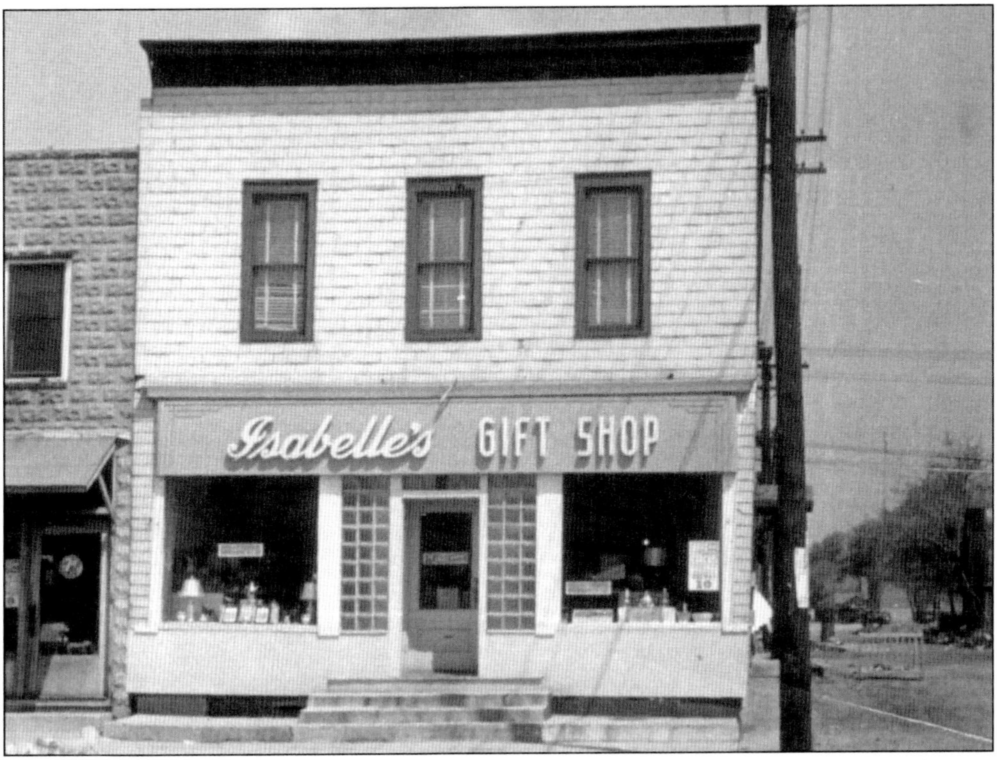

This building stood on the alley at 335 West Broadway in the 1940s. The earliest record shows that during the late 1890s, it was a hardware store and tin shop. Lambert's Lunch Room and Ice Cream Store preceded Isabelle's Gift Shop in that location. The building was razed sometime before the 1970s, and the site is now occupied by G and G Printing. (CE.)

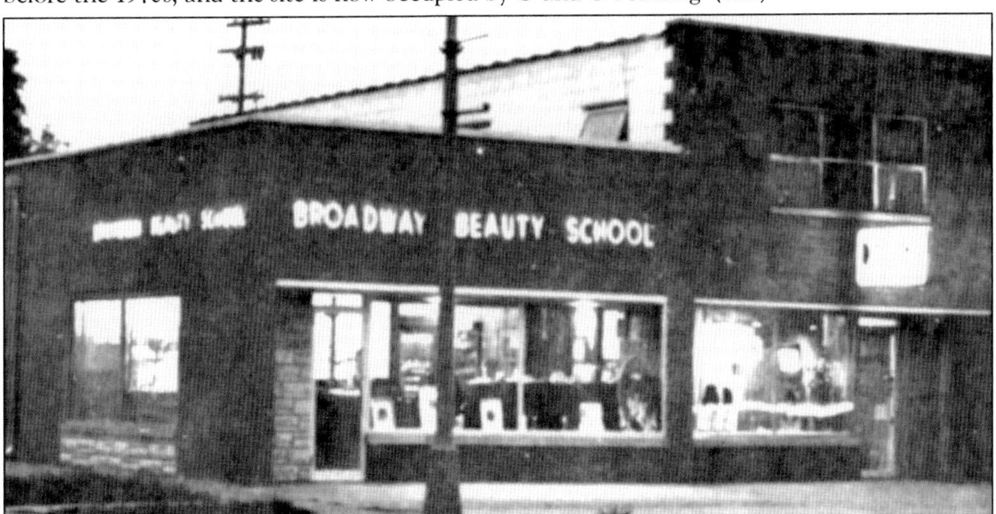

John Manning established the Broadway Beauty School on the northeast corner of North Prairie Avenue and West Broadway in 1962. Larry Kinder and his wife, Rita, took over the business in the 1970s. From 1980 to 1984, John and Janice Schoup were the proprietors. In 1996, Mark and Lorie Clark became the school's owners. A few years later, they changed the name to Trend Setters College of Cosmetology and moved to a new location. (BHS.)

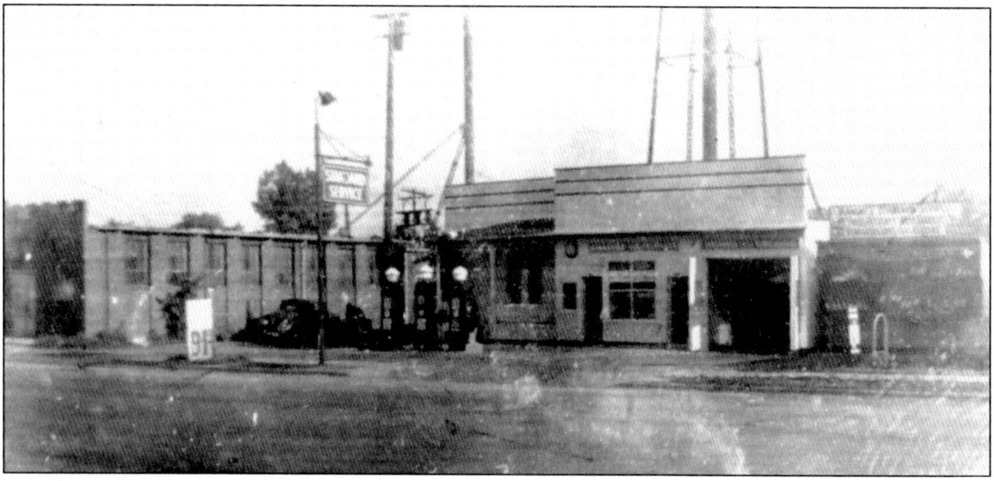

Joseph A. Biamont owned and operated this Standard Oil filling station and repair garage at 342 West Broadway during the 1940s. The old Bear Brand Hosiery building is on the left. (CE.)

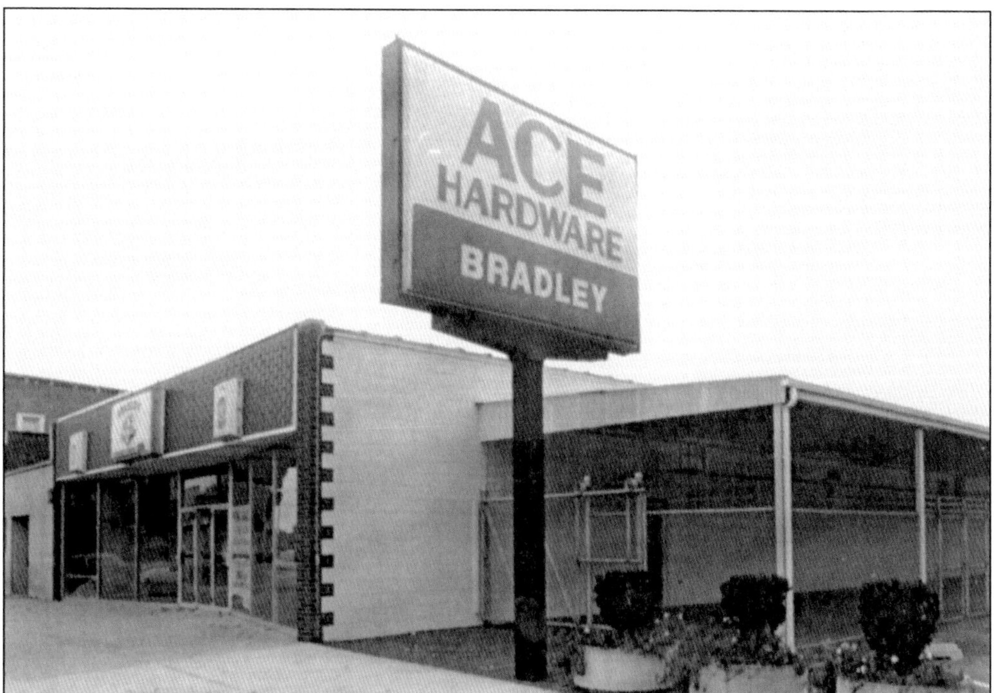

In 1960, Robert Bell moved his store from the location at 358 West Broadway to 428 West Broadway. Bell's store then became an Ace Hardware franchise. After 75 years of serving hardware customers on West Broadway, Bell's store closed in 2000. (RB.)

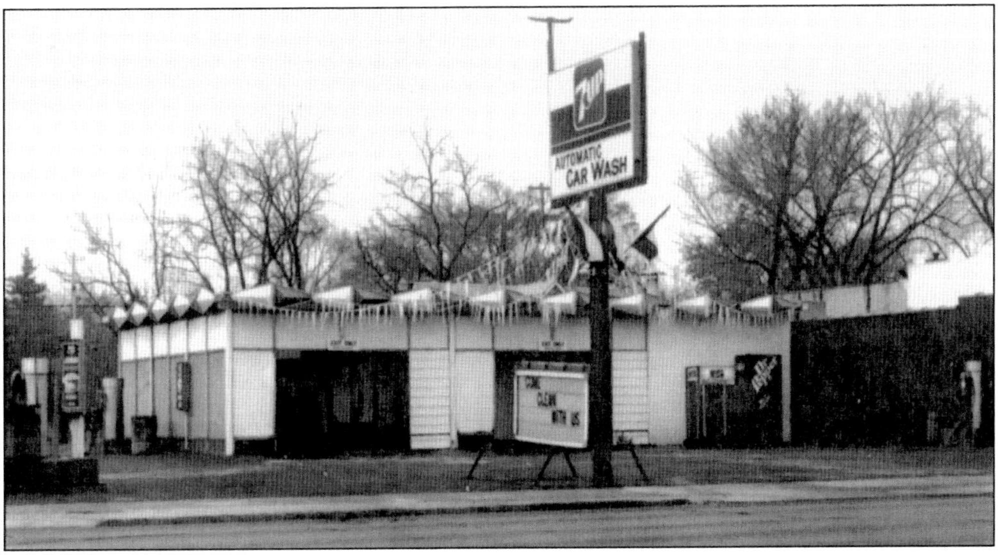

A brand new car wash in the 800 block of West Broadway in the 1960s was a novelty to Bradleyans. (RB.)

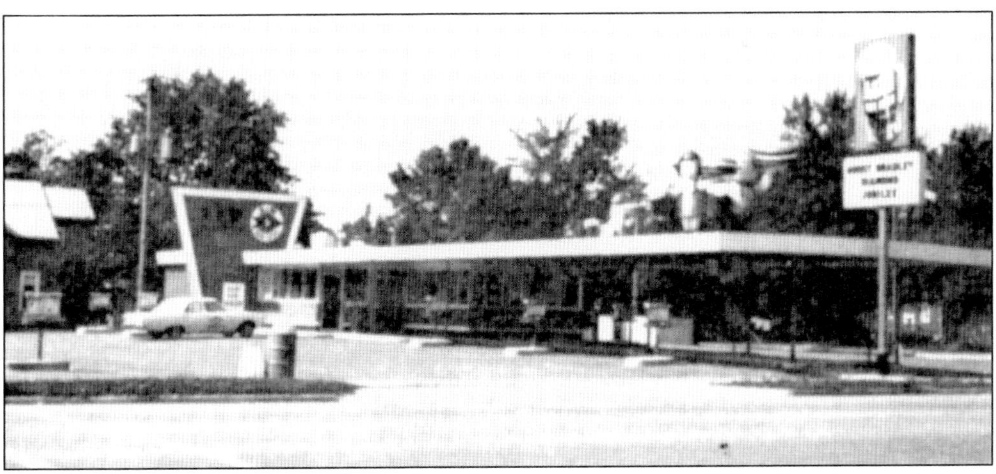

A&W Root Beer Drive Inn was located on the southwest corner of West Broadway and South Cleveland Avenue in the 1960s. It was managed by Cy and Mardell Beaupre. (BHS.)

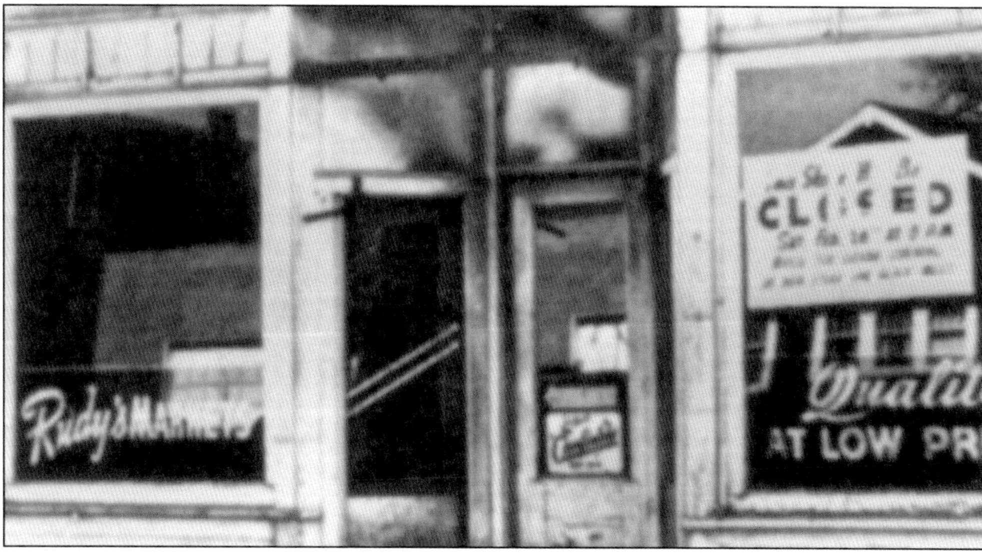

"Every man has one supreme big moment during his lifetime. This is mine," wrote Rudolph (Rudy) Jagersma in March of 1955, at the time he opened Rudy's Market (below) on West Broadway in Bradley. Bradley was Rudy's adopted home town. He had been born in Kalamazoo, Michigan. In 1936 he came to Kankakee as meat manager for the IGA grocery chain. Four years later as owner of an IGA franchise Rudy opened a store at 1245 East River Street in Kankakee, and another in what had been the A.L. Martin Grocery Market (see page 69) in Bradley (above), at 570 West Broadway. Rudy's first "supermarket" was built in Joliet in 1952. On March 2, 1955, he opened Rudy's Market in the 700 block of West Broadway in Bradley. It covered 14,500 square feet, employed 60 people, advertised 10,000 items at "everyday low prices," and the parking lot had space for 135 cars. Rudy's policy of filling management jobs with young men who he trained, and who had worked their way up through his stores enabled Rudy to build a retail grocery empire of 14 supermarkets in 12 years. Rudy's markets merged with Scot Lad Foods in 1961. Scot Lad was a Chicago wholesale food supply company. Rudy's Memorial Park on South Washington Avenue was dedicated in November 1974 by the Bradley Lions. (Above, CE; below, DM.)

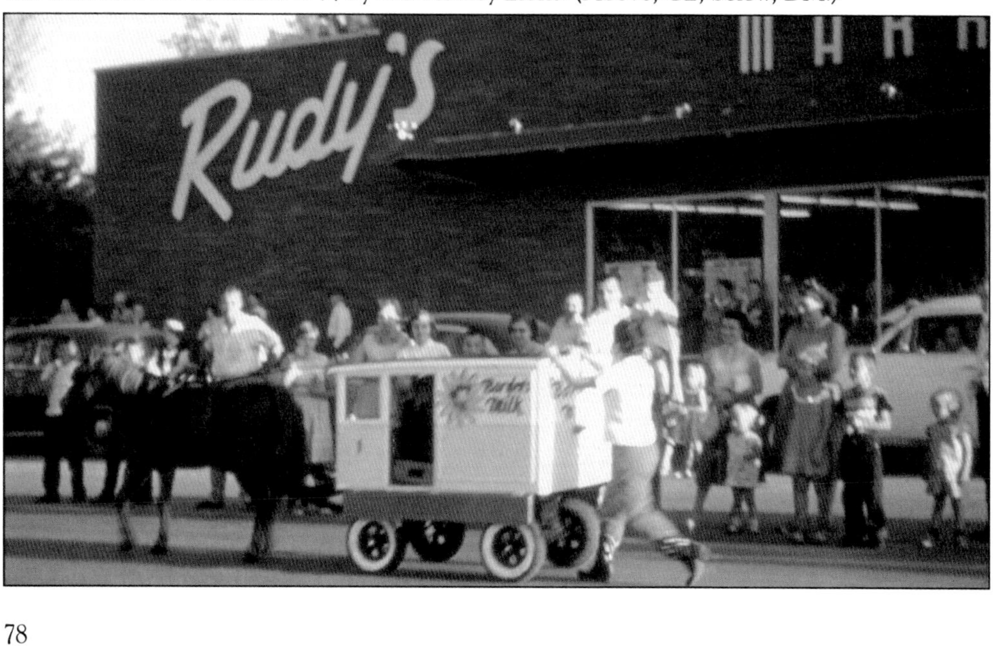

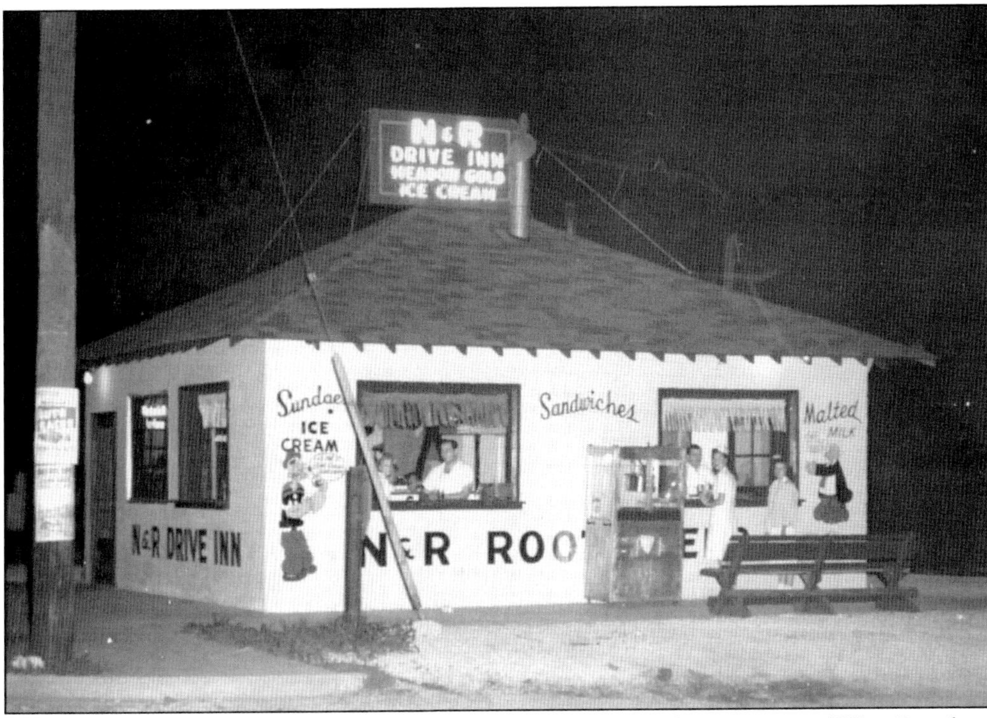

The N&R Drive Inn restaurant opened in May 1945 on the southeast corner of West Broadway and Forest Avenue. The restaurant featured curb service. It was owned and operated by Nick and Ray Colevris. Cartoon characters painted inside and outside were by Shorty Williams. Nick is on the left (below), and Dolores Falkenham is on the right. (Jeannie Dayhoff.)

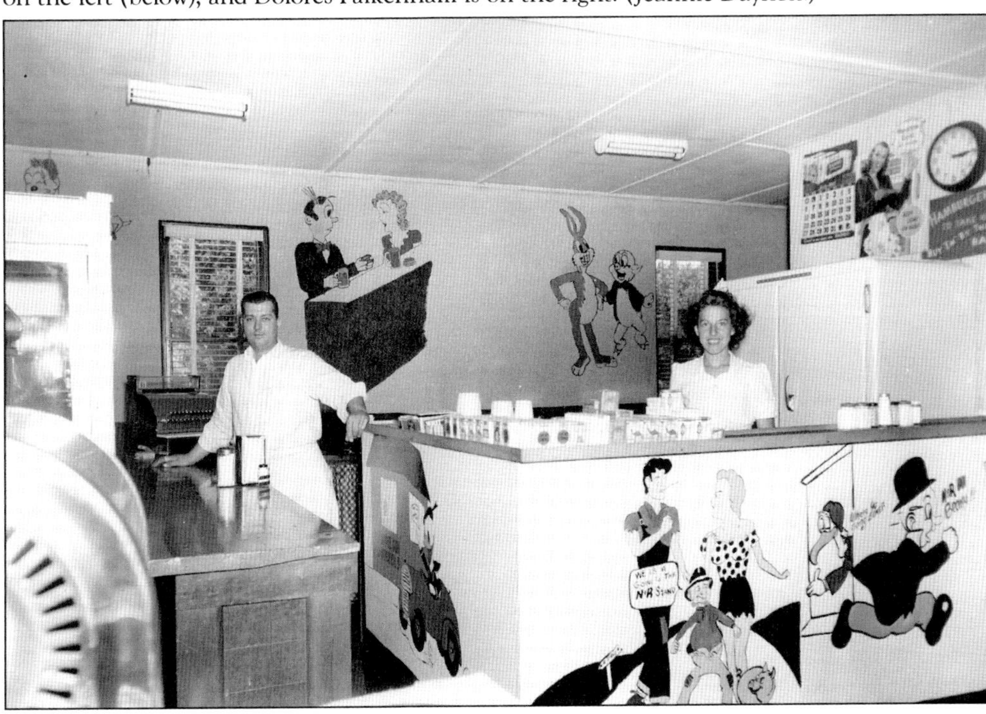

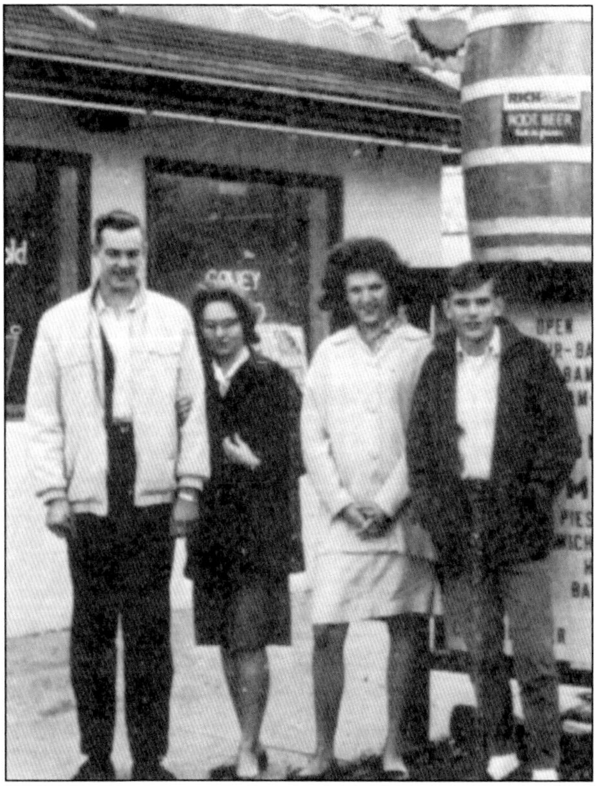

In 1961, Stanley and Lily "Lil" (Rudolph) Zajc became proprietors of what was once the N&R Drive Inn. For Lil it was the beginning of a 17-year business career as West Broadway's premier restaurateur. Seen in this 1960s photograph, from left to right, are Stanley, daughter Carol Ann, Lil, and son David S. The village honored Lil in 1980 for community service. She assisted in numerous fund-raisers, including for an ambulance for Bradley firefighters, for senior citizens' facilities at the Bradley-Bourbonnais Community Center, and for tuition for students to attend Bishop McNamara High School. In April 1981, Lil was elected to a four-year term as village clerk, but she died in 1983. The village of Bradley dedicated Lil's Park on North Street in 1984 as a tribute to her long involvement in community affairs. (BHS.)

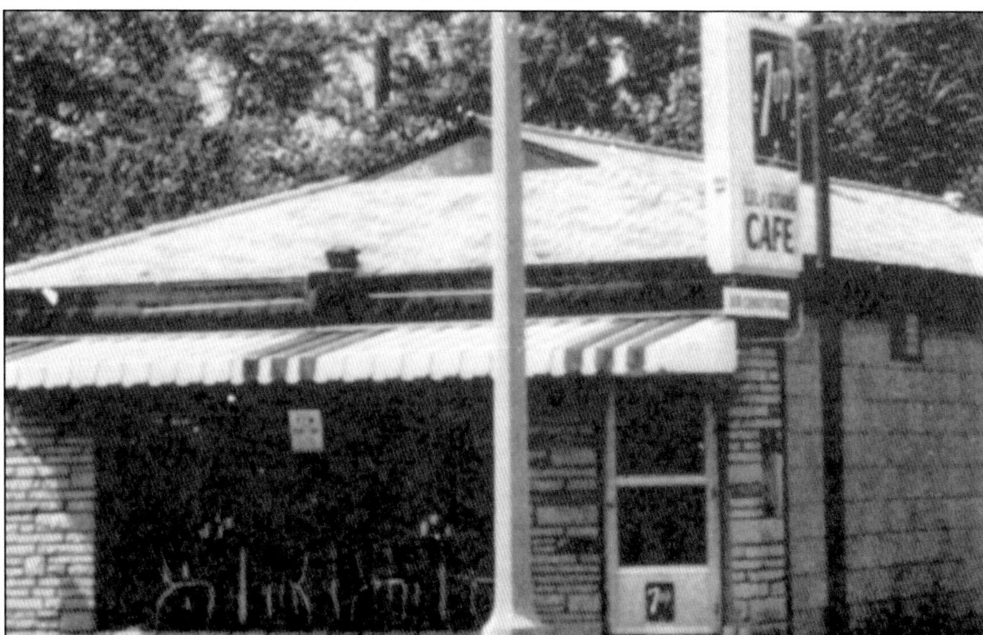

Lil and Stan's Cafe moved into the old Cox Electric Shop on the northwest corner of West Broadway and Cleveland Avenue in 1965. The new restaurant became a favorite of Bradleyans. (BHS.)

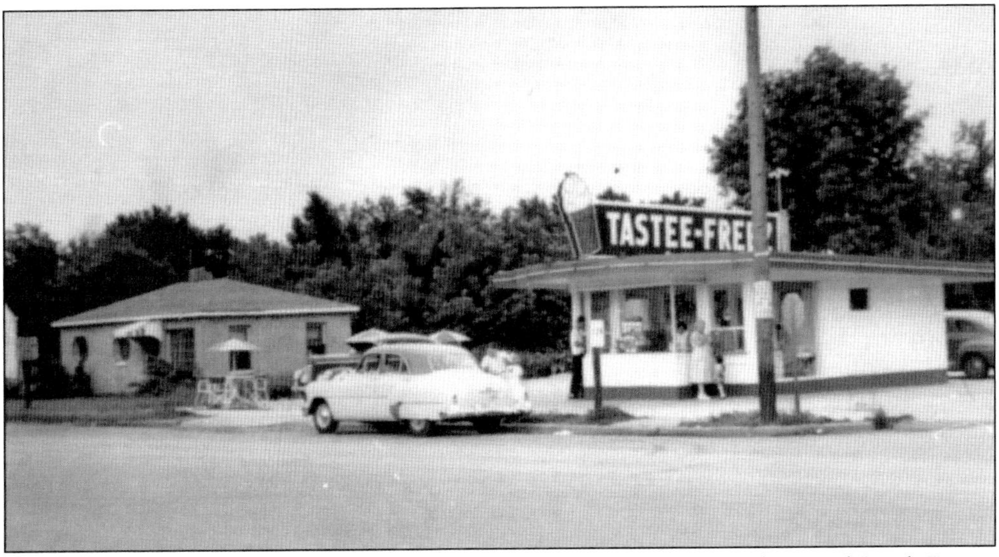

Morton McGruder bought this lot on the southeast corner of West Broadway and South Prairie Avenue in 1892, put up a building, and opened a grocery store and real estate office. This Tastee Freeze drive inn stood on that lot in the late 1940s. A few years later, Rudolph (Rudy) Jagersma bought the lot and constructed a new building to use as the headquarters for his chain of supermarkets. Today King Music occupies that building. (BHS.)

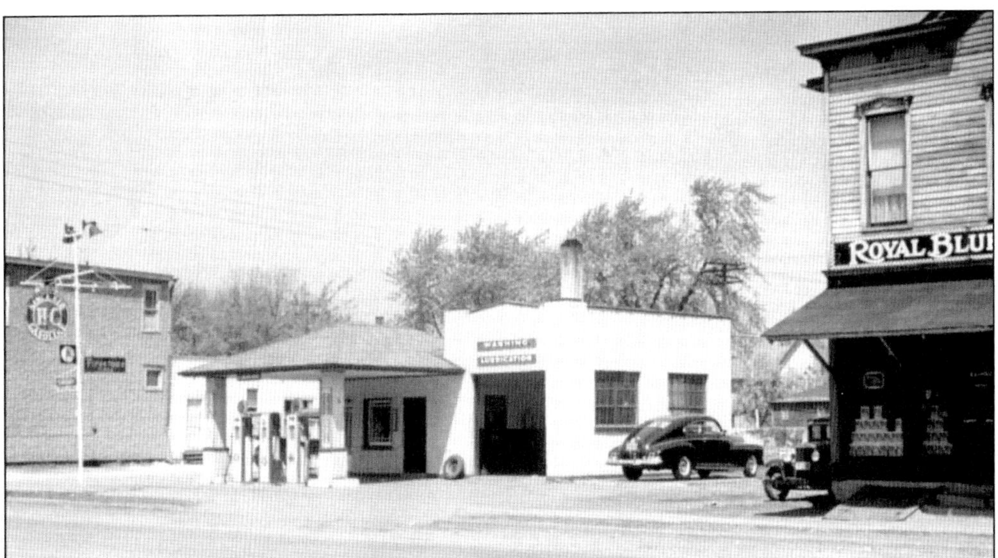

This 1940s Sinclair filling station at 517 West Broadway was managed by Henry J. Longtin. (CE.)

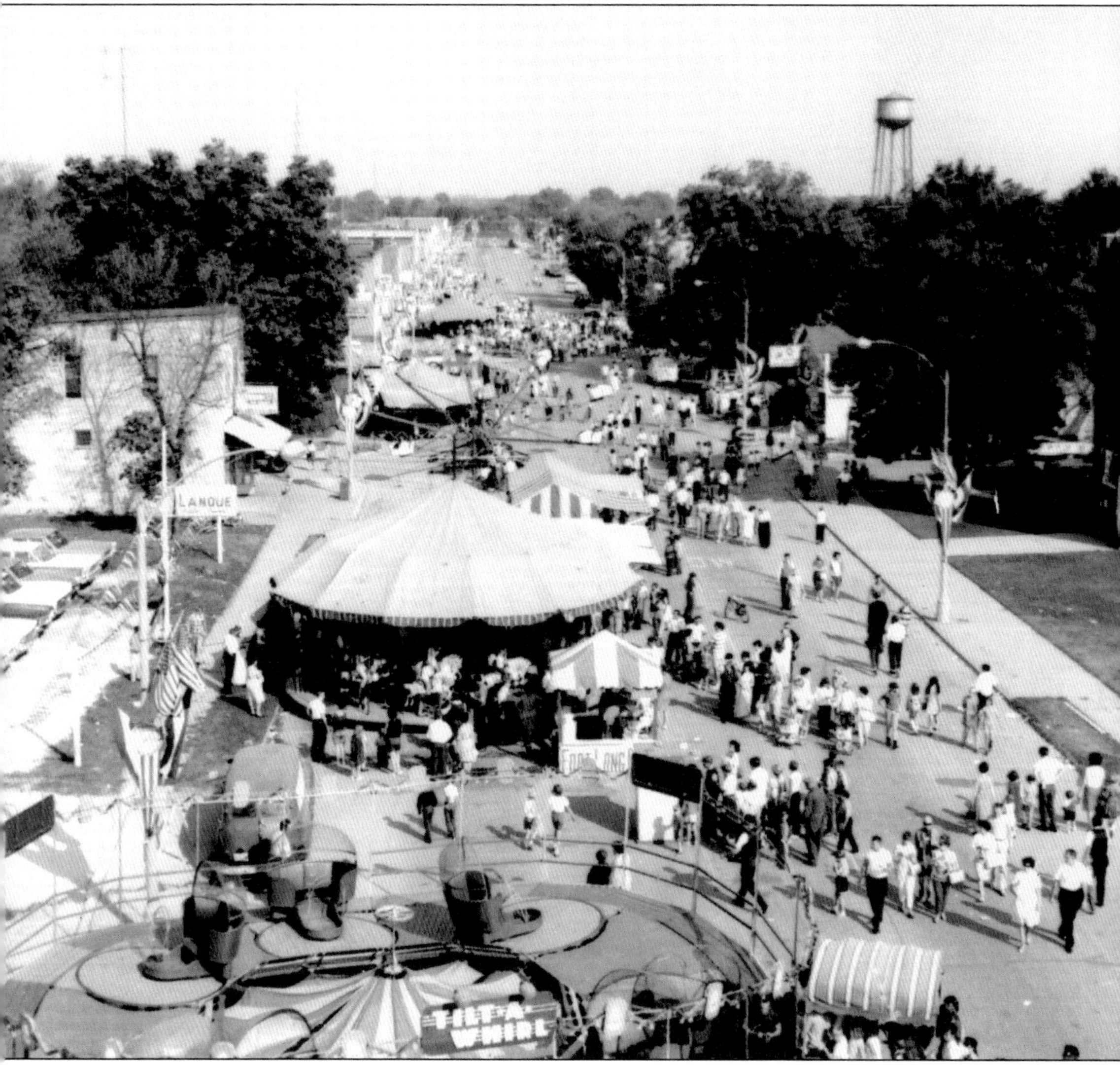

During the 1967 Diamond Jubilee, a carnival opened up on West Broadway for a week. This photograph was taken from the Ferris wheel looking east. The Evangelical United Methodist church is on the right, and Lanoue Auto Sales and Beland's Grocery Store are on the left. (Author's collection.)

Six

The Melting Pot

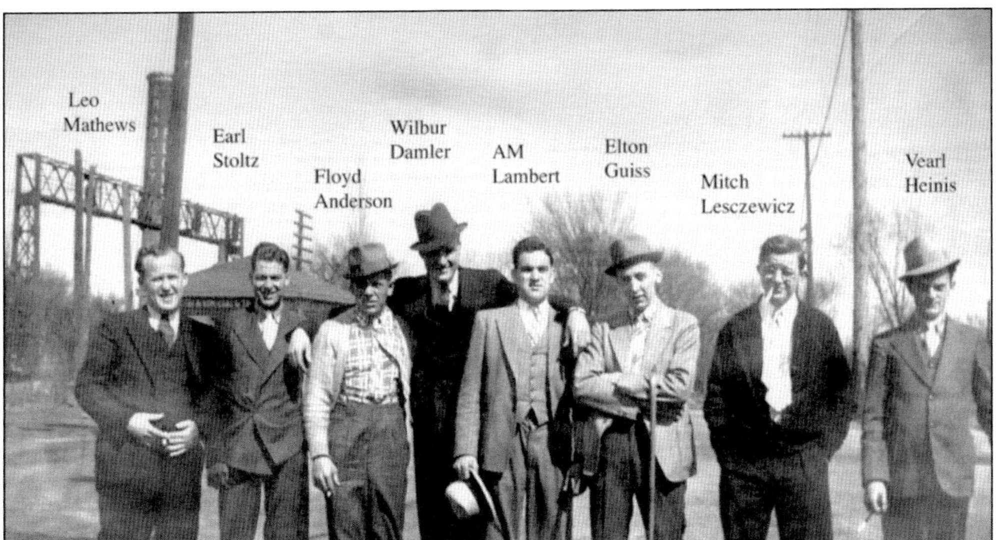

This photograph was taken at the Perry Street crossing of the Illinois Central Railroad tracks. The original David Bradley Manufacturing Company water tower is visible to the left. Among Bradley's first citizens were wealthy entrepreneurs, enterprising businessmen, and workers from all classes of society. Workers from Germany, Belgium, Scandinavia, Italy, Poland, Bohemia, and Slovenia were also drawn to Bradley by good jobs. They found that their neighbors included descendants of an established French Canadian settlement (Bourbonnais); Irish and Scottish, who had built the railroads; and also a potpourri of descendents from Yankee industrialists; immigrant British merchants; German farmers; and tidewater yeomen farmers. (James Guiss.)

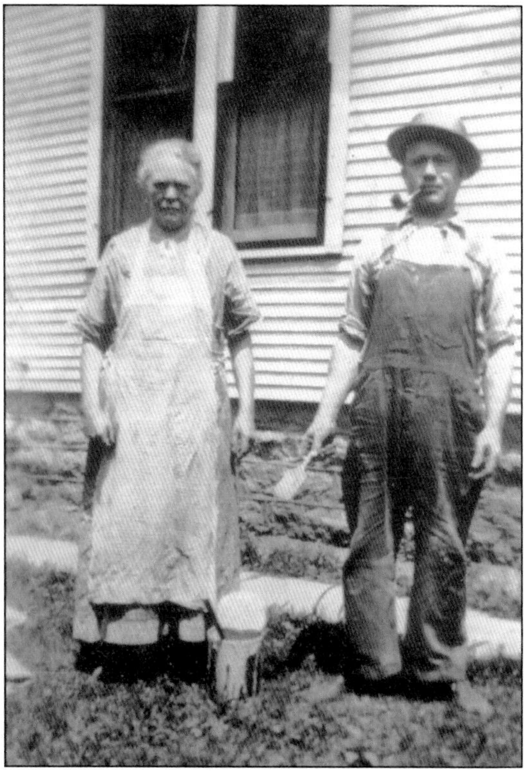

John Ott came to Bradley in 1892 from Chicago. Ott was born in 1873 at Stambach, Germany, and came to the United States at the age of 17. His wife, Mathilda (Huettner), also was born in Stambach. They were married in Kankakee on October 2, 1897. John worked at the Kroehler Furniture Company until his retirement. (Shirley Manley.)

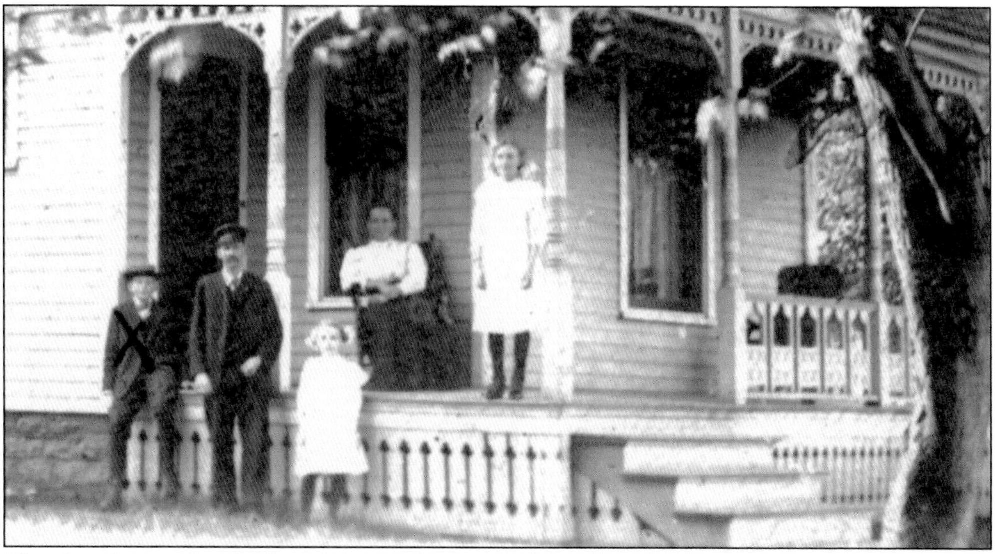

The Gonderman family, from left to right, are Earl, Emil, and Edna. On the porch are Emma and Carrie. The house still exists at 211 North Grand Avenue. (Marietta Tanner.)

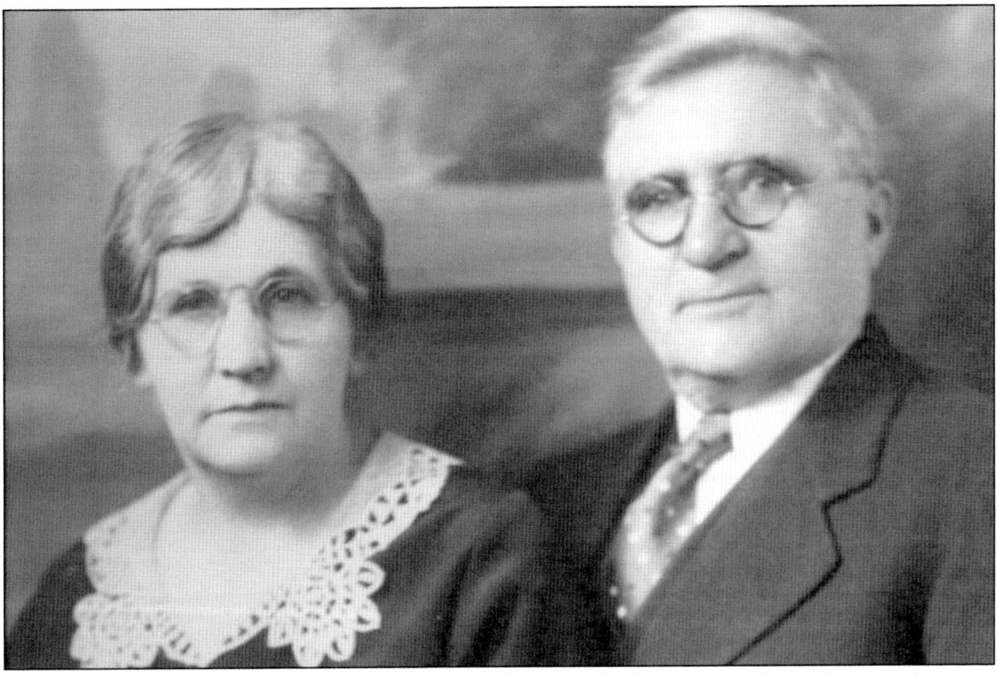

Alphonse Dolle came to Bradley in 1900 with his wife, Julie (Morel). Both were born in Alsase-Lorraine in Europe. They were proprietors of the Bradley Department Store for many years. (James Guiss.)

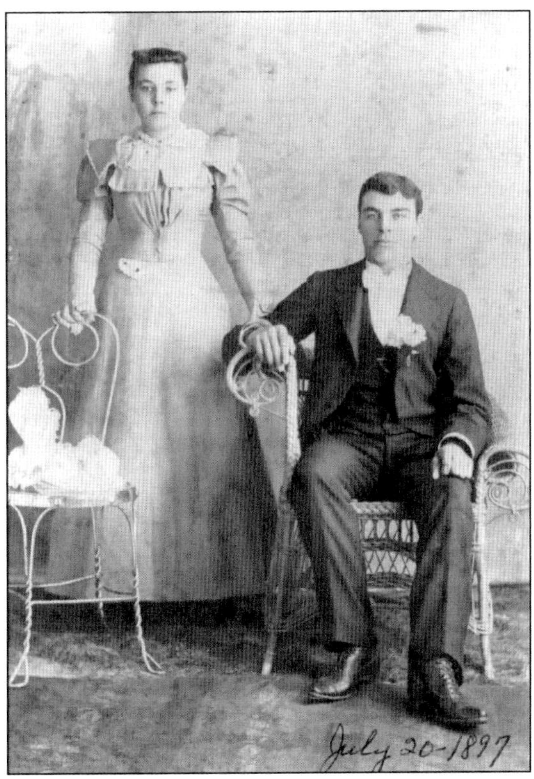

Fred and Nelda (Bergeron) Brosseau, who lived at 148 North Cleveland Avenue, were married in Ghent, Minnesota, on July 20, 1897. Both were born in Manteno. (Janice Brosseau Sims.)

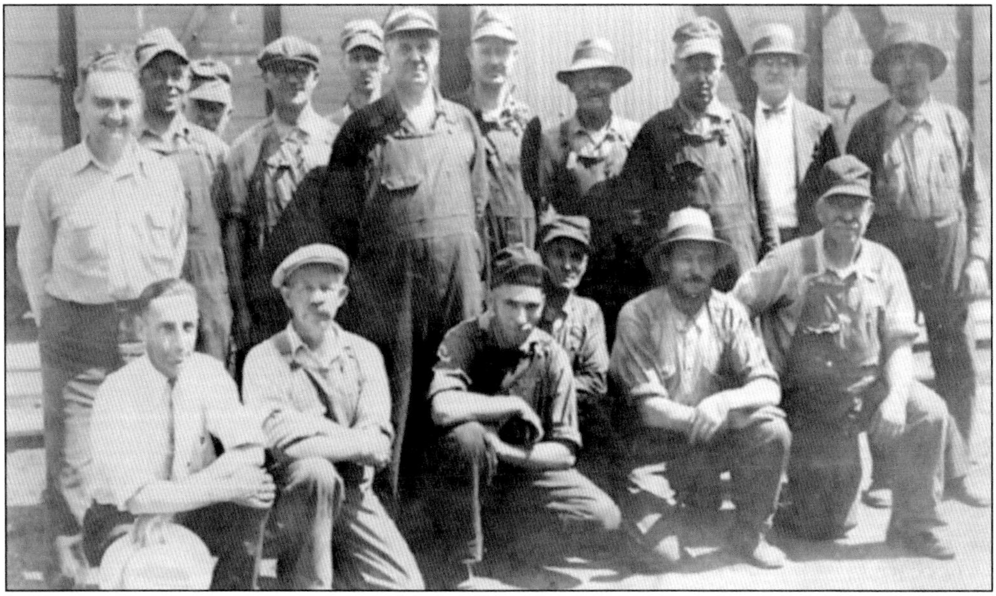

Rumors were circulating in early 1891 that the Illinois Central Railroad would make room for the 1893 World's Columbian Exposition on Chicago's lakefront by moving its shops to Kankakee. On July 16, 1891, the *Kankakee Gazette* announced that Diederich Ehrich had sold a strip of land to the railroad that was just south of North Kankakee. This photograph, taken in the 1920s, shows Illinois Central Railroad yard and shop workers and track gang members. (Author's collection.)

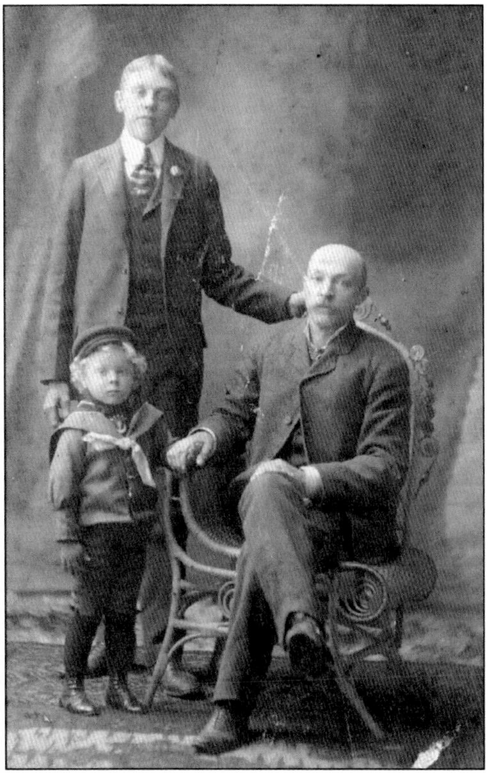

One of the immigrant families to settle in North Kankakee was the Book family (originally spelled Bouk). In this 1901 photograph, from left to right, are young Theodore Book standing in front of Oscar Book and Charles Book (seated). August J. Book came to Bradley before 1897 to work for David Bradley along with other Swedish craftsmen, including Frank Erickson, Frank Carlson, Charles Matteson, August Anderson, Otto Bolen, and Frank Gustafson. (Mary Book Schmitter.)

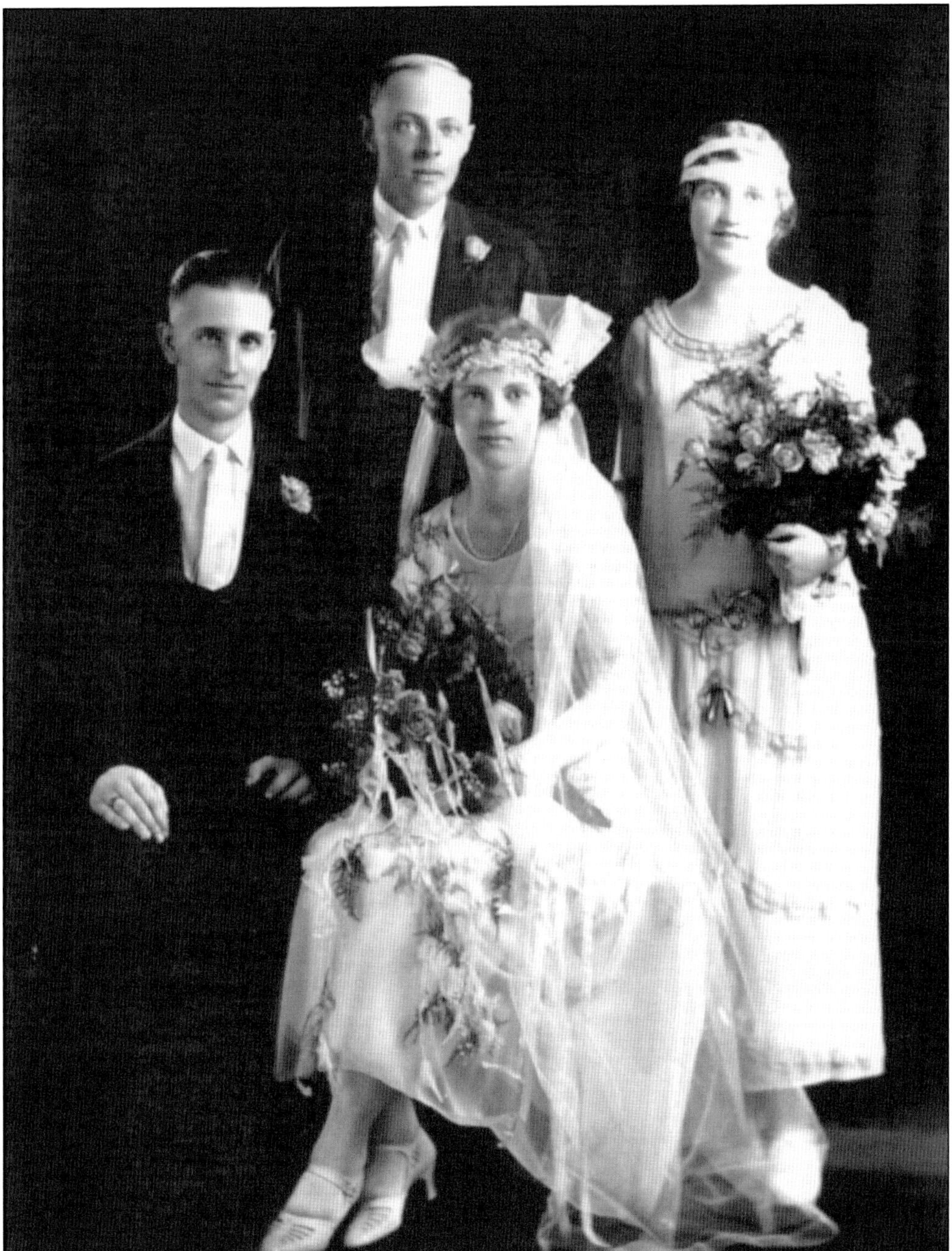

This wedding photograph was taken in 1920 or 1922. Standing are best man Theodore Book and an unidentified bridesmaid. Seated are Virgil Kinneman and Mildred Book. Kinneman became president of the Bradley village board (a position similar to mayor) in 1941. (Mary Book Schmitter.)

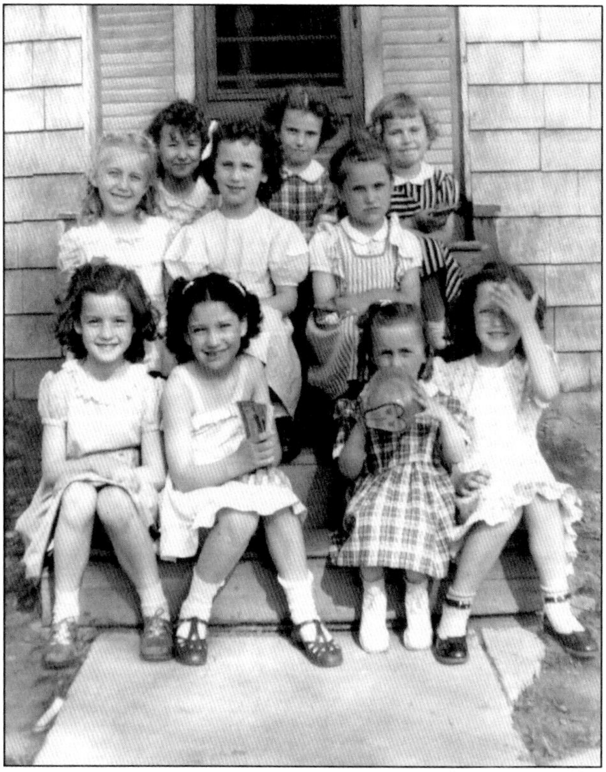

On May 4, 1949, a party was held to celebrate Janice Brosseau's seventh birthday. Pictured, from left to right, are (first row) Barbara Wilkins, Mary Marcotte, Barbara Brosseau, and Judy Benoit; (second row) Barbara Stefanich, Jane Mayotte, and Sandra Amiot; (third row) Margaret Davis, Janice, and Joanne Pakulski. (Janice Brosseau Sims.)

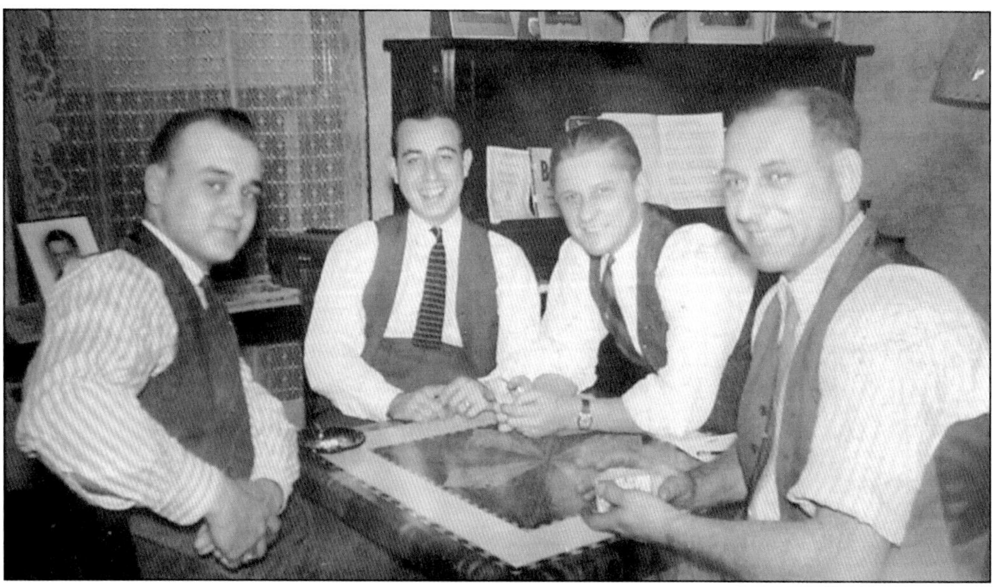

A Sunday afternoon card game on December 7, 1941, was interrupted by news of the bombing of Pearl Harbor. Someone was there with a camera to record the historic moment. Pictured, from left to right, are Bruce Hubert, Wayne Monte, Billy LeMaster, and Tony Rittmanic. Months later LeMaster was killed in an air training crash. (DM.)

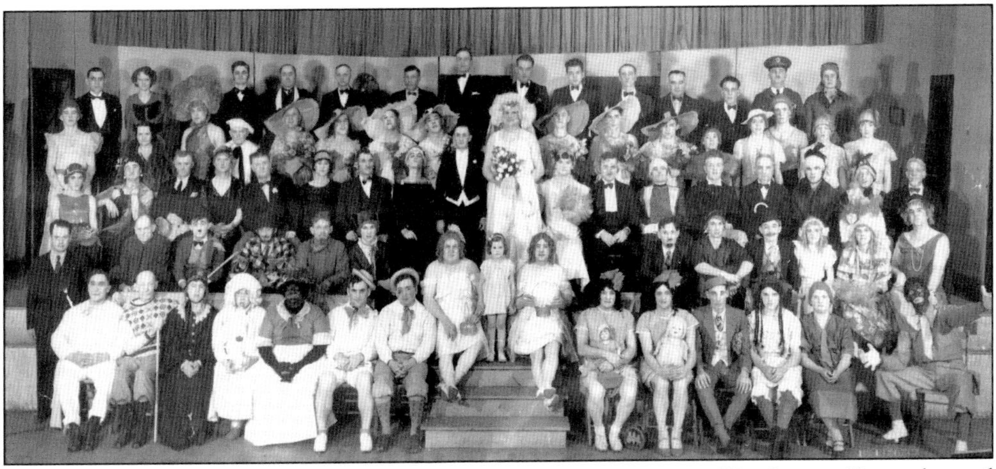

A farce, *Womanless Wedding*, staged by the Simpson-Levie Company of Bardstown, Kentucky, and Jackson, Michigan, was held December 4 and 5, 1934, at the Bradley High School gymnasium. It was sponsored by the Brotherhood of the Bradley Methodist Evangelical Church, and 70 local men were cast. Many dressed in women's clothing. The all-star cast included R. P. Welker as the leading lady and Norma June Linter as the featured dancer. Dorthea Jacob directed the production. (RG.)

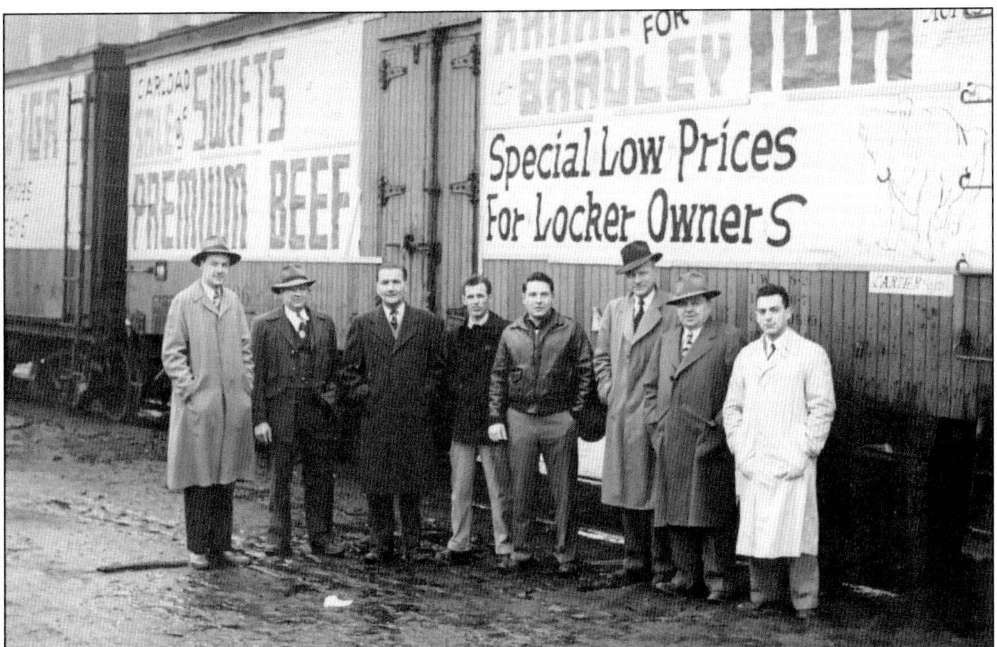

Beef by the carload was the order of the day when these grocery men had their picture taken. Pictured, from left to right, are Paul Foster; unidentified; Ray Rasmussen; unidentified; unidentified; Rudolph (Rudy) Jagersma, the owner of all IGA stores in Kankakee County; John Battaglia; and Howard Dahling. (Beverly Rasmussen.)

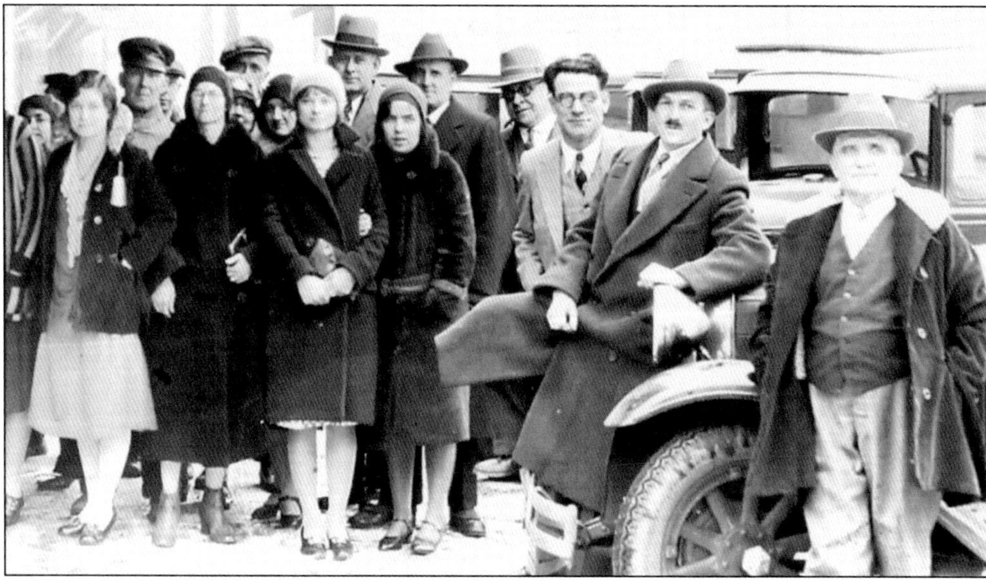

This photograph was taken at the opening of the new Dolle's Bradley Department Store in 1930. Alphonse Dolle is standing at the far right. After his death in 1939, the store, and the Bradley Appliance Store at the same address (423–429 West Broadway) was operated by his son-in-law Eldon Guiss. (James Guiss.)

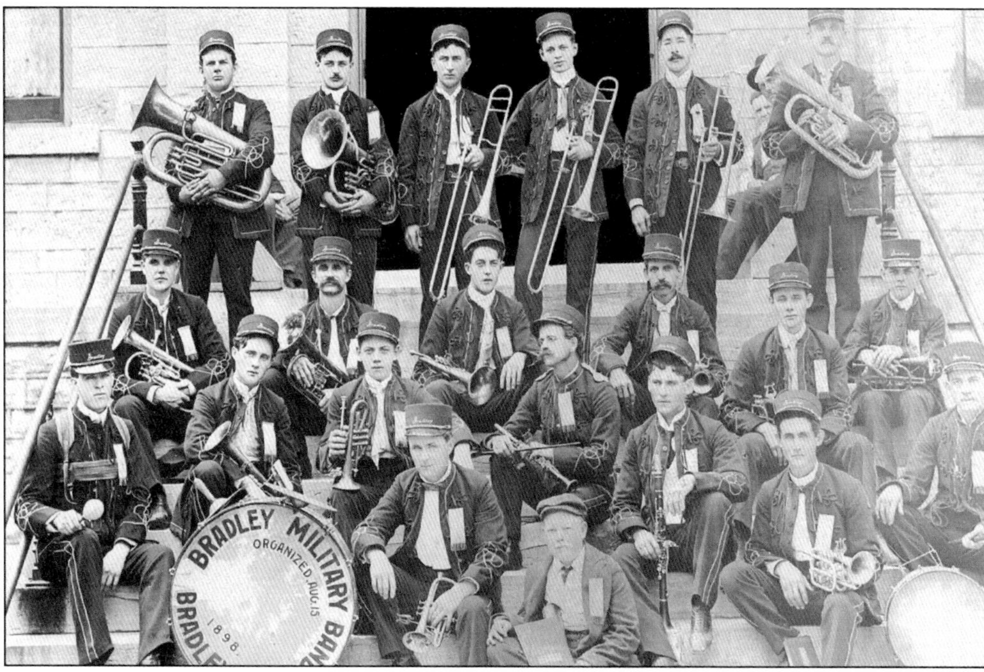

Organized by Professor Gaudiose Martineau on August 15, 1898, the Bradley Military Band came into being at the end of the Spanish-American War and existed for seven years. Besides marching in patriotic parades and playing concerts at the Bowery, an open air pavilion on the west side of Vasseur Avenue, and at a bandstand near the intersection of Broadway and Michigan Avenue, the band was a favorite to serenade passengers on the *Minnie Lillie* as it cruised on the river between Kankakee and the summer resort at Gouger's Grove (Martha Sovinski and SC.)

Seven

OF SCHOOLS AND CHURCHES

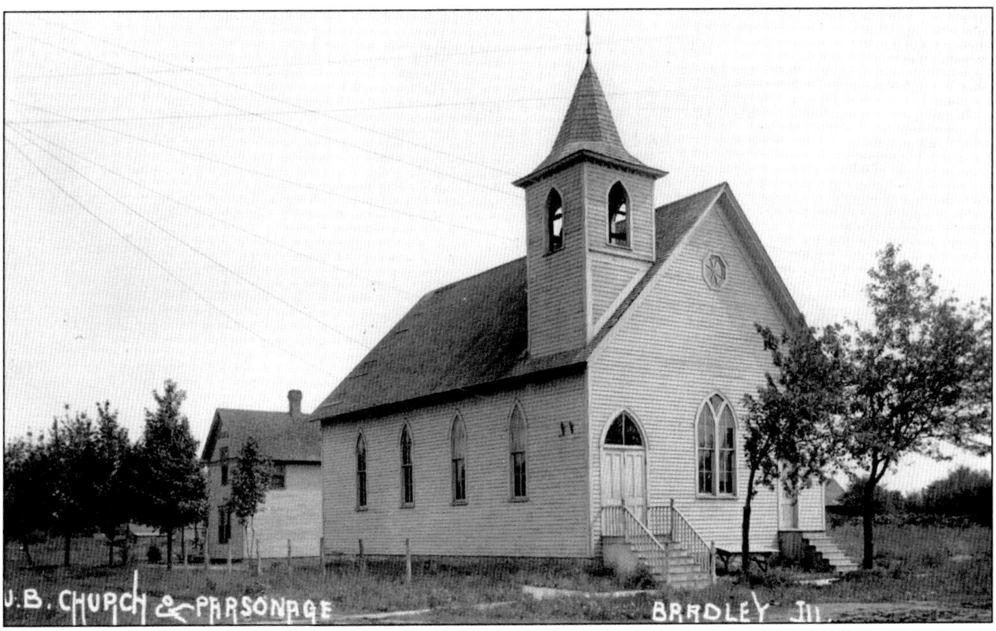

On May 3, 1893, The United Brethren from Altorff bought lot No. 1 in block 52 at 212 South Cleveland Avenue in North Kankakee and began work on their new building. In time, the United Brethren became the present day Bradley Evangelical United Methodist Church. Other early churches in the community were the Wesley United Methodist Church, which was organized in 1892 at the southeast corner of North Center Avenue and Perry Street, and St. Joseph Catholic Church, which was organized in 1904 at the 200 block of North Center Avenue. The North Kankakee grade school district was organized in 1892. Charles H. Wertz was the first board president. (Thomas J. Lindsay.)

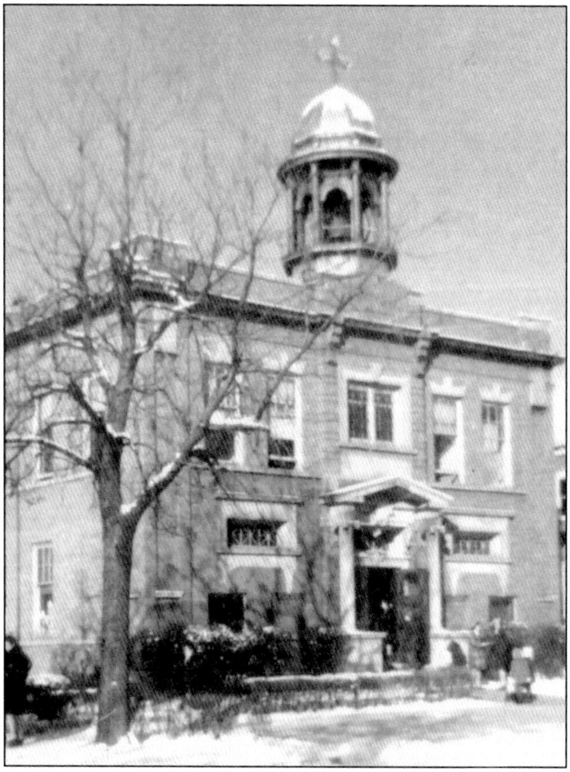

Fr. William Hackett, the St. Patrick Church pastor in Kankakee, established a mission church in Bradley dedicated to St. Joseph, the patron saint of workers, in 1900. Four years later, Chicago's archbishop James Edward Quigley elevated the mission to a parish. Several parishioners were instrumental in obtaining Fr. Joseph Avila Milot as first resident pastor. The parish census included 136 families. The first Catholic services were held in Umstead Hall on West Broadway. Services then were moved to the vacant Baptist church building at 148 North Center Avenue. Seven nationalities attended St. Joseph Church at this time, including French, Irish, Slovenian, Polish, German, Italian, and Bohemian. On January 27, 1907, a new St. Joseph church building was dedicated. It was 50 feet wide and 80 feet long and served as the church and the rectory. (CE.)

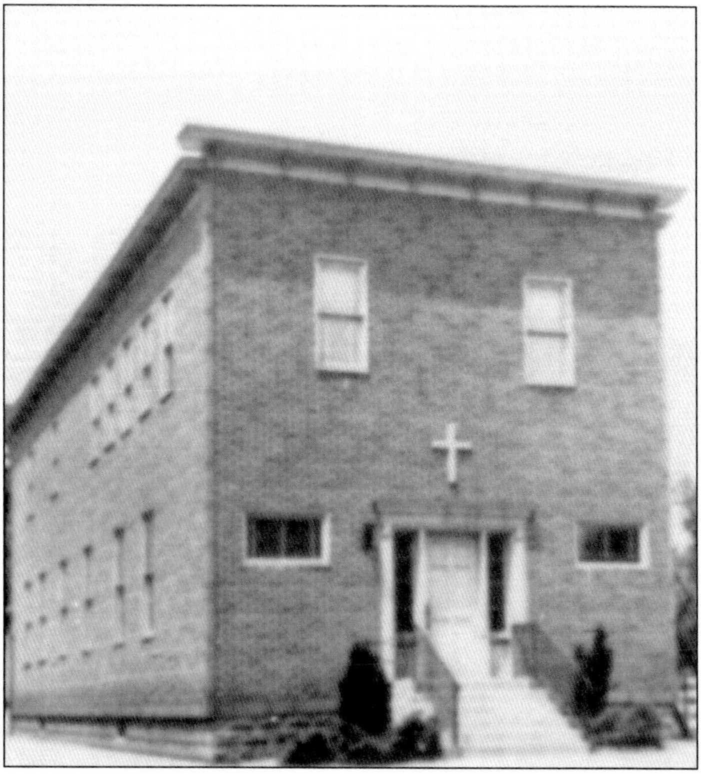

Superior Dominican Sister Mary Dionysius, Sister Mary Leonarda, and Sister Joseph Marie arrived at St. Joseph Church on August 23, 1924. They opened Bradley's first Catholic school. Classrooms were in various parts of the church building. There were 186 children in the first six grades. In the spring of 1925, Pastor Harris A. Darche received a wooden building from Bear Brand Hosiery Company. Workmen converted the building's two floors into four classrooms and an assembly hall. (BHS.)

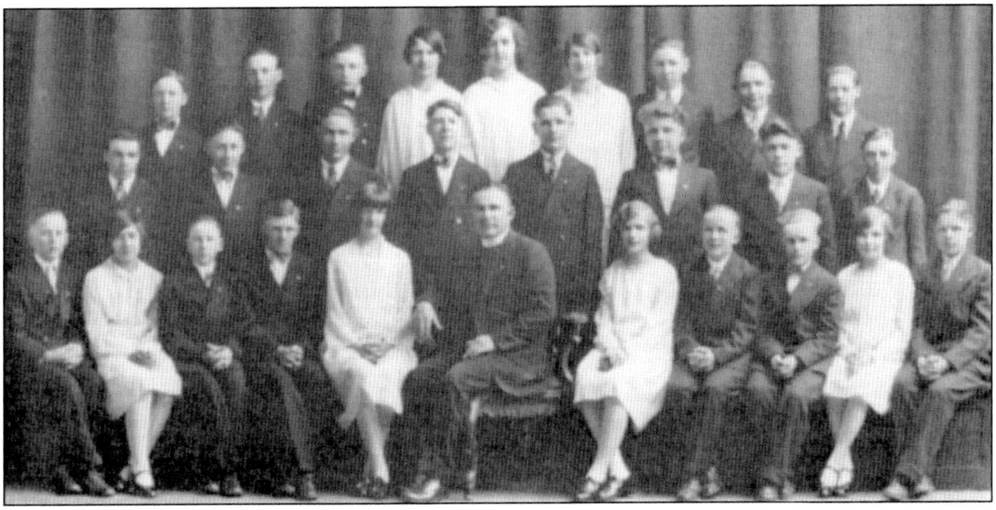

The first class to graduate from St. Joseph School received eighth grade diplomas in May 1926. Pictured, from left to right, are (first row) Paul Toliuszis, Josephine Casino, Ray Duchene, Frank Sovinski, Florence Sovinski, Rev. H. A. Darche, Eloise Lustig (Sister Mary Sabina), Leon Lambert, Leo Cavanaugh, Antoinette Lustig, and Louis Drassler; (second row) George Brosseau, Leon LeDuke, Joseph Lelehowski, Joseph Honn, Donald Goudreau, John Smietanski, Bennie Casino, and Vincent Courtney; (third row) Harry Boudreau, Francis Courtney, Alfred DeLonais, Steffie Kendziorch, Isabelle Martin, Molly Starasinich, Earl Anderson, Omer Duchene, and Earl Stoltz. (St. Joseph Grade School.)

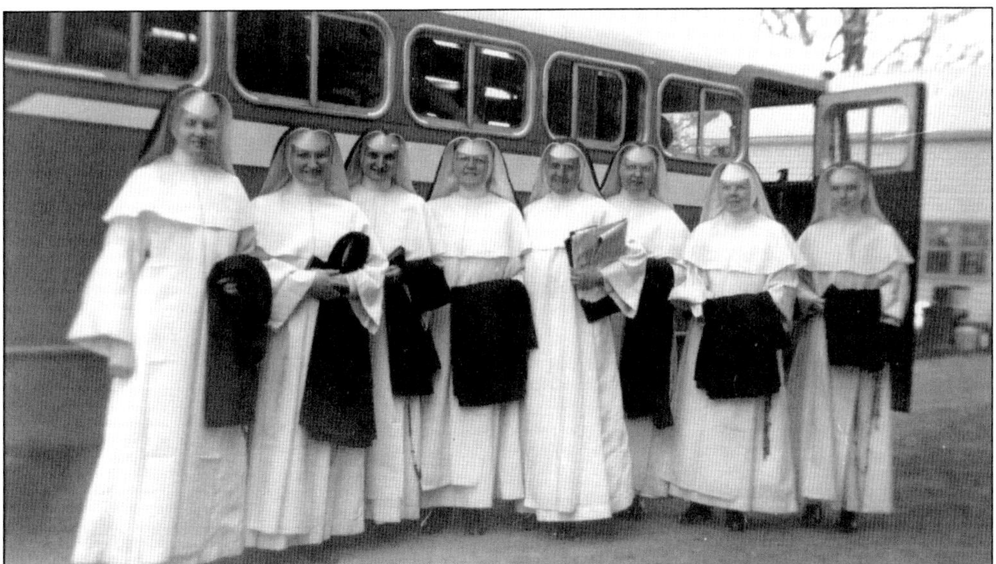

The Dominican motherhouse in Springfield assigned teachers to St. Joseph School. In 1960, the teachers, from left to right, were Sisters Lucille, Judith, Anita, Albertine, Gerold, Sabina, Catherine Marie, and Rose Margaret. (Janice Brosseau Sims.)

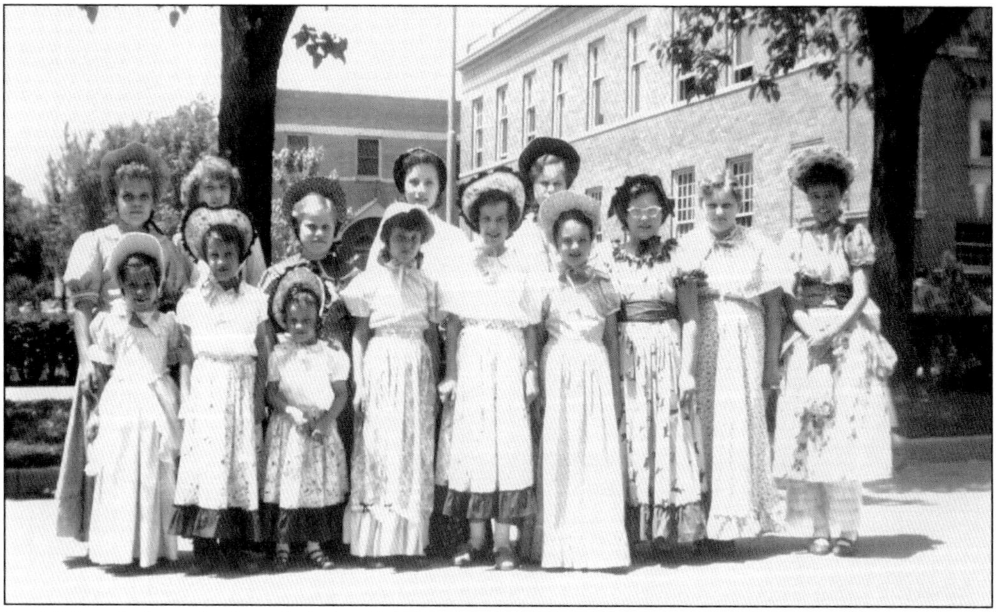

In 1953, girls from St. Joseph School's fifth grade class pose in period costumes with members of other classes probably in anticipation of the parish's 50th anniversary. (Janice Brosseau Sims.)

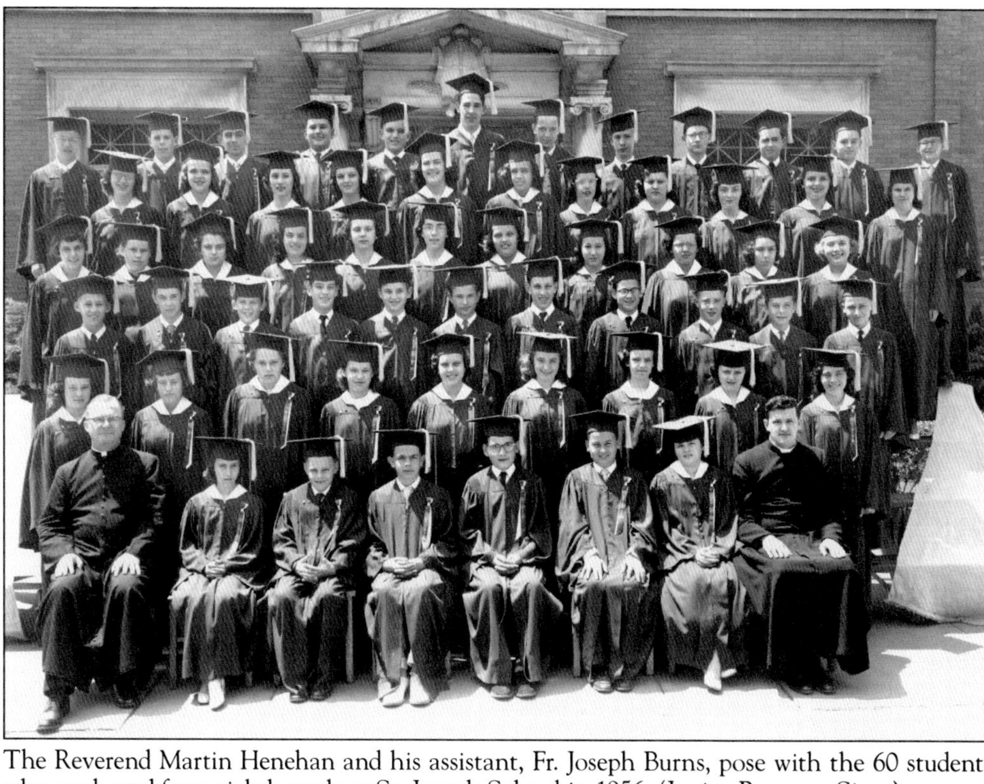

The Reverend Martin Henehan and his assistant, Fr. Joseph Burns, pose with the 60 students who graduated from eighth grade at St. Joseph School in 1956. (Janice Brosseau Sims.)

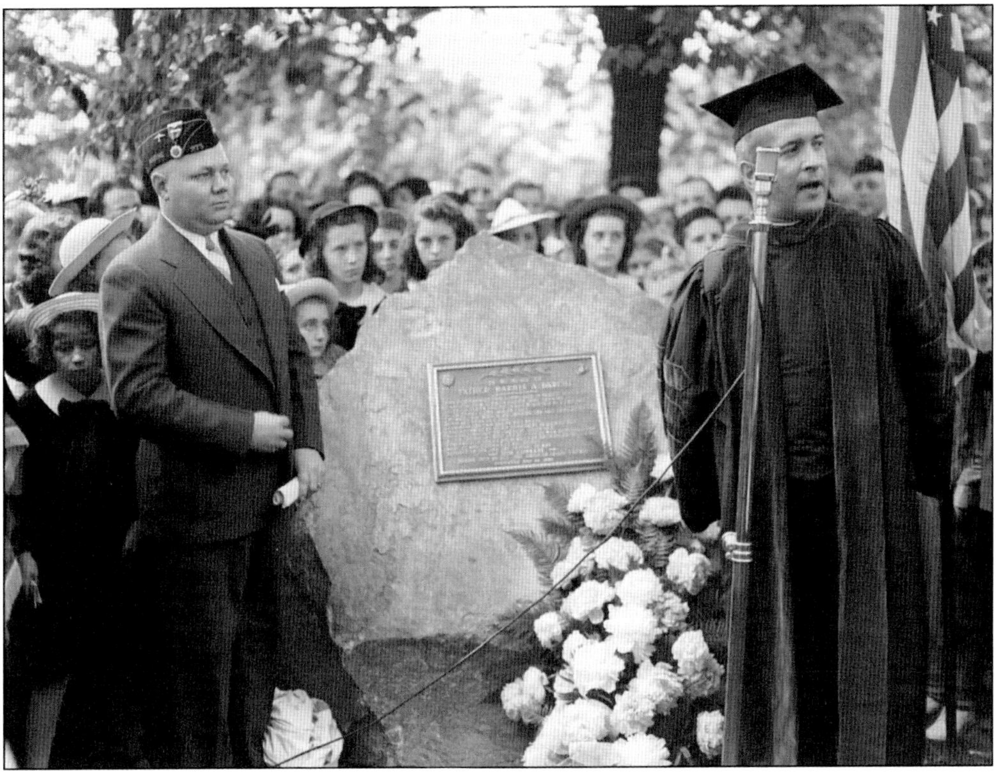

In 1923 Fr. Harris A. Darche became the sixth pastor of St. Joseph Church. He remained pastor until his death in April 1937. Darche served as a chaplain in World War I with the U.S. Marines, in the 2nd Infantry Division and engaged in three campaigns. For his valor, he received the Legion of Honor, the French War Cross, the Navy Cross, and the World War I Campaign Medal with three campaign bars. Darche also served as national chaplain for the American Legion. On May 29, 1938, on the campus of St. Viator College in Bourbonnais, Frank W. Bloom, commander of the Marine Post of the American Legion in Chicago, unveiled a memorial plaque to Darche. The Reverend E. V. Cardinal, the college's president, accepted the memorial. (Above, KCM-KDJ; right, KCM.)

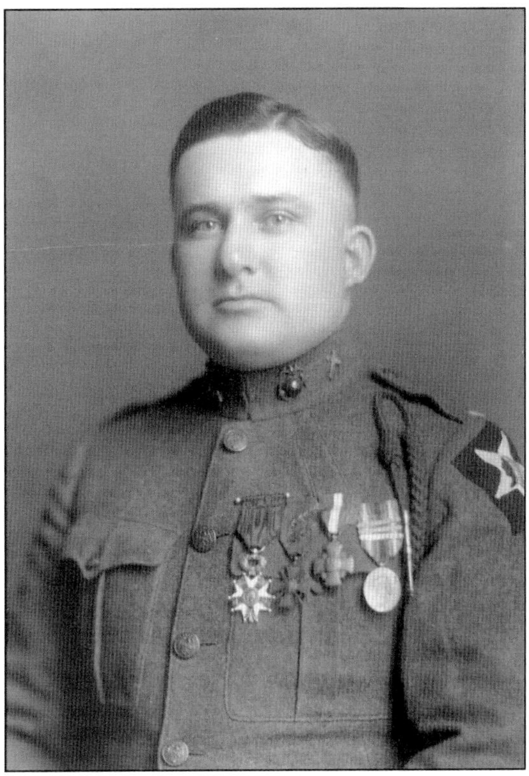

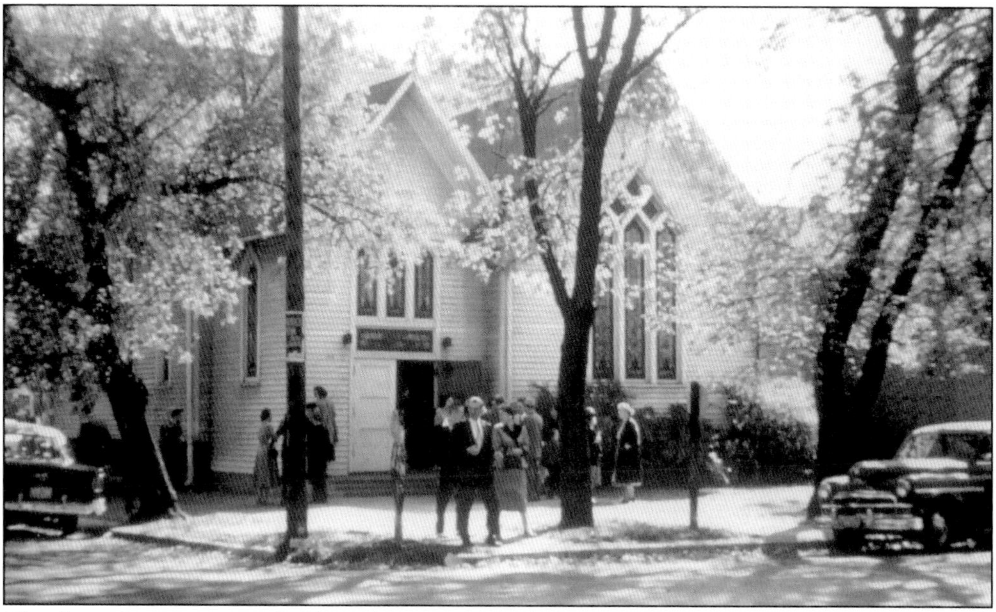

The first religious service held in this North Kankakee Wesley United Methodist Church at 196 North Center Avenue was on June 4, 1893. Shortly before October 1957, the congregation had moved to a new building. St. Joseph Church bought the old church and used it for classrooms until 1964. (RS.)

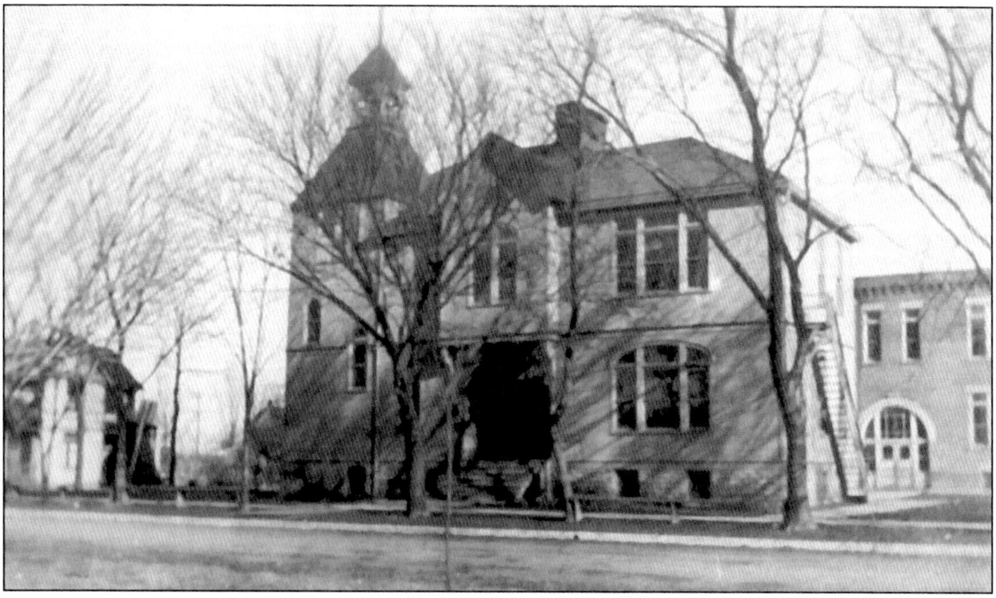

After the first North Kankakee School District was organized in December 1892, classes were held in the Wesley United Methodist Church. An elementary school building was constructed in 1894. In 1898, a wing was added to the east side of the building. The second floor classrooms were used for second- and third-year high school students. Further additions to the school were made in 1910 and 1912. The old school was replaced by a new central school building in the early 1960s. (BHS.)

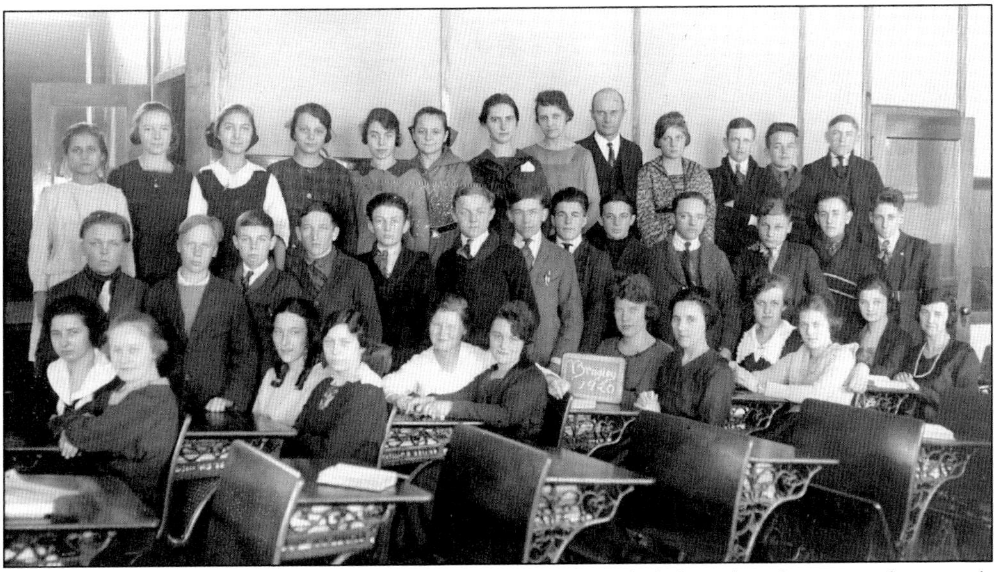

Students from the seventh, eighth, and ninth grades are included in this classroom photograph from 1920. Standing in the third row is teacher ? Greer (seventh from right), teacher ? Alden (sixth from right), and superintendant of schools ? Robinson (fifth from right). (Mary Lou Walsh.)

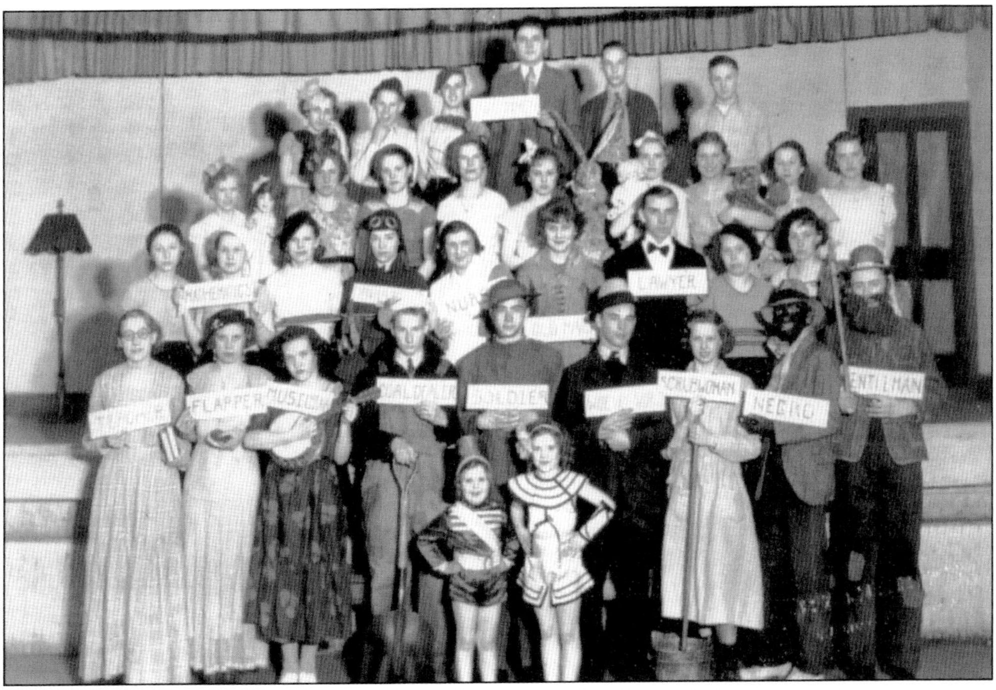

In the play or program photographed here, the students hold signs indicating various avocations and occupations. (BHS.)

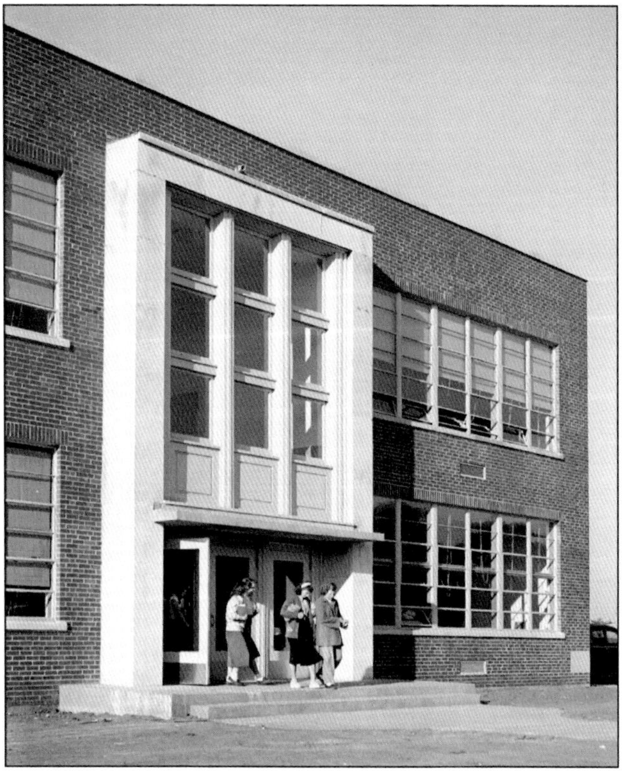

A new Bradley High School opened on North Street in September 1949. It had six regular classrooms, two science rooms, a home economics room, typing room, bookkeeping room, library, manual training shop, and offices. The gymnasium opened on December 1. There were 263 students enrolled. A superintendent and 11 teachers made up the faculty. The 1950 graduating class numbered 40. In 1955 an addition was made to the building. Further additions were built in 1962, and 1966. (KCM-KDJ.)

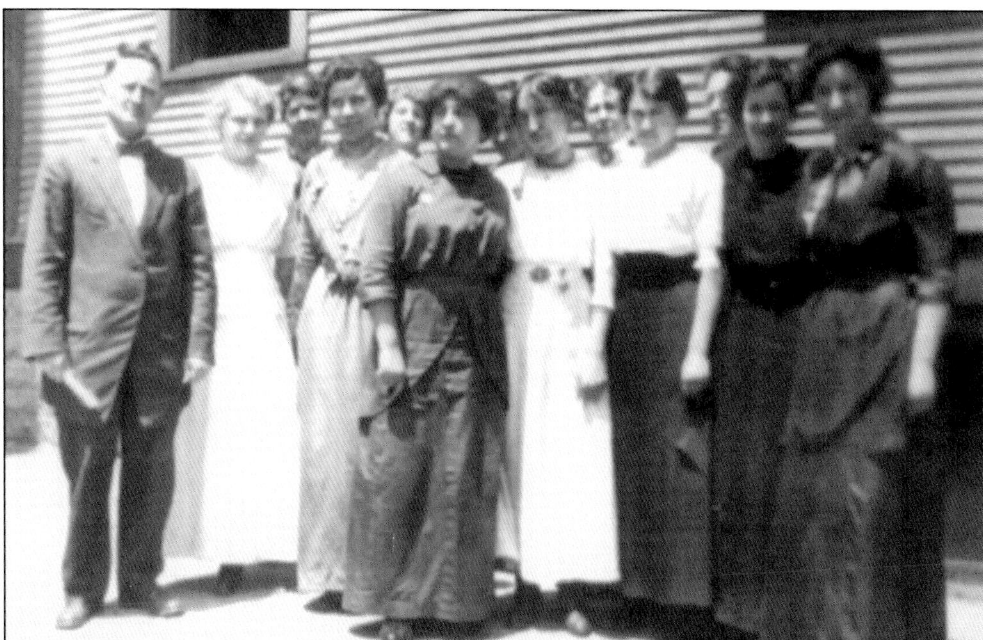

An unidentified teacher and students appear in this 1920 photograph. (BHS.)

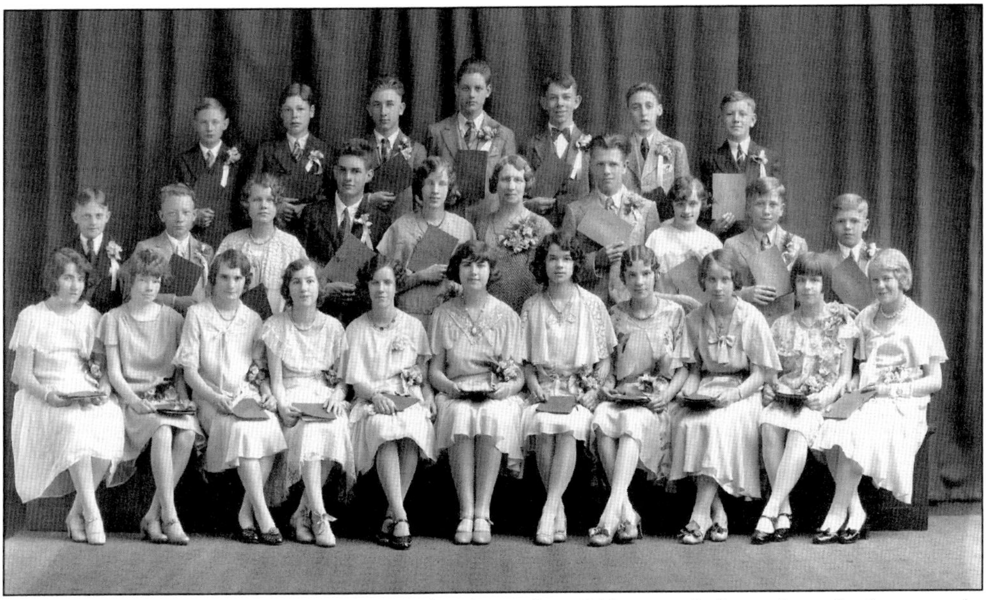

A graduating class of Bradley High School in the 1920s posed for a formal photograph. (James Guiss.)

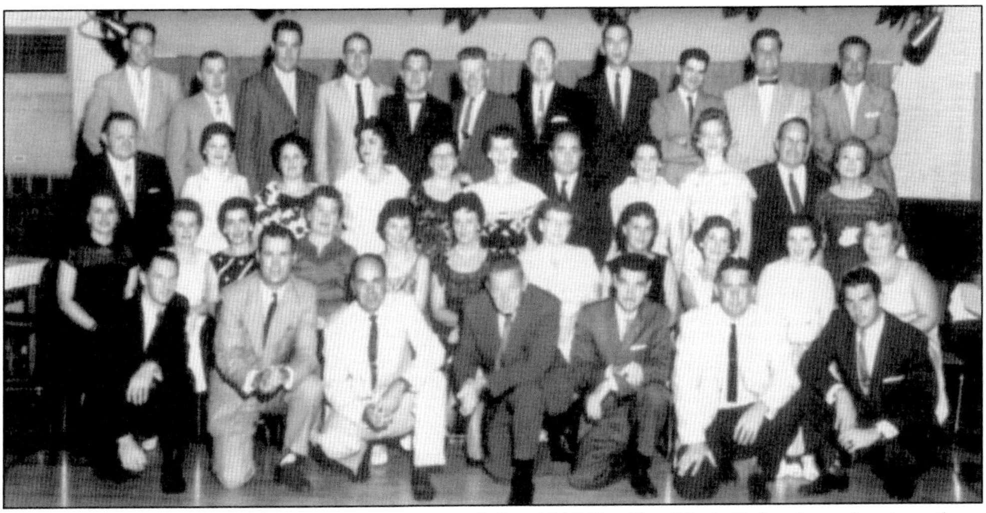

This is a photograph of the 20 year reunion of the 1940 Bradley High School graduating class. From left to right are (first row) Tom Ketcik, LaVern Hahs, Earl Jones, James "Pete" Laffey, Clarence Stoltz, Robert Grass, and Cas Mitchell; (second row) Shirley Heinze Toby, Frances Sanor, Arlene LaGesse Mitchell, Alpha Engelhardt Ketcik, Mary Martin, Betty Kassman Martin, Dorothy Outsen, Leota Roush Stoltz, Darlene Marlaire, Doris Hahs, and Geneva Amiot; (third row) Stanley Leszczewicz, Wanda Dominick Grass, Nelda Stump. Celeste Johnson, Rita McCleary, Anna McCue, Jesse McCue Jr., Anna M. Laffey, Shirley Jones, Ruel Hall, and Frances Hall; (fourth row) Charles Toby, Elmer Stump, Leonard Martin, Robert Martin, Hal McCleary, Eugene Marquis, Raymond Outsen, Lloyd Marlaire, Francis Amiot, Raymond Sanor, and Donald Johnson. (BHS.)

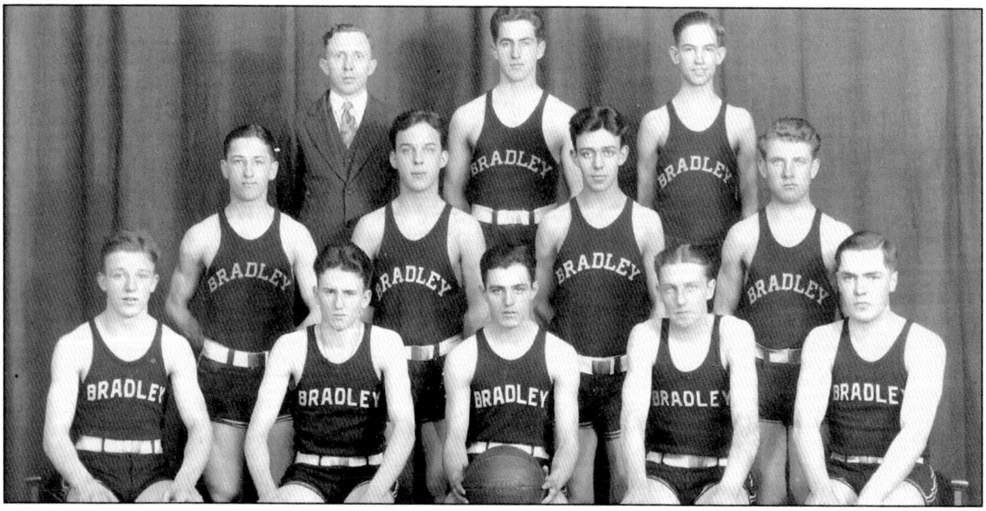

Pictured is the 1926–1928 Bradley High School basketball team. From left to right are (first row) Frederick Hasemeyer, Edward Huddelston, Everell "Tiv" Monty, Everett Hayes, and unidentified; (second Row) Edward Dressler, three unidentified; (third row) coach Oscar Young, unidentified, and unidentified. The 1927–1928 team established a number of school firsts, including playing in a Christmas tournament at Illinois Wesleyan College in Bloomington, having a single game scoring record of 23 points set by Fred Hasemeyer, and having a record 20-win season. During the 1928–1929 season, the first Kankakee County tournament was held, where Bradley lost its first game to Reddick High School, 27-17, and finished fourth. The next two county tournaments saw Bradley finishing second to St. Anne Community High School. (DM.)

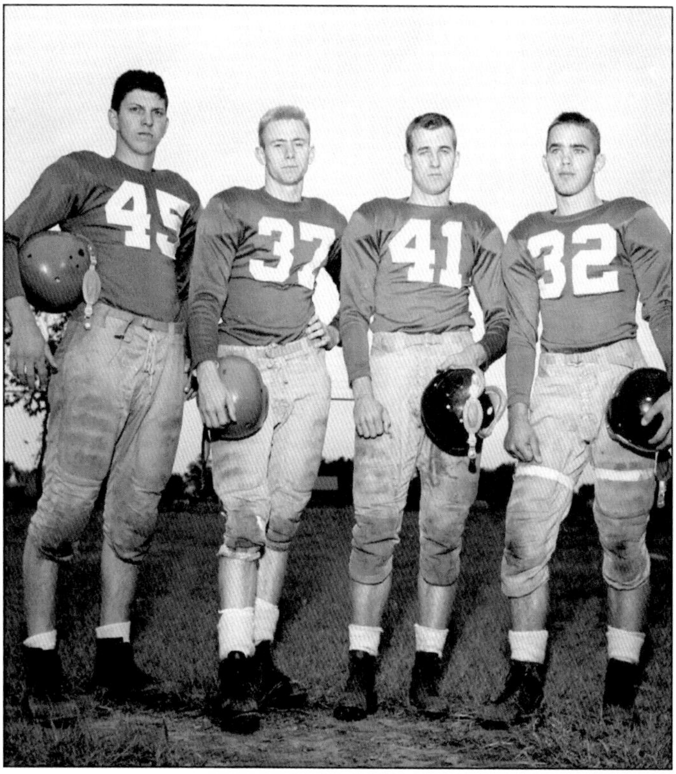

This photograph shows Bradley High School football team members from the 1949–1950 school year, including (from left to right) senior quarterback Francis Pechauer, fullback Jack Thaden, right halfback Joseph Henry Wertz, and left halfback Gerald Decker. The 1949–1950 school year became memorable not only for the opening of the new building, but also for many other activities. The football team completed an undefeated season by rolling up an amazing total of 308 points (state record) to their opponents' 27, and they led all state teams in scoring. The 308 points is also a record for points scored in one season. (KCM-KDJ.)

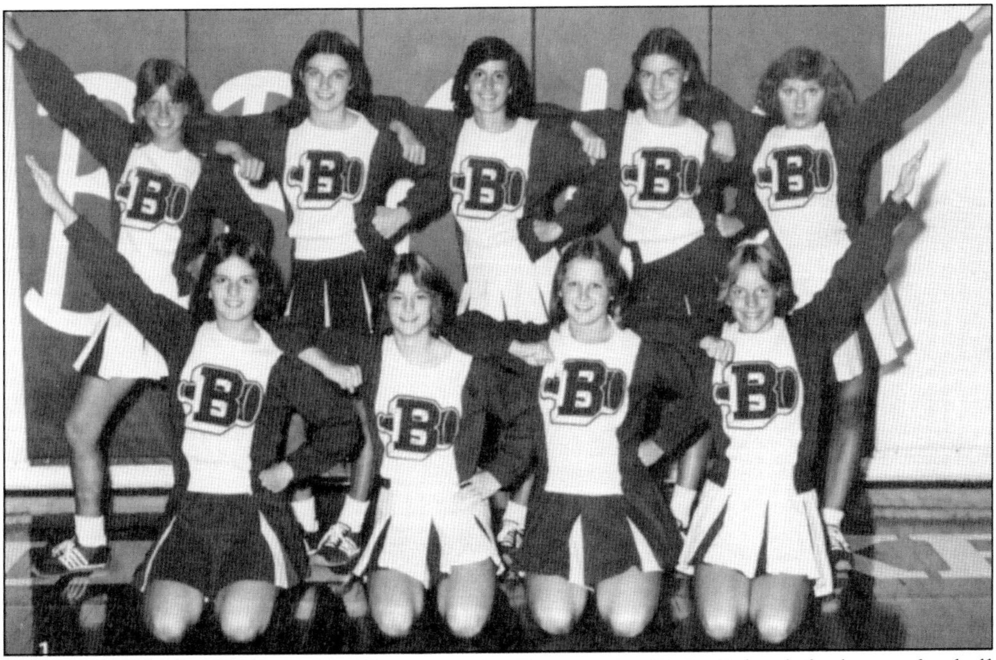

Pictured here, the 1978 Bradley-Bourbonnais Community High School freshman football cheerleaders, from left to right, are (first row) Sue Yates, Karla Boudreau, Gail Johnson, and Sherrie Sims; (second row) Sandy Hart, Christy Larkins, Kathy Bowman, Jodi Rasmussen, and Tammy Landry. Not pictured was Missy Klopp. The sponsor was Betsy Weber. This photograph is from the 1978 *Bradleyan*.

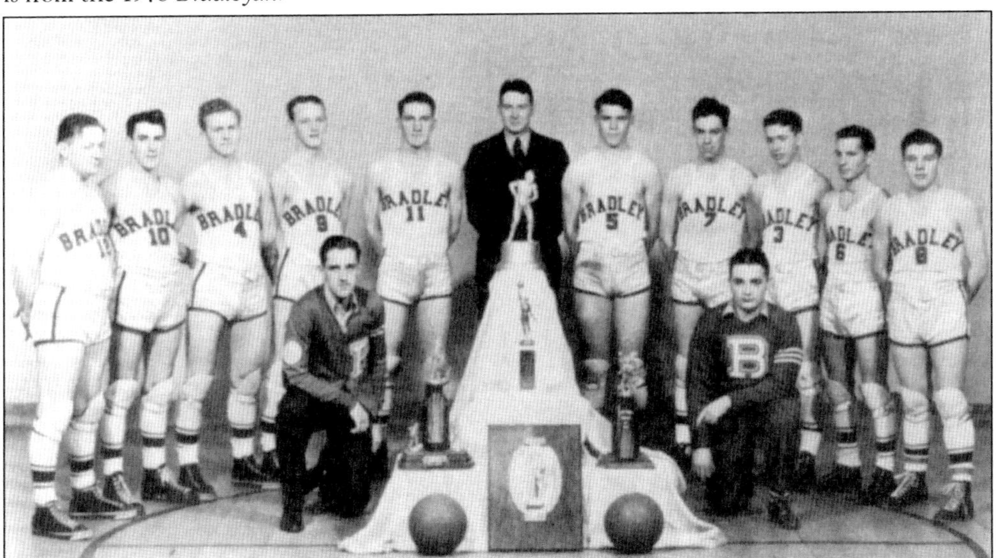

The 1938–1939 Bradley High School varsity Boilermaker basketball team was the first Bradley team to make it to the state finals in Champaign. The players, from left to right, are (first row) manager Harvey Hackley and manager Jesse McCue; (second row) Stanley Lesczewicz, Robert Martin, Roman Smietanski, Mark Marlaire, Charles Voorhees, coach James Laffey, LaVern Hahs, Leonard Martin, Fred Beach, V. Wasetis, and Leon Slovikoski. This image if from the *Bradleyan*. (KDJ.)

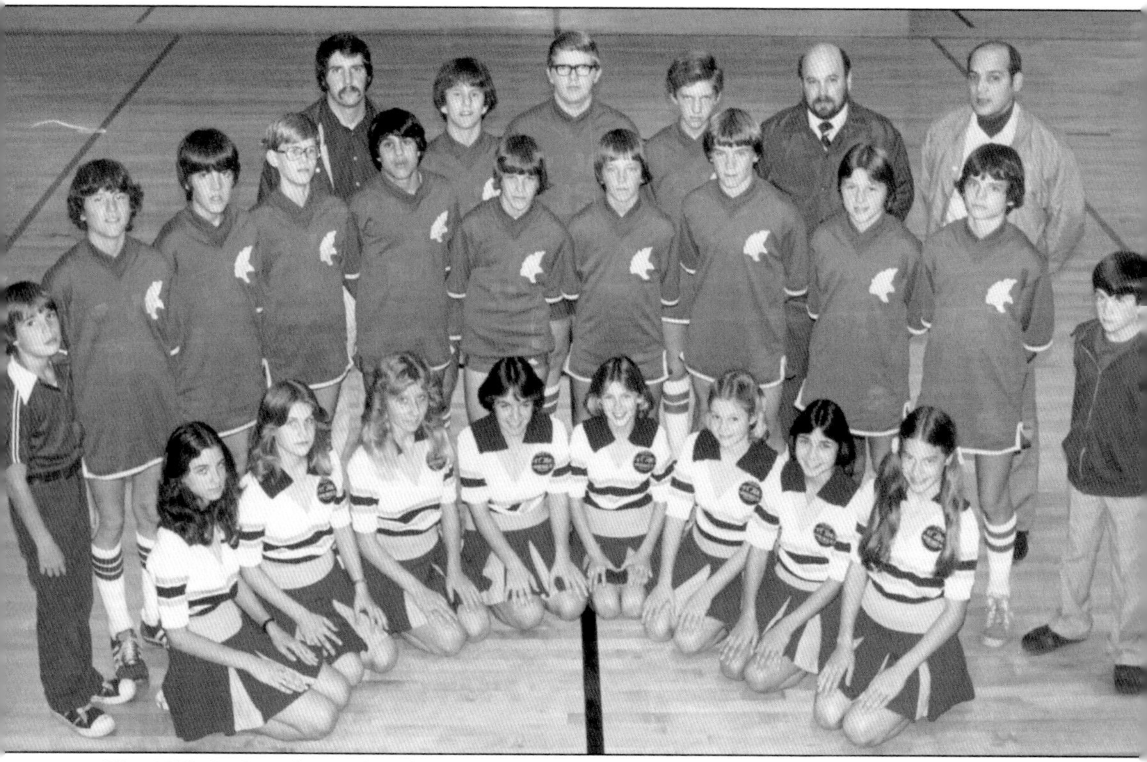

The 1979 St. Joseph Grade School Vikings "heavyweight" basketball team and cheerleaders are shown here. Coaches, in the third row, are Dennis E. Glenzinski (left), Jerry Balthazor (second from right), and Larry W. Barbee (right). (Author's collection.)

Eight

Dedication and Participation

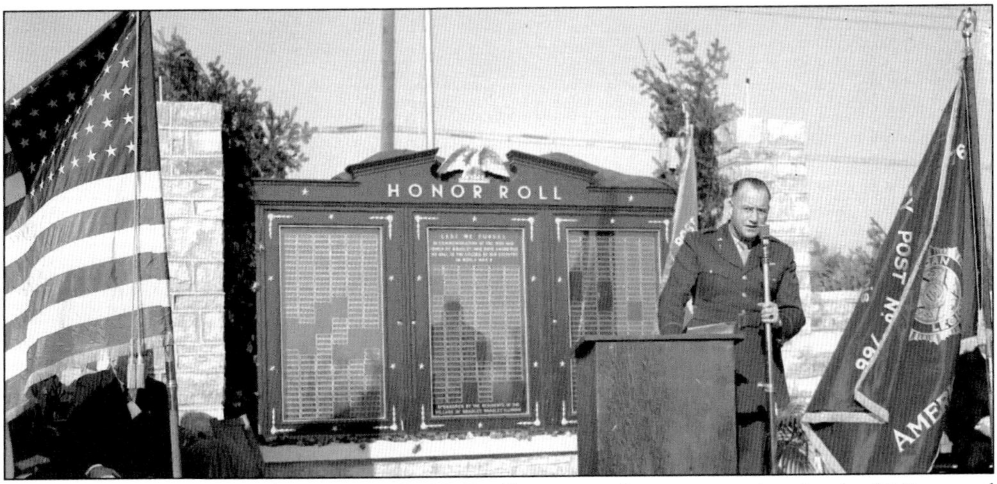

A memorial containing the names of 487 Bradley men who were serving in the U.S. armed forces was dedicated in Legion Park on Sunday, November 11, 1944. The principle speaker at the dedication was Maj. Norman S. Gillispie. He stressed the point that America was the melting pot of the world and that our fighting men are a combination of many nationalities. Many named on the memorial were descendants of Bradley's immigrant population, men such as Capt. Anthony Stefanich. Stefanich commanded Company C, 505th Parachute Infantry Regiment. He would be remembered as one of the most decorated infantrymen of World War II. Stefanich was mortally wounded on September 18, 1944, while attempting to save injured comrades near Groesbeek, Holland. Among the honors he earned during his military career were the silver star, bronze star, and two purple hearts. Grateful Dutch villagers in Groesbeek dedicated the bell tower of a small church (now a museum) to Stefanich's memory. By the end of the war Bradley was ranked third highest in ratio of armed service members to community population. A total of 520 Bradleyans became World War II veterans. Nineteen men had made the supreme sacrifice. (KCM-KDJ.)

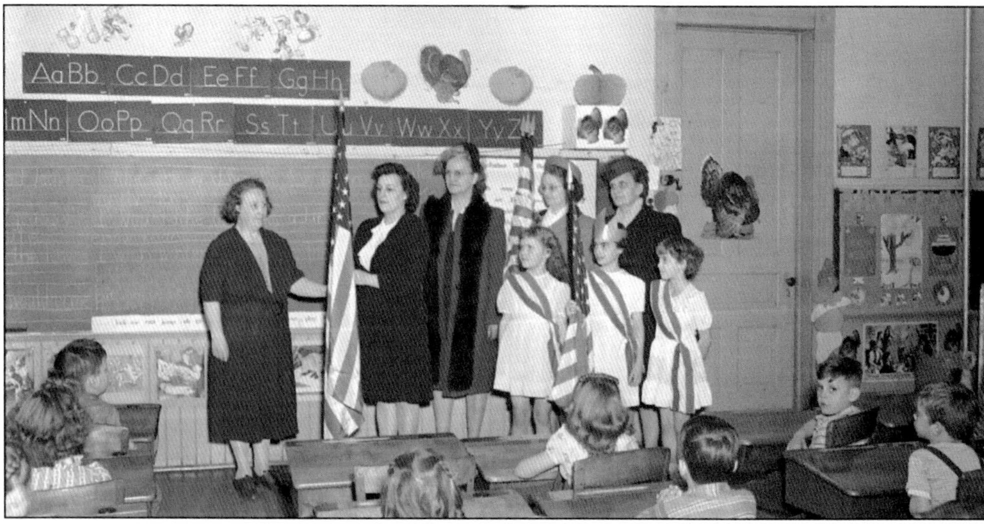

During the fall of 1947, the Bradley American Legion Auxiliary donated 17 American flags to three Bradley schools. At the Bradley Elementary School, first and second grade teacher Ms. Knox received a flag from Cecilia Tutewiler, auxiliary Americanism chairman. To the right of Tutewiler are Pearl Dorks, Daisy Eby, Louise Chamness, and junior auxiliary members Donna Marie Tutewiler, Jacquelyn Gulczynski, and Shirley Chamness. (KCM-KDJ.)

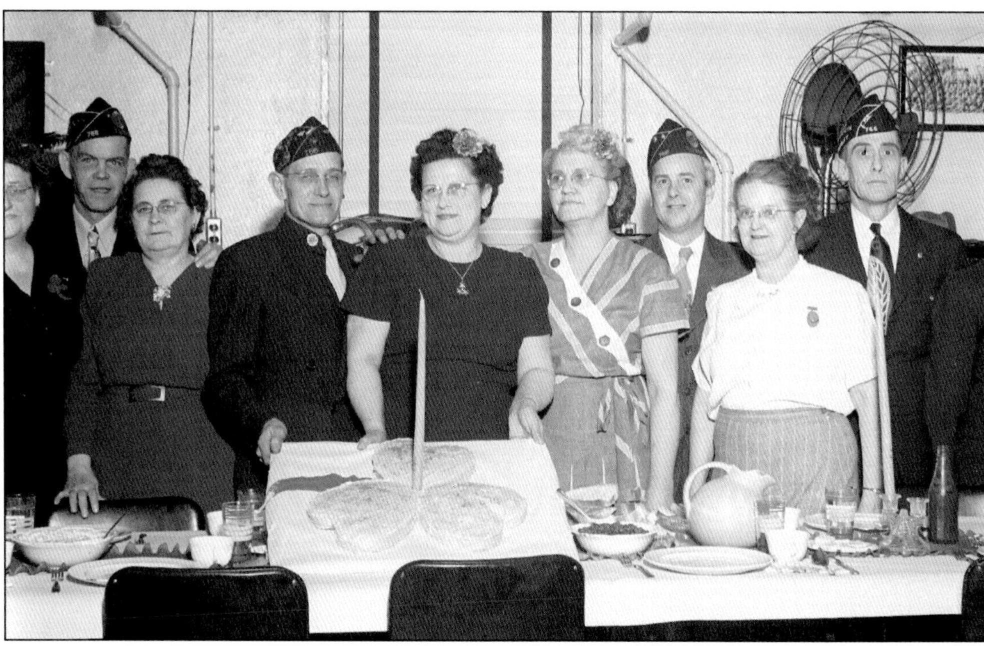

American Legion Post 566 commander James Eby and auxiliary president Marie LaFine (center) presided over a dinner dance on St. Patrick's Day in 1949. (KCM-KDJ.)

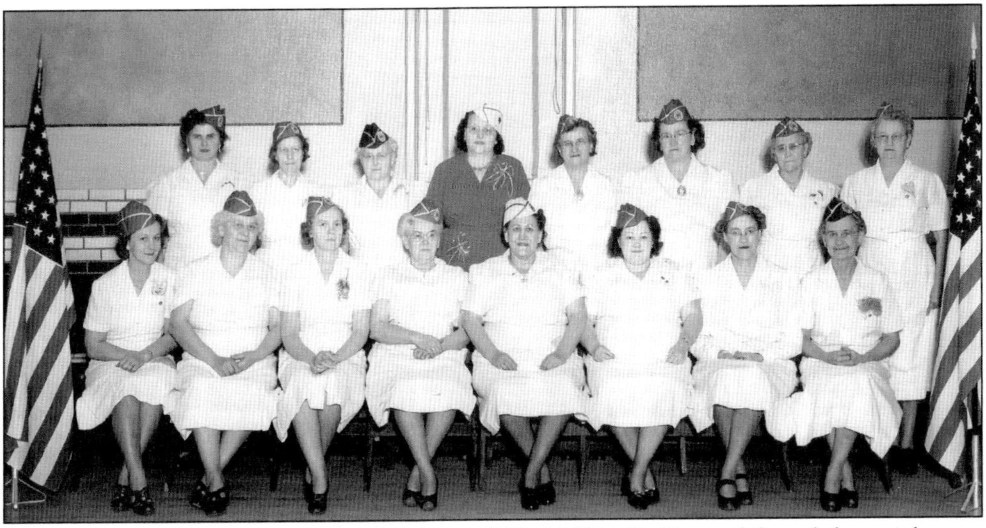

These are members of the Bradley Mothers of World War II. Pictured from left to right, are (first row) Lorraine Vogelsang, Gertrude Stelter, Mildred Kinneman, Jessie Lehnig, Rose Larson, Erma Ashline, Minerva Rochelle, and Denise Betourne; (second row) Elizabeth White, Zelma Beland, Blanch LeDuke, Leota Sanor, Charlotte Krizan, Jennie Menard, Myrtle Hubert, and Ida Atkins. Two members, Rosetta Alwine and Pearl Dirks, are not pictured. (DM.)

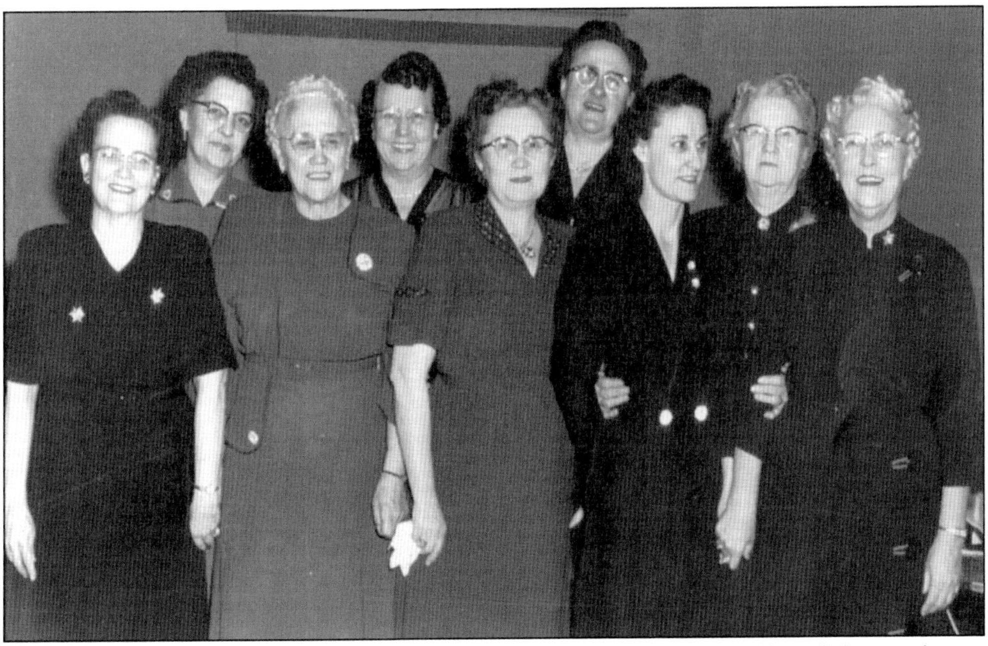

Pictured are the Bradley Royal Neighbors of America from the 1940s. From left to right are Blanche Rittmanic, Loretta Falkenham, Myrtle Hubert, Mildred Vaughn, Irene Reilly, Genevieve Lenfert, Bertha Haack, Ida Atkins, and Cora Shimanik. The local Royal Neighbors of America Pansy Camp 1129 was founded on September 7, 1898, with 21 charter members. (DM.)

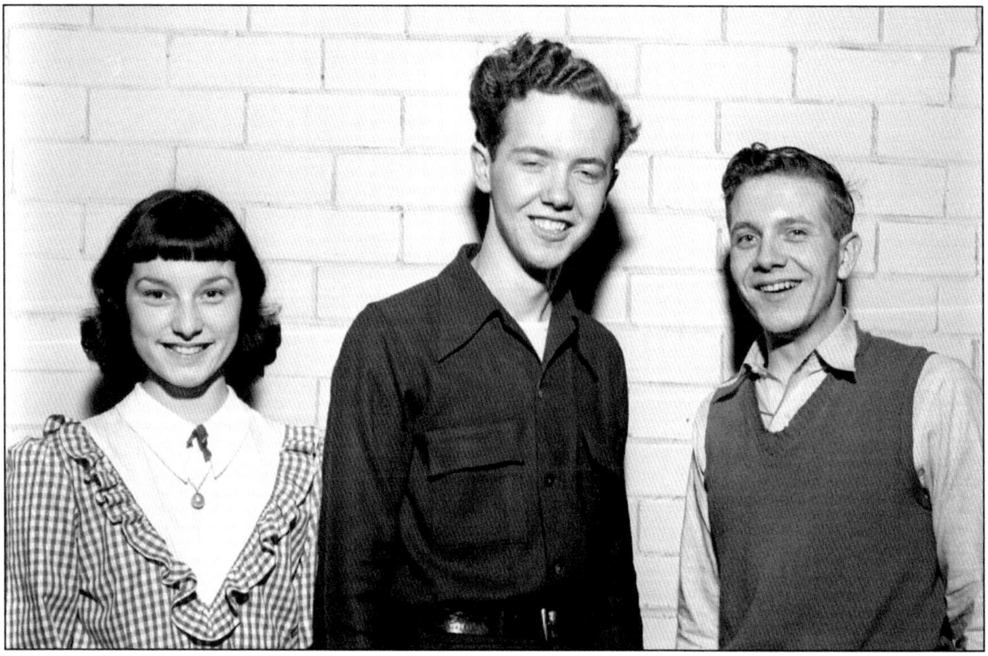

Dale Hale (center), an 18-year-old Bradley High School senior, won first place Saturday, April 12, 1949, in an oratorical declamation contest held at the University of Illinois. He competed against 12 other orators from six districts. Second place went to Jack Maddrell of Freeport, and Shirley Brown of Geneseo placed third. (KCM-KDJ.)

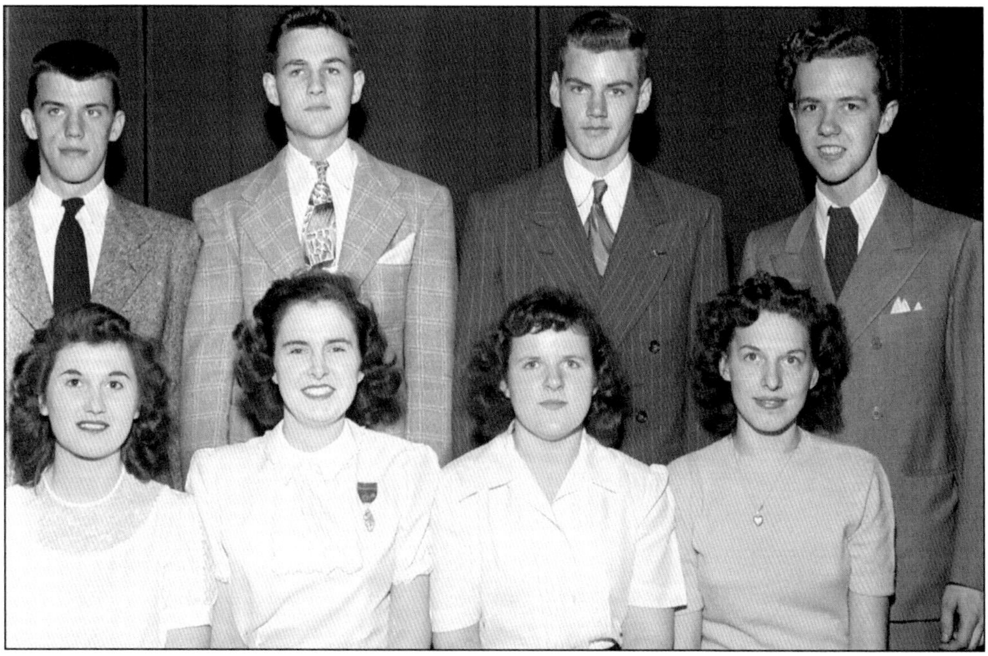

The Bradley High School Mixed Ensemble is represented in this newspaper photograph from April 1949. Pictured, from left to right, (first row) are Margery Kirchner, Beverly Nicoson, Patricia Hasemeyer, and Dolores Falkenham; (second row) Joseph Sykes, Ronald Dusenbury, Dennis Rasmussen, and Dale Hale. (KCM-KDJ.)

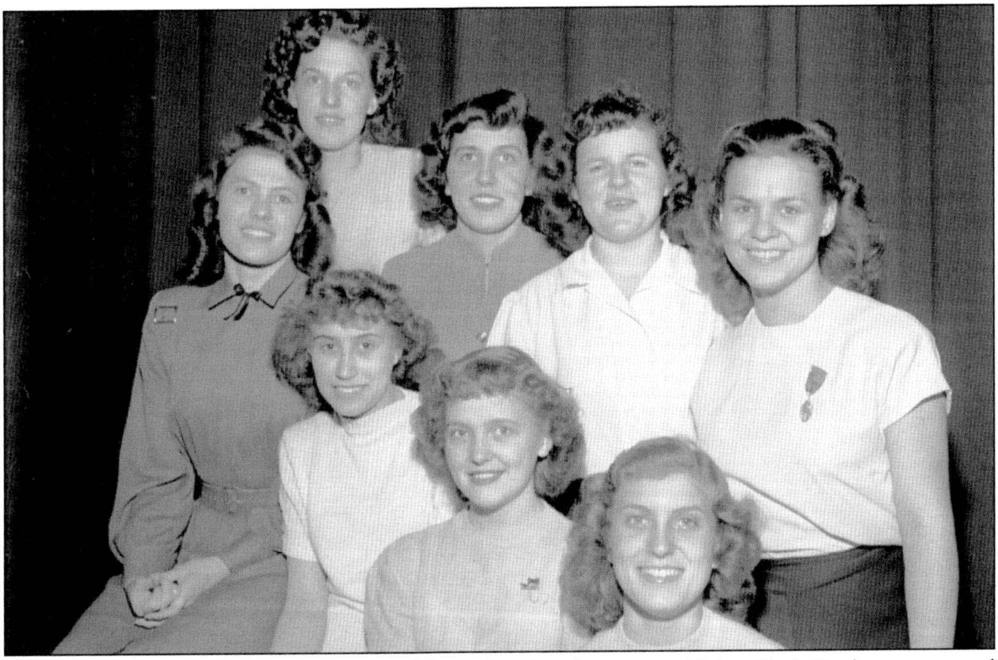

The Bradley High School Girls Ensemble under the direction of Mrs. Carl Hughes competed in the state music finals in April 1949. Pictured, from left to right, (first row) are Lois Johnson, Delores Altenbrunn, Joyce Anderson, and Sharon Smith; (second row) Dolores Falkenham, Marilou Meents, Patricia Hasemeyer and Jeanne Smith. (KCM-KDJ.)

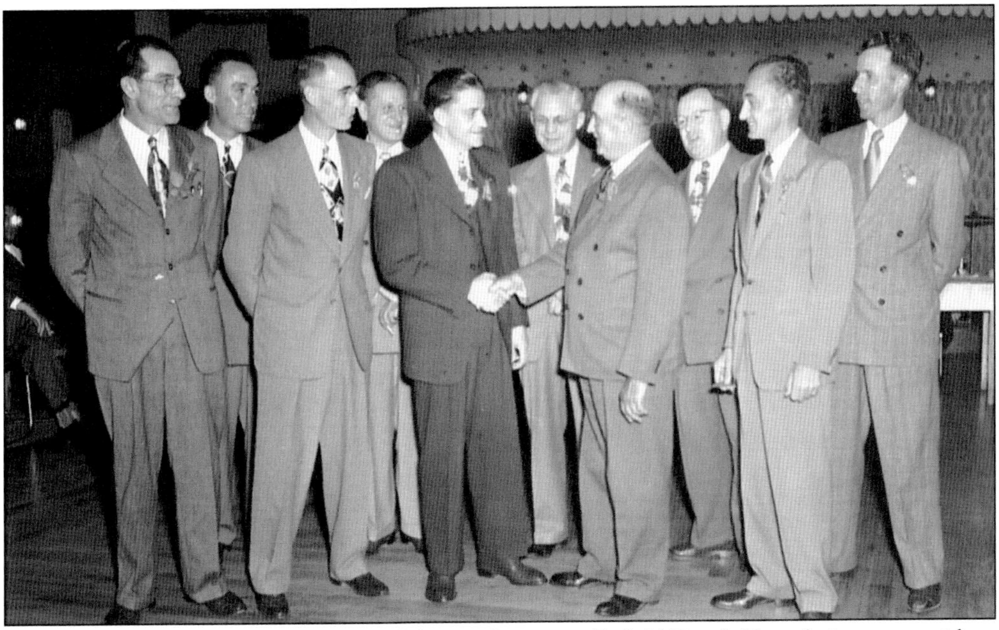

On June 9, 1948, the Bradley Lions Club members installed Al Finefield as their new president during a ceremony conducted by district governor Everett Mitchell of Morris. Finefield is on the right shaking hands with outgoing president Ray Magruder. Looking on, from left to right, are Urban Boudreau, Theodore Martin, Everett Mitchell, Roy Shapiro, Frank C. Benoit, Weldon Wadleigh, Edward Douvia, and Arthur Martin. (KCM-KDJ.)

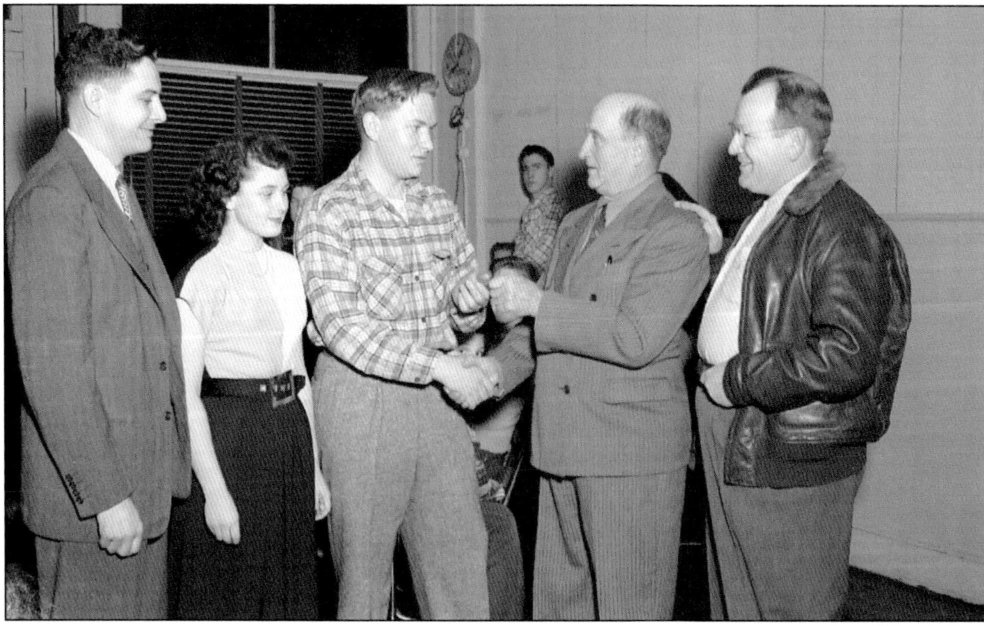

The Bradley Youth Center had been closed for several months before being reopened on Thursday, December 16, 1948. Lions Club president Al Finefield presented the key to the center's building, located on West Broadway, to youth group president Orville Hoffman. Looking on, from left to right, are Dr. W. J. Mayo, Jackie Gustin, and Weldon Wadleigh. The reopening of the youth center was made possible by the Bradley Lions and the Community Chest. (KCM-KDJ.)

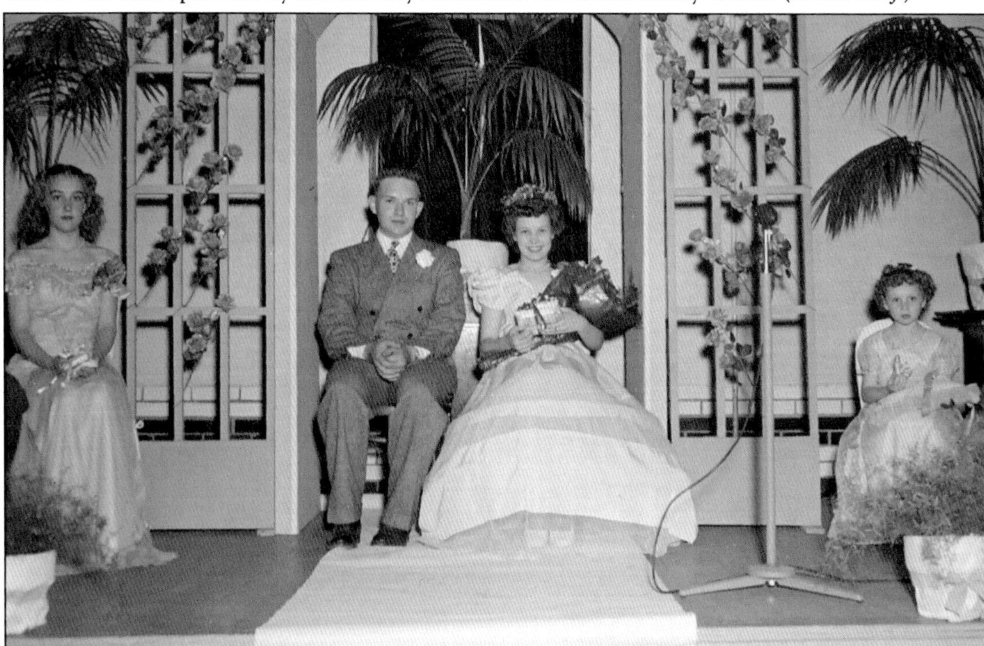

The chosen king and queen for a Bradley Youth Center benefit dance, which was held on April 22, 1949, at the Bradley American Legion, were Orville Hoffman and Violet Kagle. Donald Boudreau, chairman of the advisory board, and his committee made the arrangements for the affair. (KCM-KDJ.)

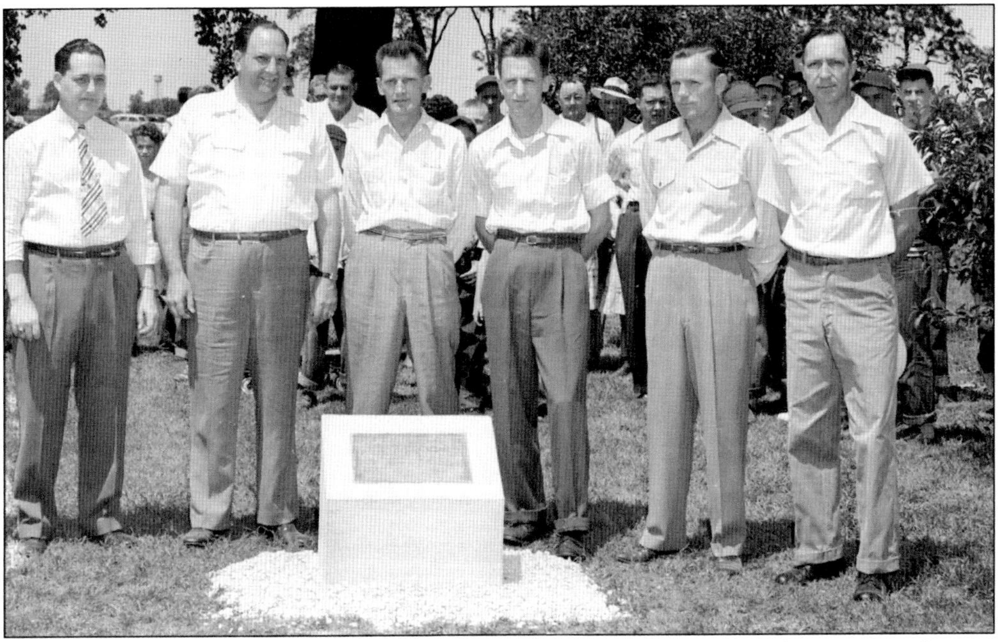

A tract of 3.5 acres across North Street, north of the David Bradley Manufacturing Works, was dedicated as a park on Saturday, June 4, 1949. The park was to be used by Bradley employees and their families. Standing behind the stone marker are members of the park committee. From left to right, are Gordon Wright, Donald Bell, Frank Sovinski, Van Emigh, Charles Pangle, and Frank Schultz. Not shown is Lawrence Dionne. (KCM-KDJ.)

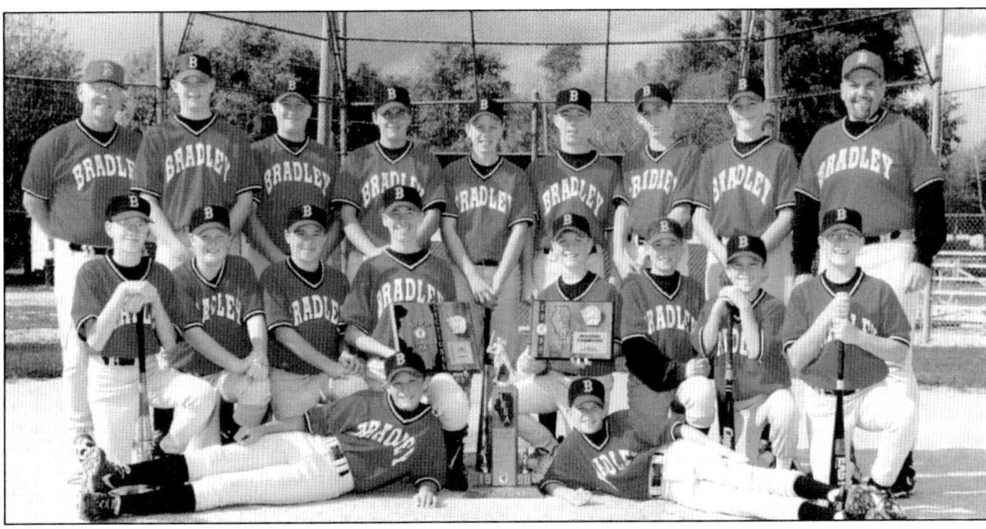

These are the 1998 Illinois Elementary School Association Class AA state champions, the Bradley Central Grade School Knights. Pictured, from left to right, are (first row) Reid Savoie and Tyler Grace; (second row) John Marcek, Cam Corcoran, Anthony Vieceli, Kyle Arthur, Nick Reid, Jared Martin, Andrew Hartman, and Matt Davis; (third row) coach Robert Long, Josh Hackley, Nick Pangle, Ben West, Andy Turrell, Roger Kilman, Scott Wills, Brandon Cotter, and coach Todd Schweizer. (RG.)

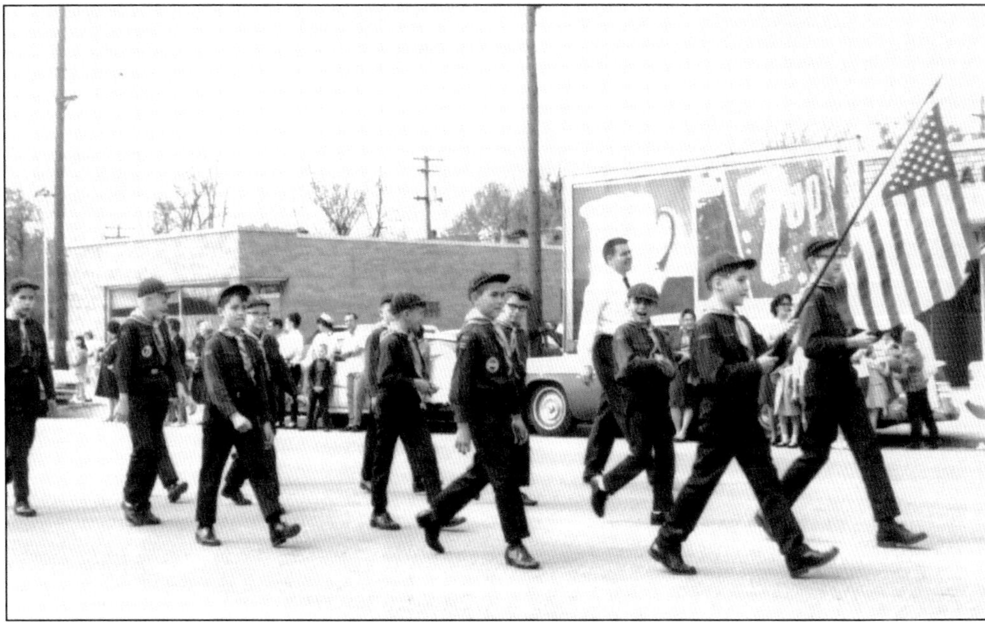

Bradley Cub Scouts march in a 1960s Loyalty Day parade. (Author's collection.)

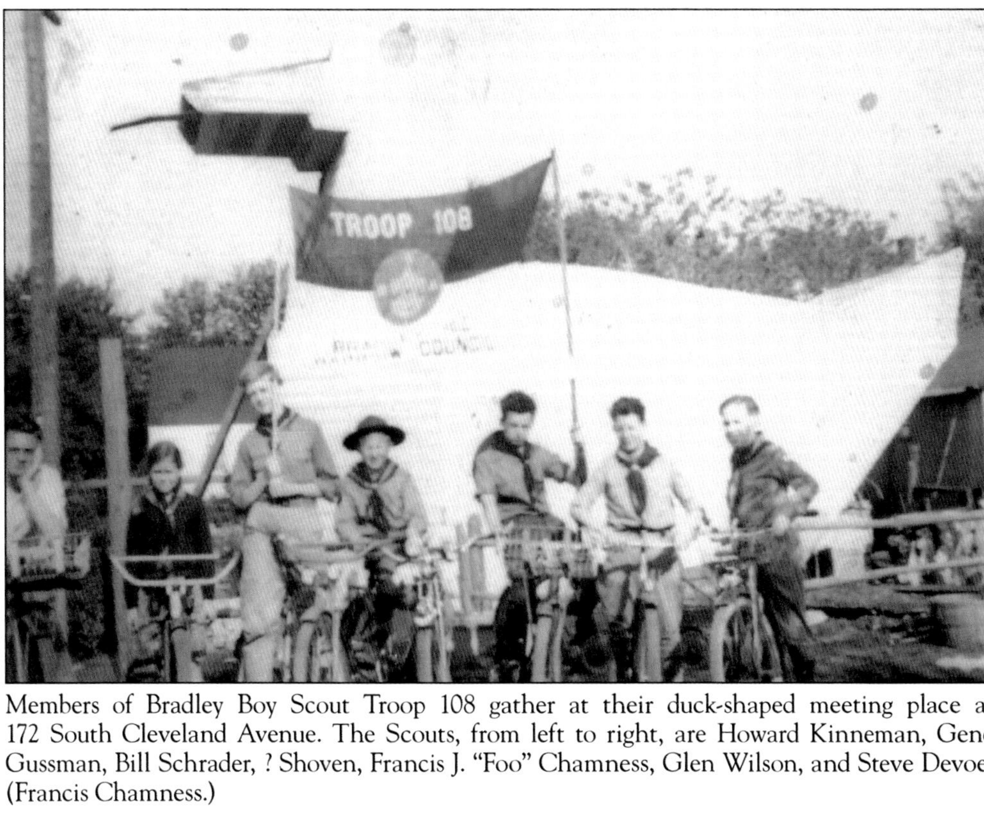

Members of Bradley Boy Scout Troop 108 gather at their duck-shaped meeting place at 172 South Cleveland Avenue. The Scouts, from left to right, are Howard Kinneman, Gene Gussman, Bill Schrader, ? Shoven, Francis J. "Foo" Chamness, Glen Wilson, and Steve Devoe. (Francis Chamness.)

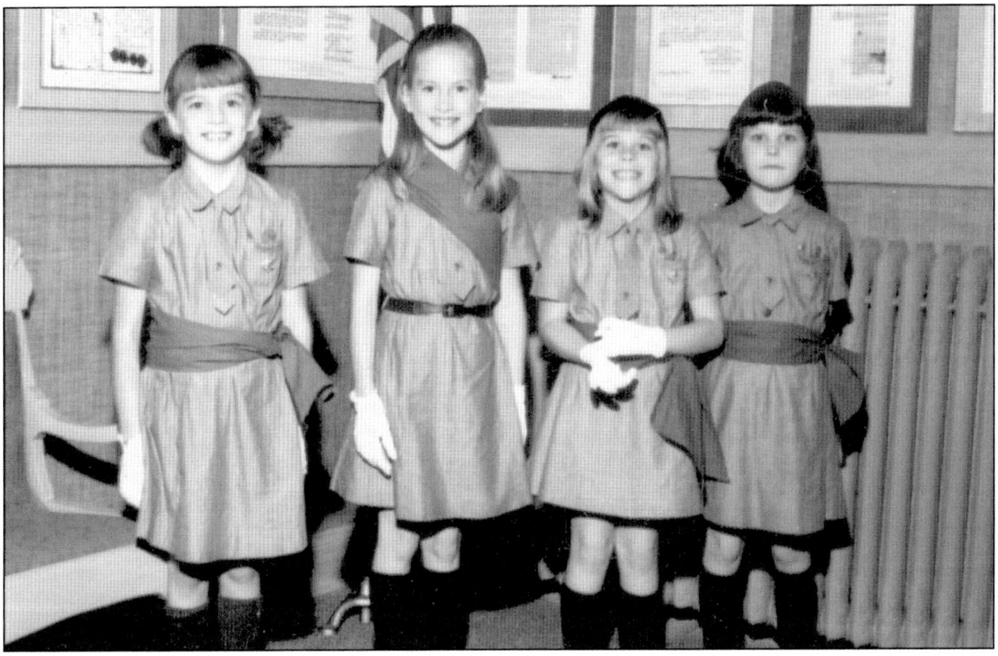

Members of the St. Joseph Brownie troop participated in the dedication of a Freedom Wall at the Kankakee Public Library in 1967. The Exchange Club of Kankakee sponsored the installation of the freedom documents. From left to right are Diana Montague, Patricia LaFontaine, Alice Johnson, and Julie Goodman. (Author's collection.)

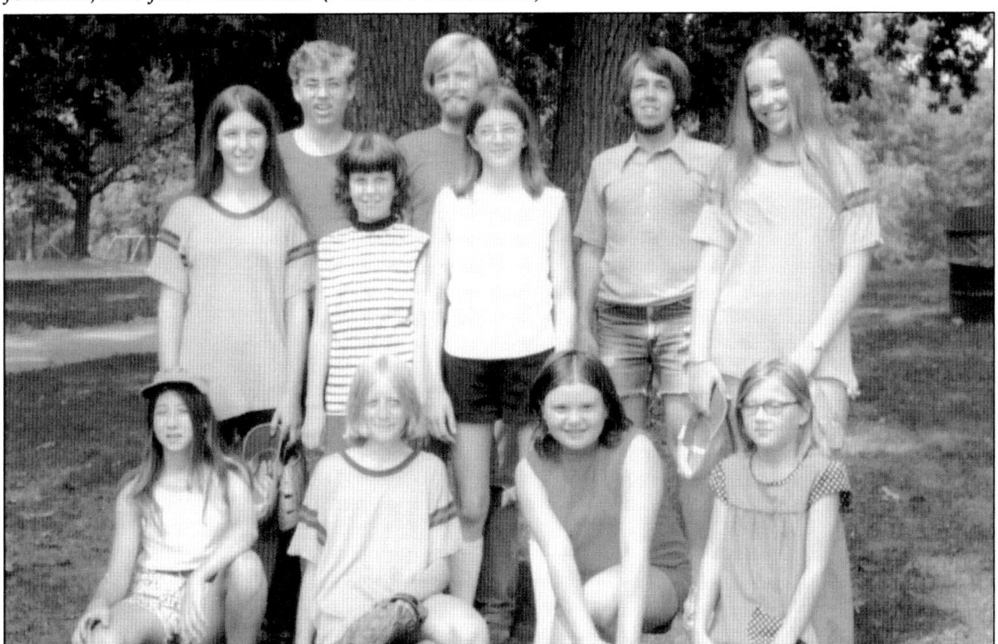

This is the 1968 Bradley-Bourbonnais Petticoat League, Plante-Kerger softball team. Pictured, from left to right, are (first row) Darla Strawn, Mary Johnson, unidentified, and unidentified; (second row) unidentified, Julie Goodman, Diane Montague, and Jayne Spencer; (third row) unidentified, coach James Ciaccio, and coach David Ciaccio. (Author's collection.)

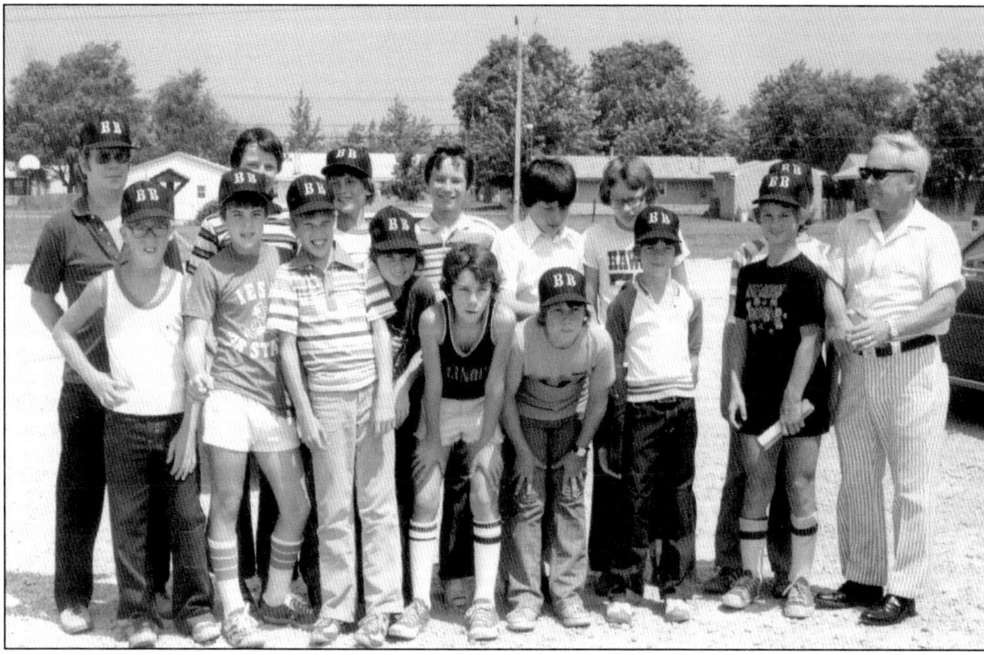

These newly chosen members of Bradley-Bourbonnais All-Stars Little League team came from several Little League teams in Bradley and Bourbonnais. The All-Stars would compete in the 1978 Illinois state finals, and place second. Jack Jones (second row, left) and Leon Pommier (second row, right) were the coaches. (Author's collection.)

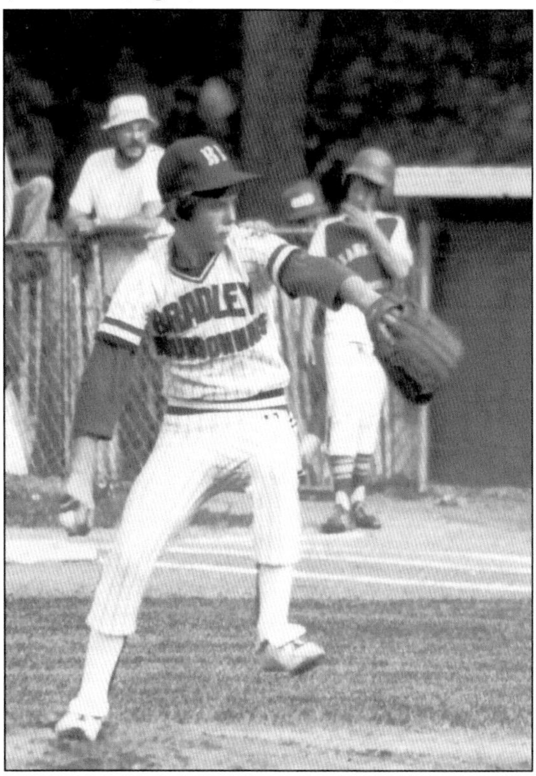

Scott Goselin pitched for the Bradley-Bourbonnais All-Stars Little League team in 1978. He then played ball for Olivet Nazarene College, and in the late 1980s, was a member of three Atlanta Braves minor league teams including the Durham Bulls, in Durham, North Carolina. During his career with the Braves organization he played at various times all three infield positions. Scott is now the superintendent of Bradley Elementary School District 61. (Author's collection.)

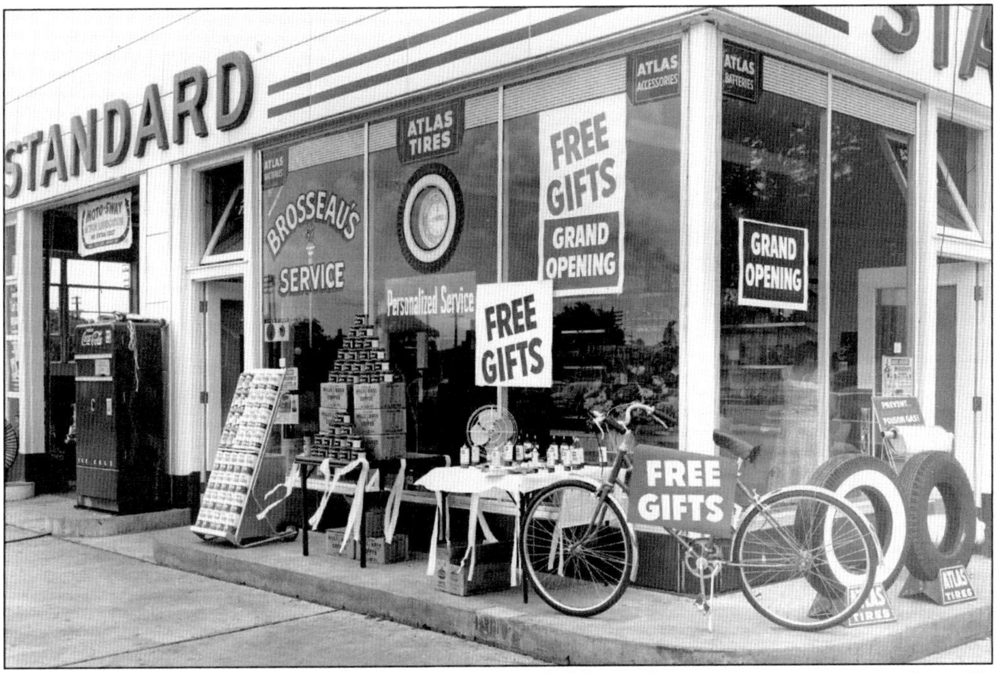

Armond E. Brosseau's new Standard service station held grand opening ceremonies on June 18, 1954. It was located at 195 East Broadway on the northwest corner of South Schuyler. Brosseau was a Bradley businessman for over 40 years. (Janice Brosseau Sims.)

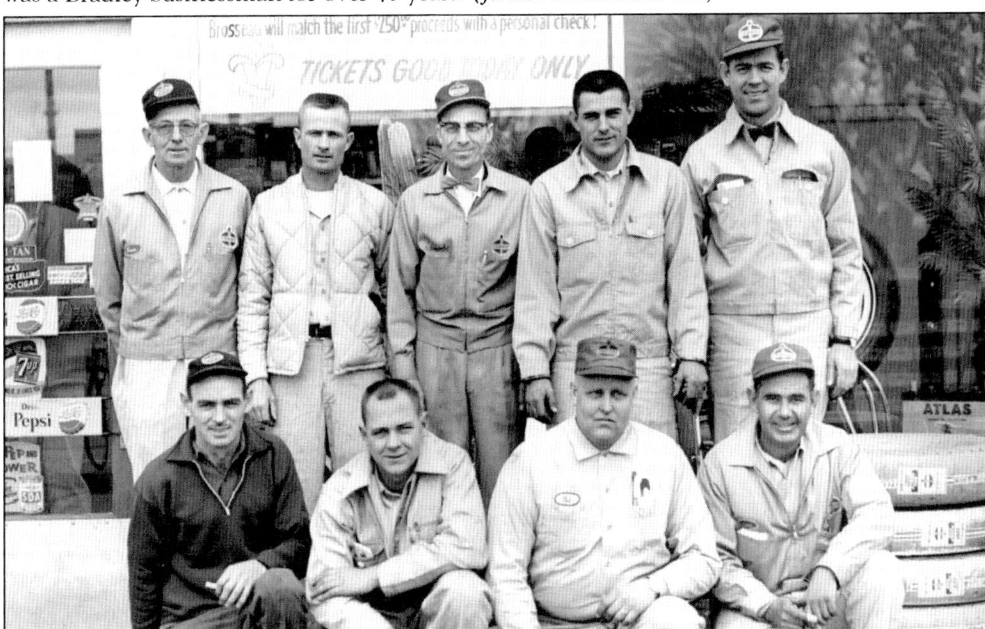

A full service gasoline station in the 1950s required workers to pump gas, change oil, repair tires, and mechanics had to work on automobiles. Employees at the Brosseau station, from left to right, are (first row) Frank Moody, ? Hawking, Ed Burr, and Charles Reynolds; (second row) Vernon Fuss, Charles Curwick, Armond Brosseau, Clarence LeDuke, and unidentified. The station closed in 1980. (Janice Brosseau Sims.)

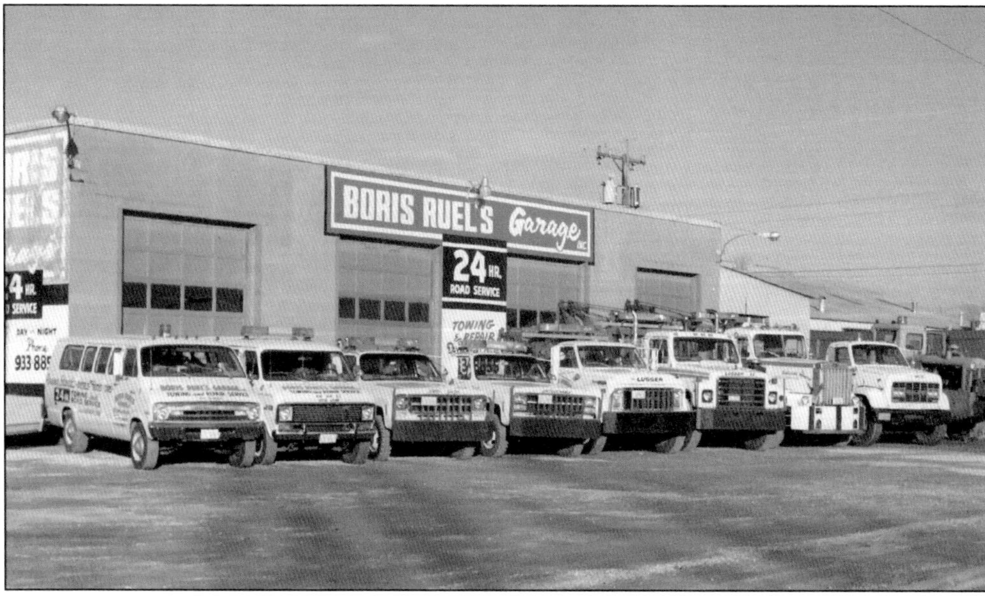

In 1962, Boris A. Ruel opened Boris Ruel's Garage and Towing Service on State Route 52. He was born on August 24, 1914, in St. George to Joseph and Leah (Senesac) Ruel. During World War II, Boris served as a paratrooper in the Philippines. He is seen on the left in the first row in the 1967 photograph below. He died in 1987. (Boris Ruel Jr.)

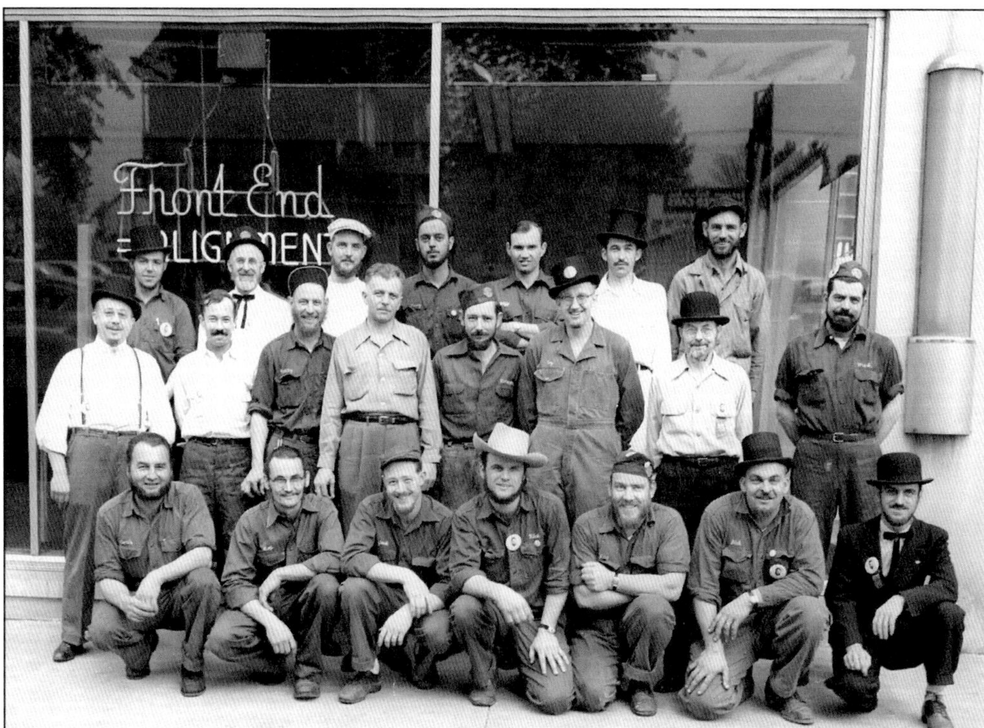

Nine

The Elected and the Appointed

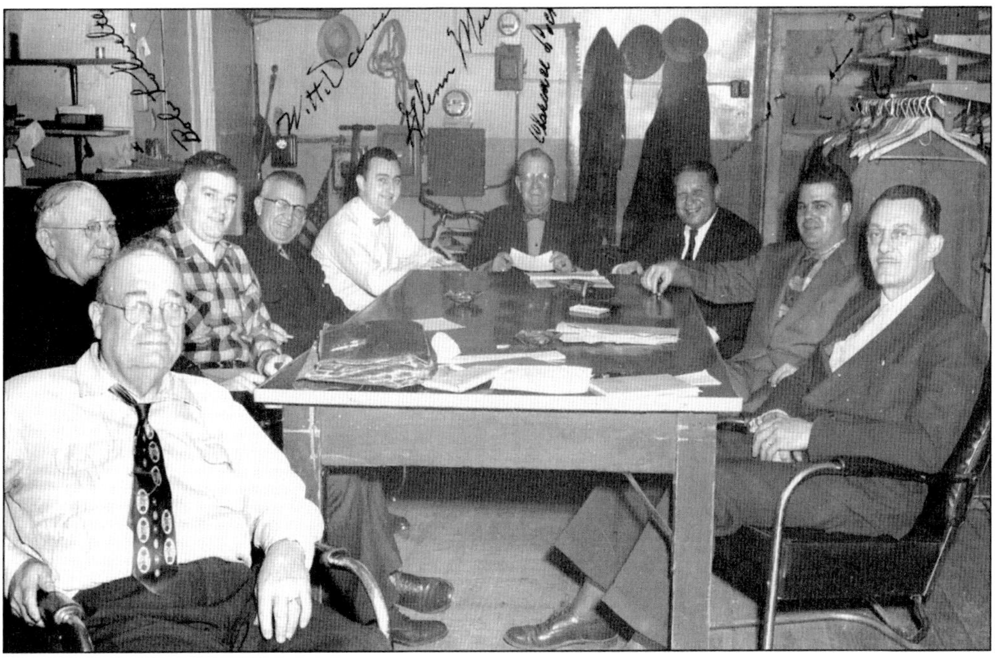

A photographer was present at the January 18, 1954, board of trustees meeting in the old Bradley Village Hall, with board president Clarence A. Lock presiding. Pictured, clockwise from bottom left, are treasurer George Marlaire, trustee George Beckhelm, trustee Robert Kolwelter, trustee Witt Davis, trustee Glenn Mulligan, president Clarence A. Lock, attorney Samuel H. Shapiro, trustee Tiff Coash, and trustee Ed Slovinski. Shapiro was elected lieutenant governor of Illinois in 1960 and 1964. He became governor when Otto Koerner resigned in May 1968 to become a judge on the United States Court of Appeals for the Seventh Circuit. (SC.)

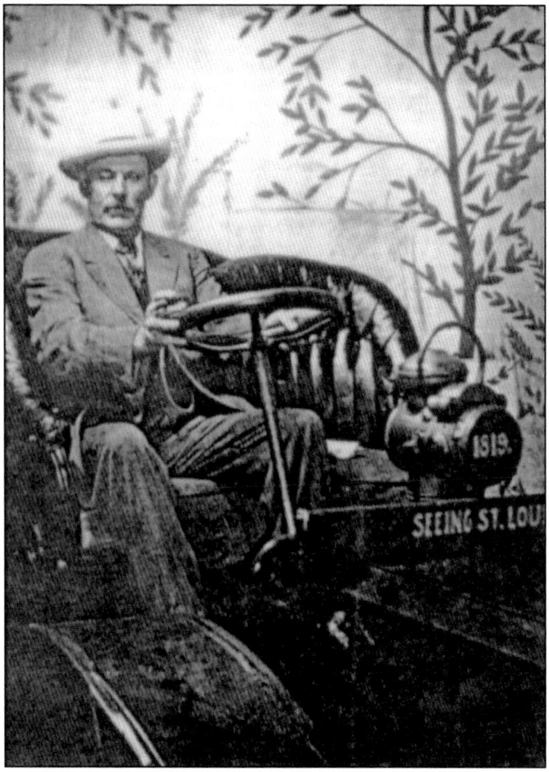

Among other settlers who moved to Bradley in the early years was John McAndrews, who was born in Pekin. McAndrews's name first appeared in Bradley records on April 20, 1901, after he had been elected to the village board. A year later, he became president of the board and served in that office for one year. McAndrews had factories in Piper City, Illinois, and at Walkerton and LaCrosse, Indiana, which were building dredge boats for use in channelizing the Kankakee River. It appears McAndrews attended the Saint Louis Louisiana Purchase Exposition in 1904, where this photograph was taken. (Marietta Frogge.)

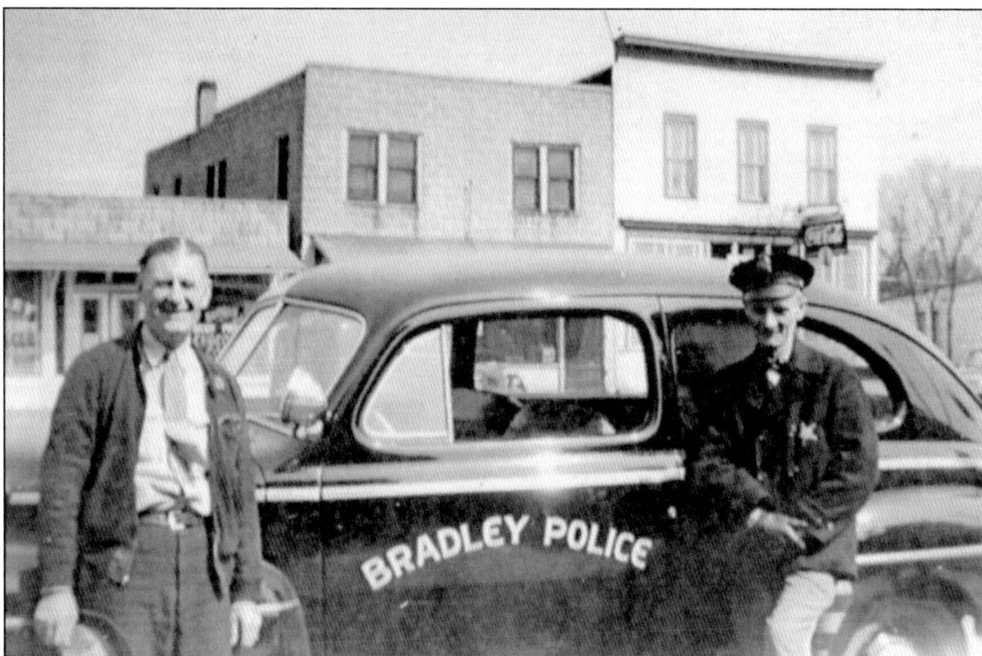

Bradley mayor Clarence A. Lock and officer August Webb pose with Bradley's first police car. (CE.)

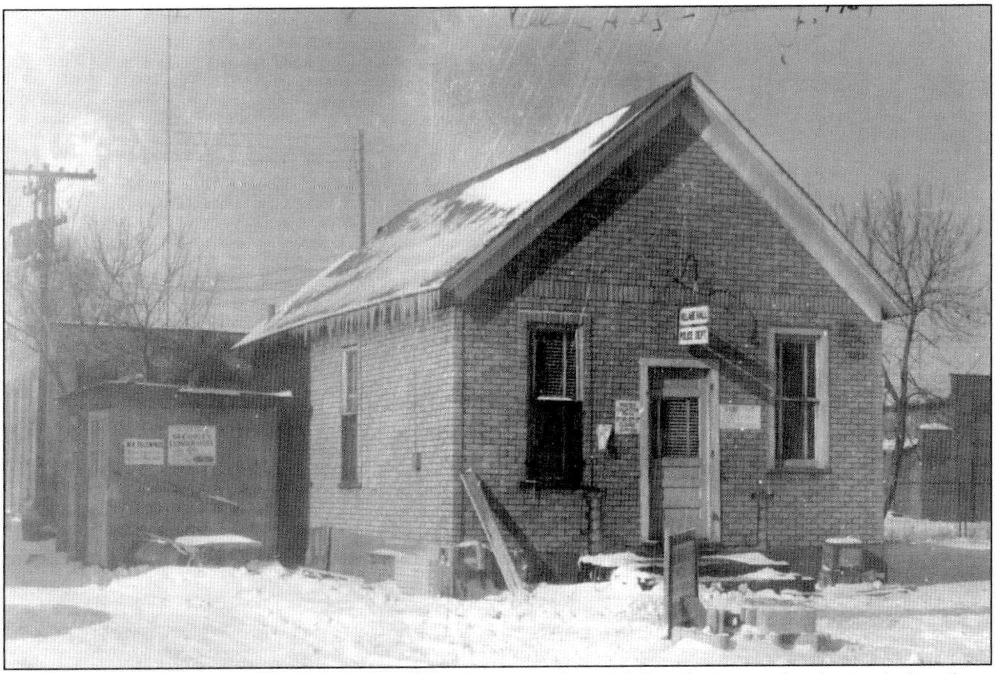

On November 18, 1892, J. Herman Hardebeck donated lot 16, block 40, to North Kankakee for a town hall. It was built between 1893 and 1895. This photograph was taken in January 1954, just before the old building was demolished. (SC.)

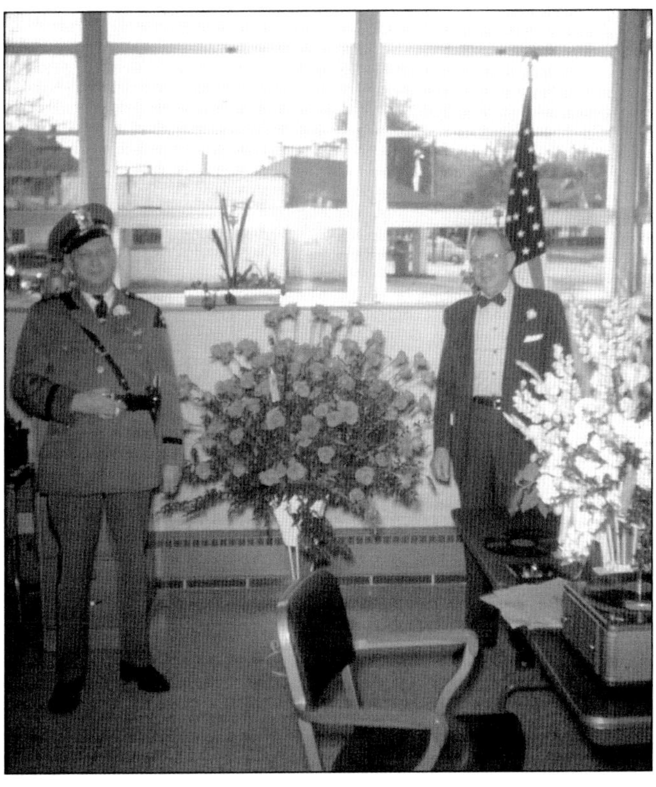

This photograph of Police Chief Harry Stutz and Lock was taken in 1956 in the new municipal building. O. L. Martin and Son had been awarded the contract to construct the municipal building in March 1954. Lock was in his second term, having defeated Virgil Kinneman in April 1949. Stutz was appointed chief of police in May 1953. (DM.)

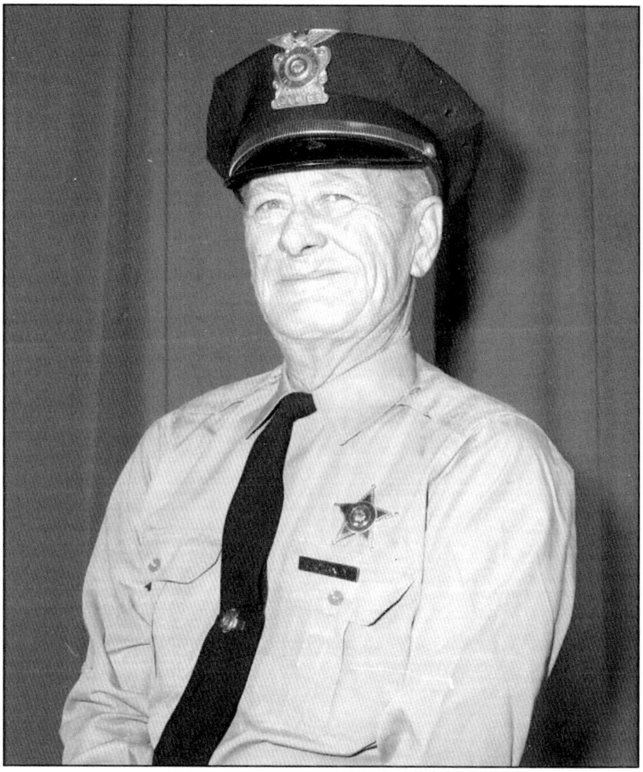

John Carney began his career as a police officer in 1934. In 1958, the Bradley village board appointed Carney acting chief of police. He resigned in January 1962 and became superintendent of safety. At the time Carney became police chief, there were only two regular officers on the police force. When he retired there were five. Carney served in World War I and World War II. (SC.)

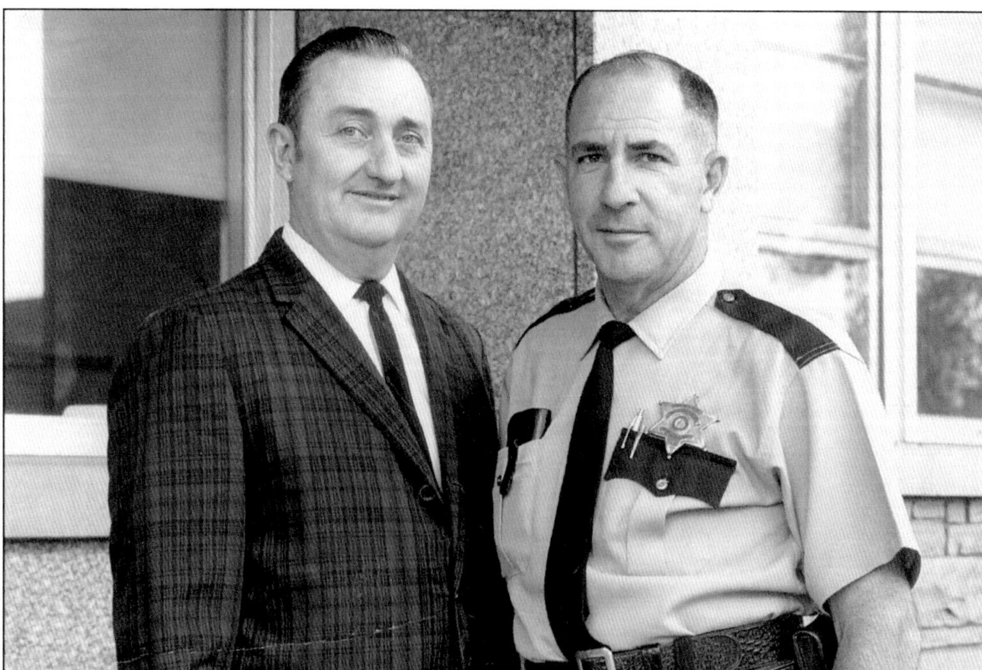

Edward Mulligan became mayor of Bradley when Mayor William Barwegan resigned on November 21, 1960. Upon the resignation of Carney in January 1962, Mulligan appointed a former village trustee, Robert Martin, as chief of police. (SC.)

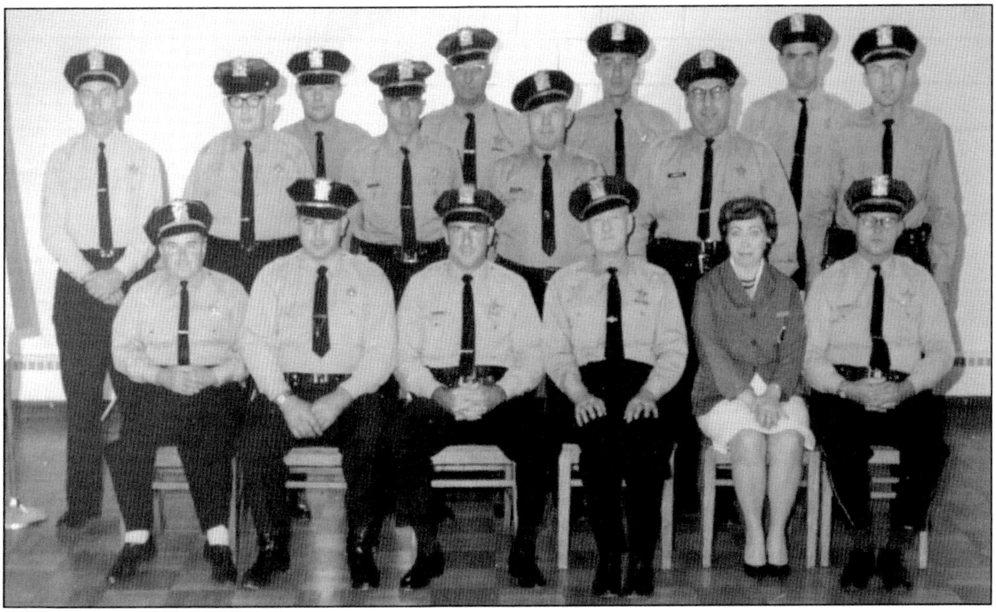

There were 16 members of the Bradley police force in 1966. Pictured, from left to right, are (first row) Leonard Pelehowski, Roland Cappalano, chief Robert Martin, Carney, Florence Cole, and Harold Knickerbocker; (second row) officer Stanley Rattin, officer Randy Kolwelter, officer John Wilkins, officer Donald Lancaster, officer Gerret Osenga, officer Merwin Shear, officer Richard Brosseau, officer Thomas Lambros, officer Delmar Douglas, and officer Ralph Thompson. (SC.)

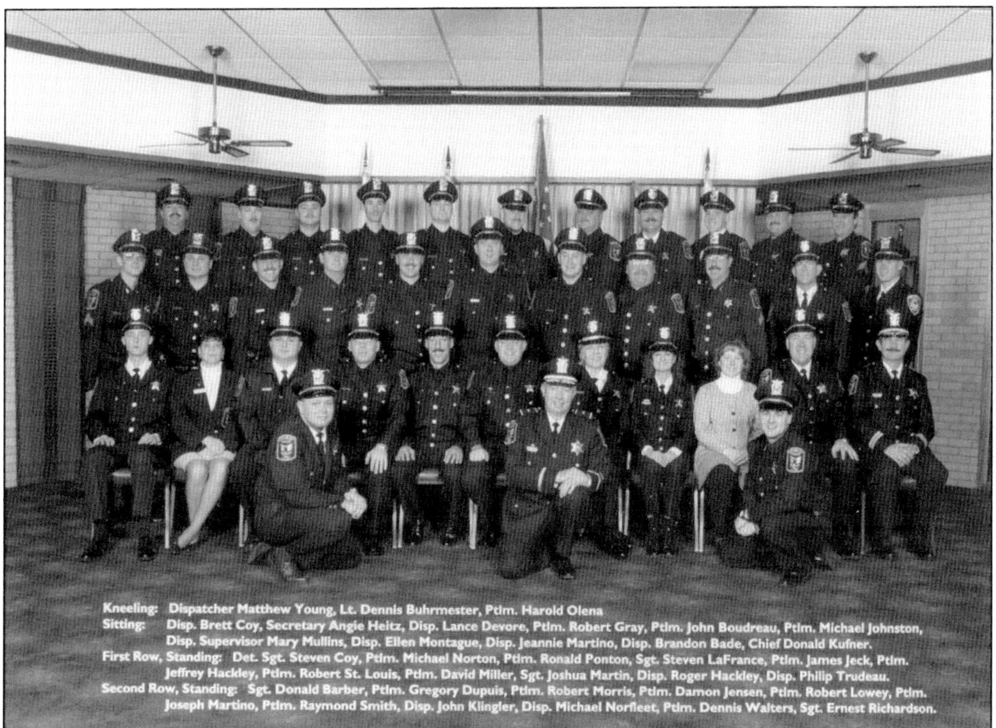

By 1997, the Bradley police force had grown to 36 members. (RG.)

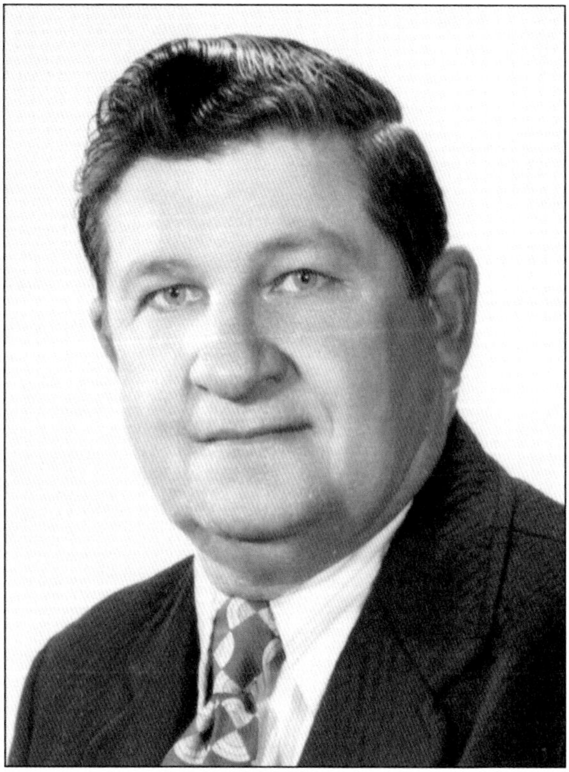

On April 27, 1981, defeated village mayor Howard Duchene swore in the newly elected Kenneth Hayes. Although the major manufacturers in Bradley were in financial trouble and unemployment was high, Hayes was instrumental in launching an era of economic development. He engineered the paving of residential streets in east Bradley, established a new metropolitan sewage system, promoted urban renewal, and negotiated the addition of Northfield Square shopping mall to the village. (BHS.)

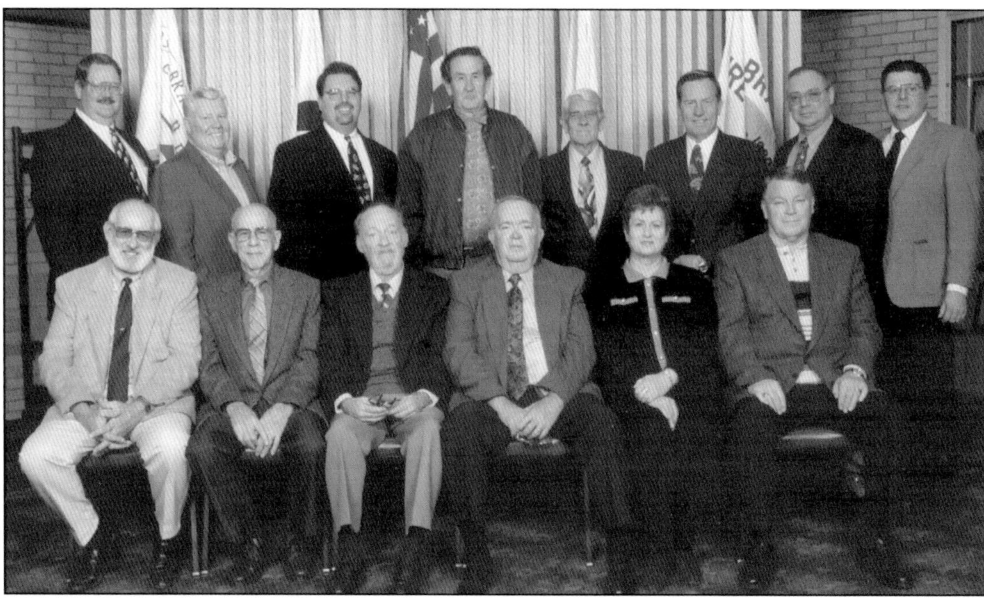

Retired police officers who had served the village of Bradley gathered in the boardroom of the village hall to have their picture taken on November 21, 1997. They attended the funeral of Will Lewis, an officer killed in the line of duty. Pictured, from left to right, are (first row) Jack Dugan, Robert Martin, Jack Polk, Donald Fitts, Catherine Bergan, and William Willis; (second row) are James Greenstreet, Paul Lovell, John Fitts, Delmer Douglas, Donald Lancaster, Leroy Eich, Stephen Alvey, and Ryland Gagnon. (RG.)

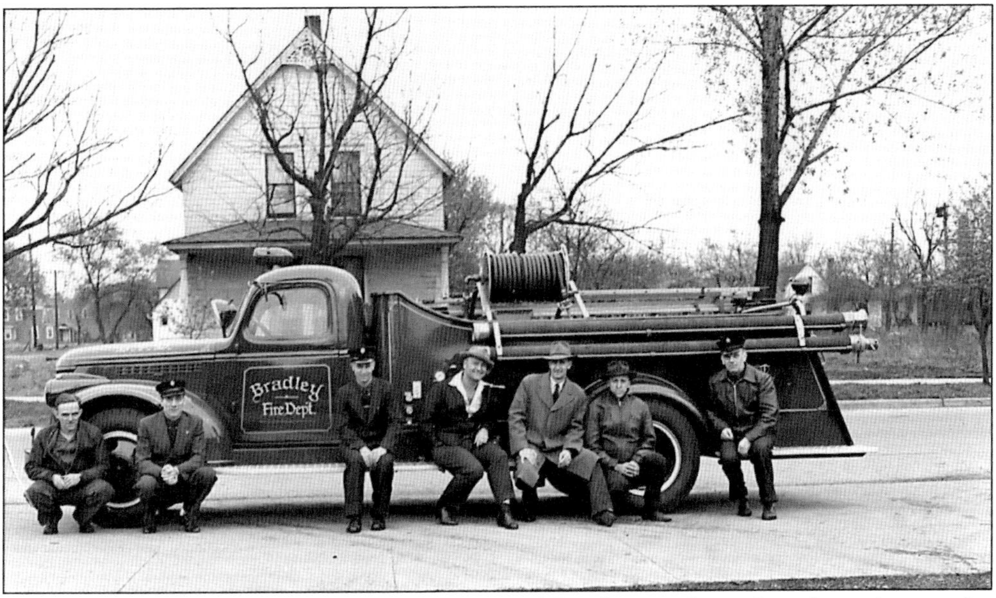

In April 1945, Fire Chief Peter Kolwelter assured Bradley residents that the volunteer fire department's new 500-gallon pumper truck with a 250-gallon booster tank would help to lower village fire insurance rates by about 20 percent. The new truck replaced a 1924 Reo. Pictured, from left to right, are fireman Warren Brickle, fireman Urban Boudreau, fireman Meddie Guimond, assistant chief Walter Heinze, mayor Virgil Kinneman, fireman Bernard LaMontagne, and fireman Charles Ponikvar (KCM-KDJ.)

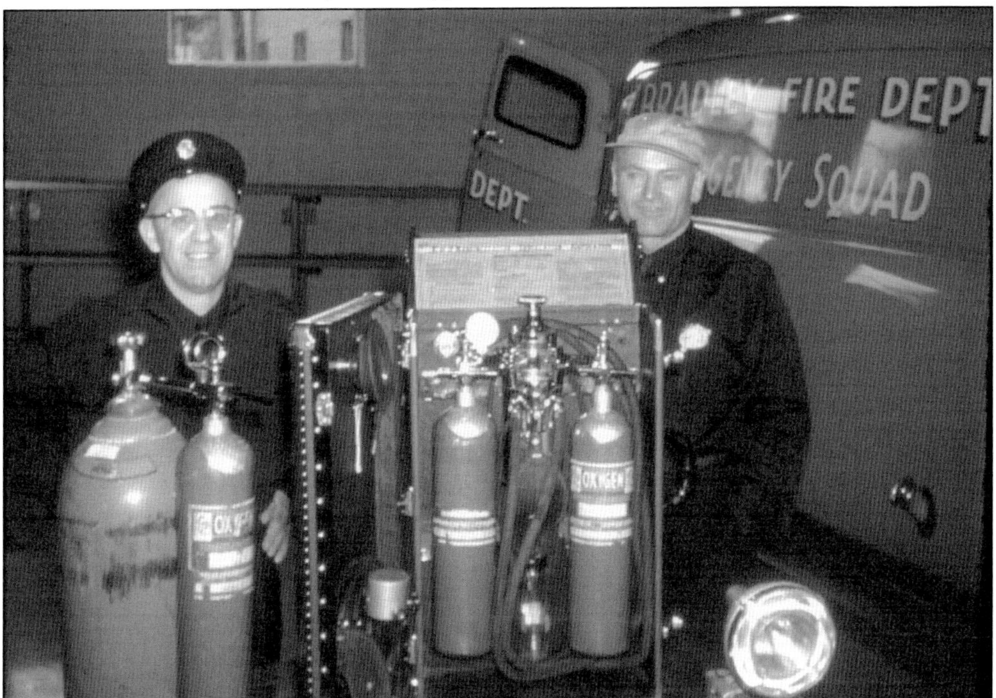

Two members of the Bradley Fire Department rescue squad, George Rambo and John Matthews, display the department's newly purchased equipment and truck. (DM.)

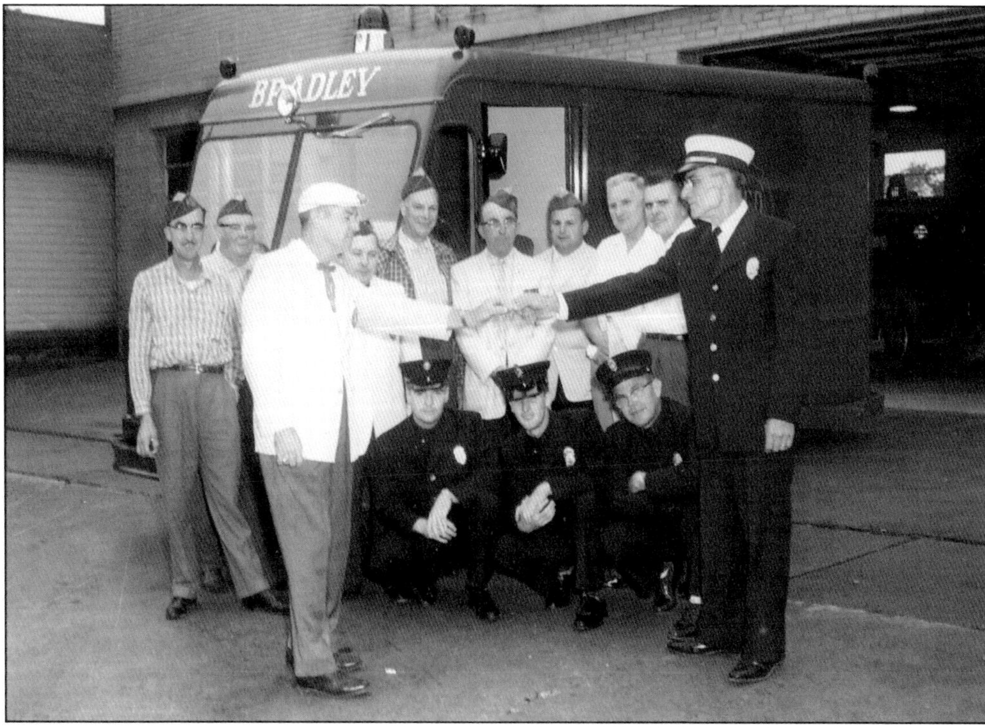

This photograph shows the president of the Bradley Lions Club handing the Bradley fire chief the keys to the new inhalator truck. The truck was purchased in 1960 with funds raised by the Lions Club. Pictured, from left to right, are (first row) Lions Club president Donald Boudreau, William Travis, James "Fuzz" Travis, ? Ragouse, and fire chief Urban Boudreau; (second row) two unidentified, Elmer Stump, unidentified, Clarence B. Chambers, William Bennett, and two unidentified. (Bradley Fire Department.)

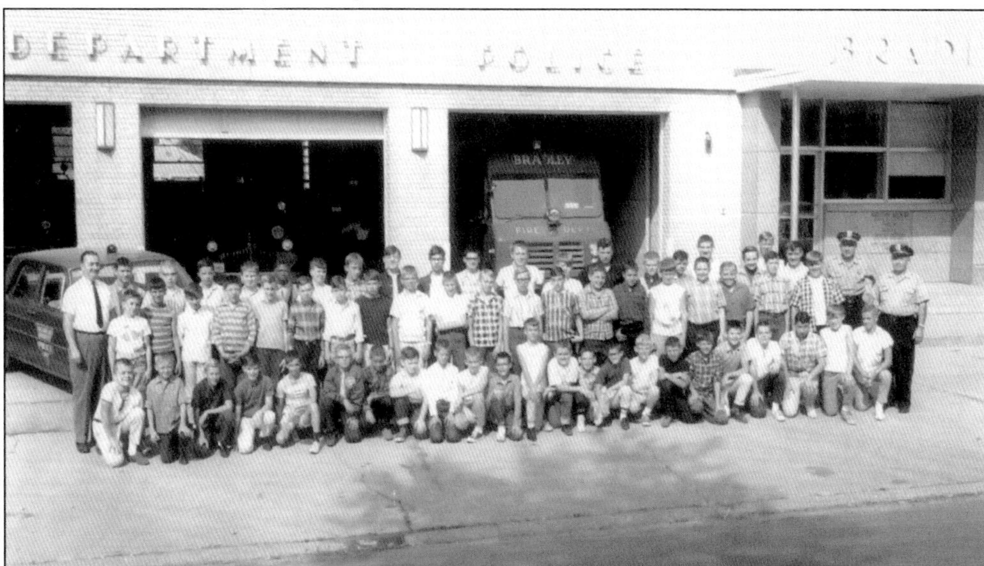

Schoolboys are shown here after receiving a tour of Bradley's fire department in 1966. Mayor Glenn Mulligan is on the left. Urban Boudreau is the fire chief. (SC.)

Ten

PRESERVING A HISTORY

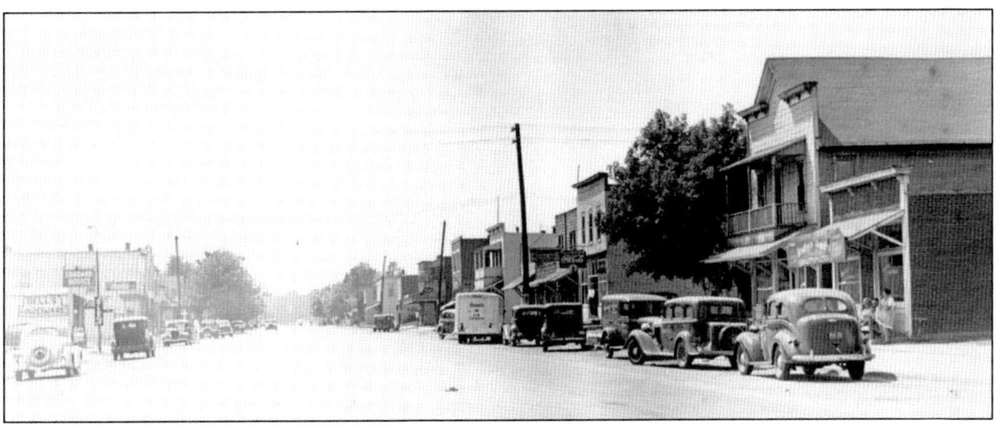

The Potawatomis came into the Kankakee River valley in the late 1700s. They remained until the mid-1830s. Two treaties with the United States, one in 1832 and another in 1833, surrendered the Potawatomi estate in north-central Illinois and required the population to move to reserves west of the Mississippi River. The region's pioneering history begins with the arrival of Thomas Durham, Noel LeVasseur, and others in the 1830s; the history of Bradley begins some 55 years later, when J. Herman Hardebeck, a land broker, capitalized on farm failures and industrialization. (KCM.)

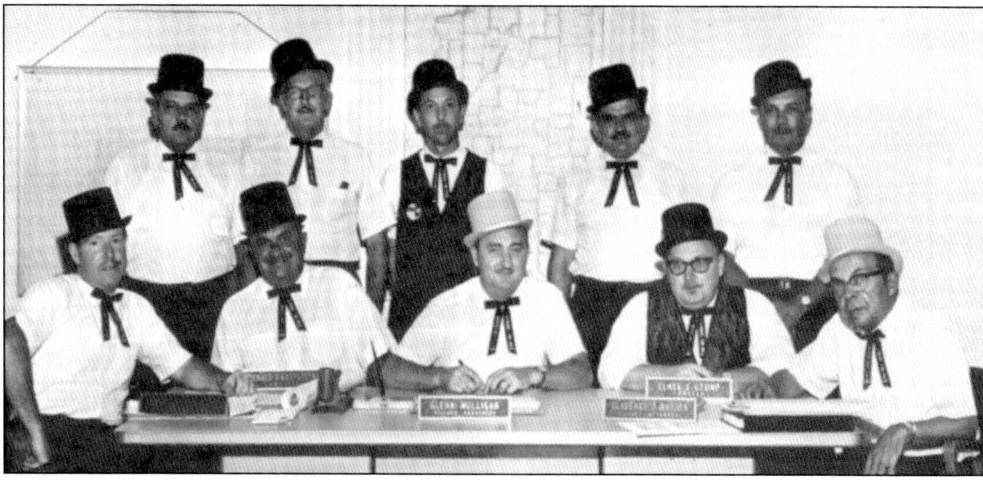

The 1967 Bradley Board of Trustees dressed up to celebrate Bradley's Diamond Jubilee. Pictured, from left to right, are (first row) trustee Howard Duchene, trustee Donald Chaplinski, village president Glenn Mulligan, trustee Elmer Stump, and trustee Clarence Hayden; (second row) trustee Leon Slovikoski, trustee John Ross, trustee Lawrence Denoyer, trustee Vince Menard, and trustee John Kessler. (BHS.)

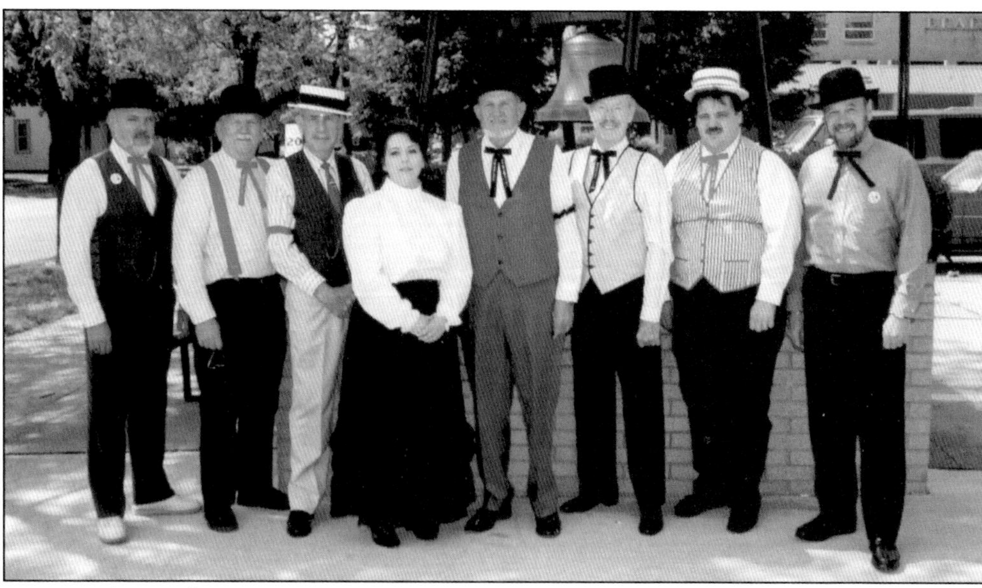

In 1992, the Bradley Board of Trustees dressed up for a centennial celebration. From left to right, are trustee Carl Erickson, trustee William Ponikvar, trustee Robert Martin, trustee Kathy O'Conner, and village president Kenneth Hayes, trustee Howard Duchene, treasurer William Zajc, and trustee Jerry Balthazor. (RG.)

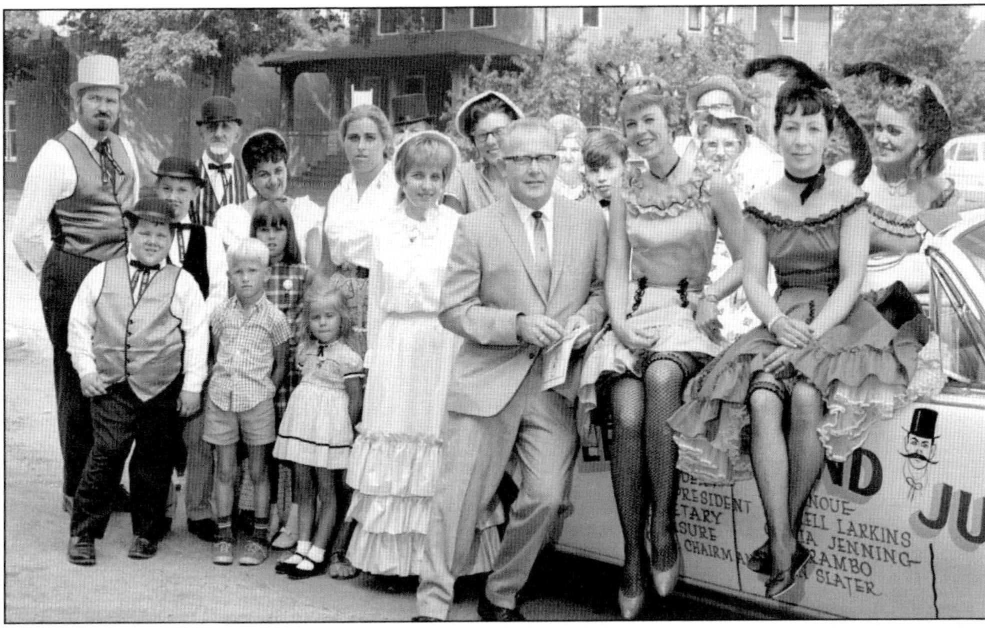

As Bradley prepared for its Diamond Jubilee in 1967, residents of the village, beginning in late July, participated in dress-up day once a week. Attempts were made to duplicate the styles of the Gay Nineties. During the week of celebration, August 30 to September 4, many events were scheduled, culminating in a grand parade and a historical pageant. Visiting a group of costumed revelers (center) is Mayor Thomas Ryan of Kankakee. (KCM-KDJ.)

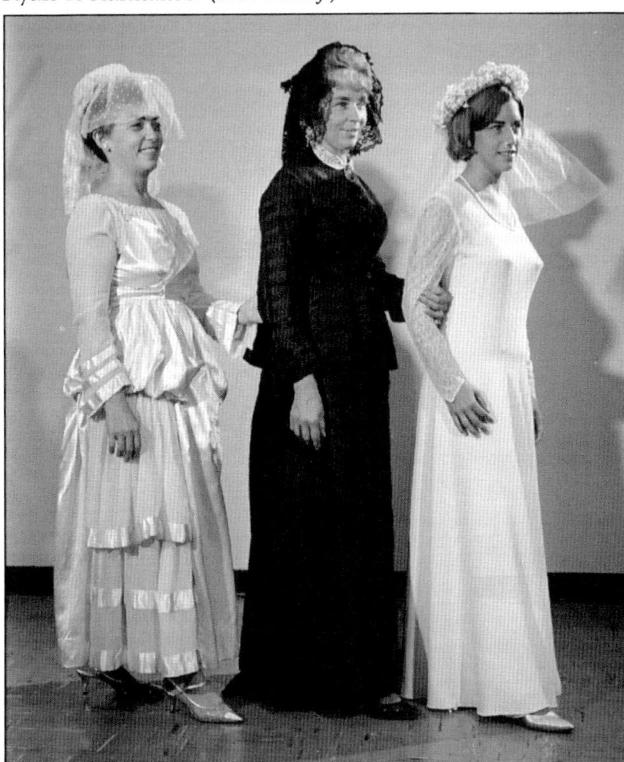

A fashion show held during Bradley's Diamond Jubilee featured wedding gowns through the years. On left is Olivia Mahoney, wearing a wedding dress that her mother had worn in 1916. Glenna Benoit (center) modeled a brown, woven, silk textured, two-piece wedding suit that was originally worn by Lavinia Kirby Hudson at her wedding in 1860. Libby Mahoney is dressed in her mother's 1948 wedding gown. (KCM-KDJ.)

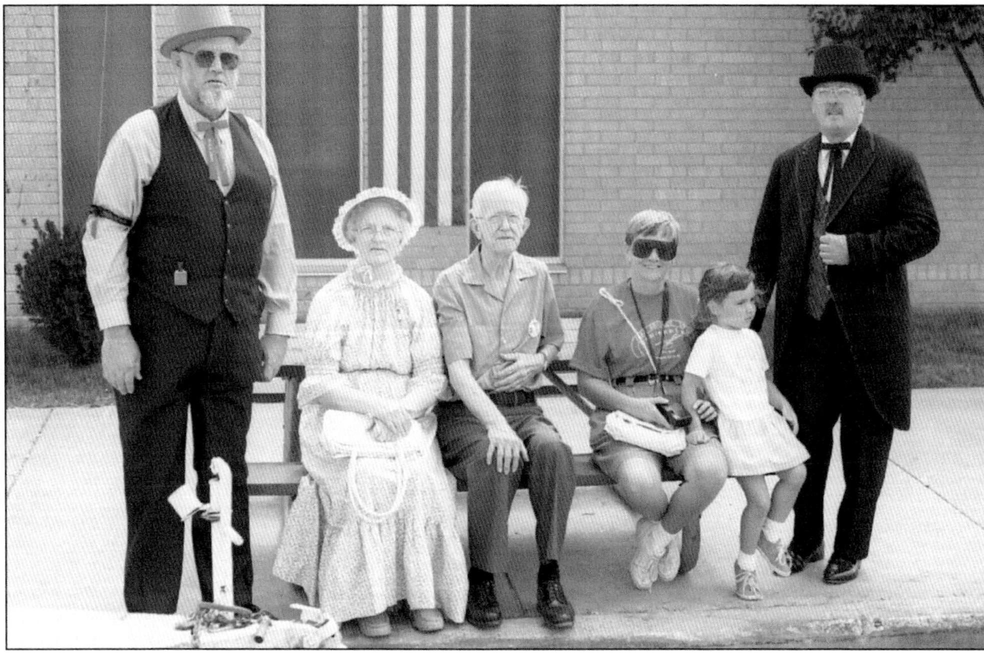

Seated on the bench waiting for centennial festivities to begin are, from left to right, Helen Maier with husband George Maier, daughter-in-law Mary Maier, and Caitlyn Vidas. George Maier is the grandson of Bradley's founder, J. Herman Hardebeck. On the left is Clint Bisping, who impersonated J. Harley Bradley, and on the right is Maier's son William dressed as Hardebeck. (Author's collection.)

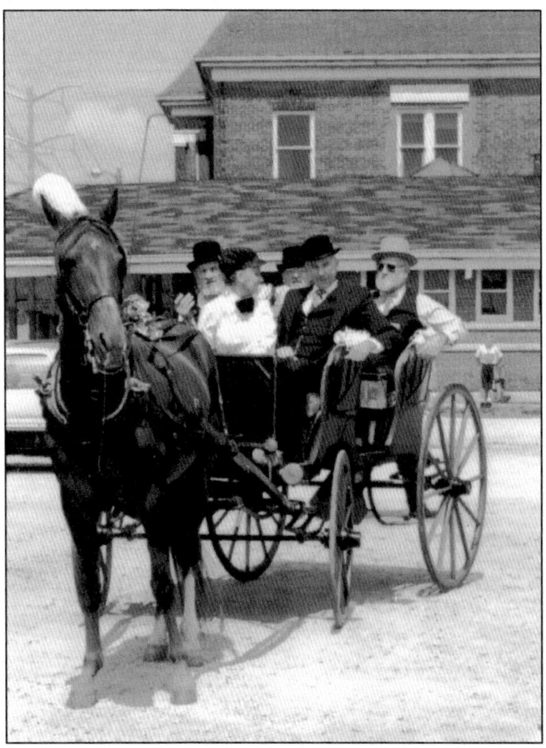

A reenactment of the arrival Bradley and Hardebeck in Kankakee on April 12, 1895, took place on the first day of the centennial at the Kankakee depot. The two men dressed as Bradley and Hardebeck were escorted by Bradley mayor Kenneth Hayes and Kankakee mayor Russell Johnson and were serenaded by Dave King's Nickel Plate Band in the style of the 1890s. The dignitaries were then whisked off to Bradley in a horse-drawn buggy. (Author's collection.)

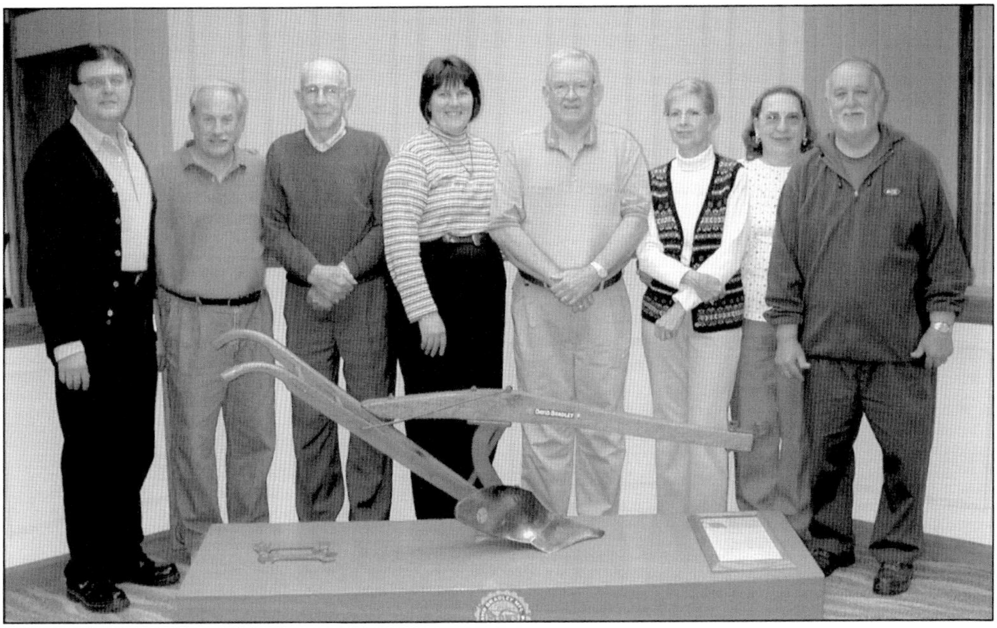

The Bradley Historical Society was established in March 2003 through the efforts of village trustees Robert Martin and Robert Redmond. Charter members of the society posed for the camera behind a David Bradley plow. From left to right are Ryland Gagnon, Redmond, Martin, Gail A. Hayes Schultz, Robert Simpson, Marcia Stang, Nelda Ravens, and Donald LeBran. Another charter member, Vic Johnson, is not shown. (RG.)

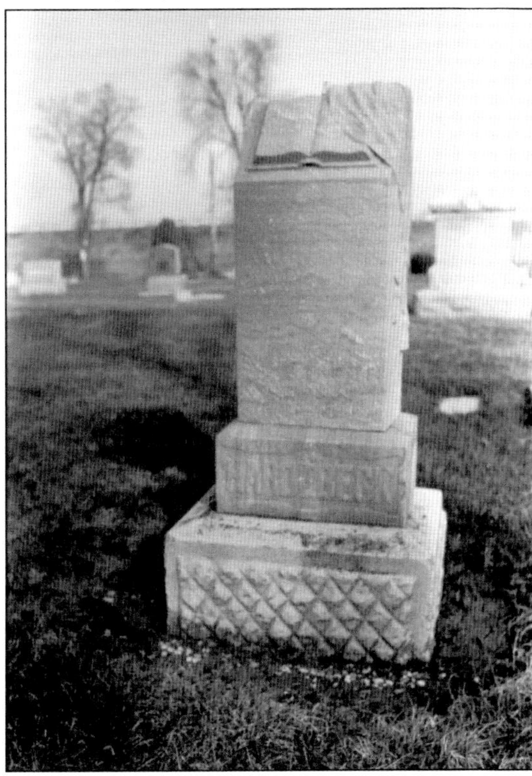

Hardebeck died on April 30, 1911, at the age of 68 in Switzer City, Indiana. After a wake held in the residence of his son-in-law Frank J. Maier on Grand Avenue in Bradley, Hardebeck was buried in Kankakee's Mount Calvary Cemetery. Few people in Bradley today know who Hardebeck was or what he accomplished. But back in 1891, *Kankakee Gazette* publisher Charles Holt admired Hardebeck's enterprising spirit so much that he compared him to Moses leading Kankakee businessmen out of the wilderness. "J. Herman Hardebeck!" said Holt, "You're a boomer from way back, and ought to ride in a carriage the rest of your days." (Author's collection.)